REINVENTING IRELAND

D1233717

CONTEMPORARY IRISH STUDIES

Series Editor Peter Shirlow (School of Environmental Studies, University of Ulster, Coleraine)

Also available

James Anderson and James Goodman (eds)
Dis/Agreeing Ireland
Contexts, Obstacles, Hopes

Colin Coulter
Contemporary Northern Irish Society
An Introduction

Graham Ellison and Jim Smyth
The Crowned Harp
Policing Northern Ireland

Marie-Therese Fay, Mike Morrissey and Marie Smyth
Northern Ireland's Troubles
The Human Costs

Paul Hainsworth (ed.)
Divided Society
Ethnic Minorities and Racism in Northern Ireland

Denis O'Hearn
Inside the Celtic Tiger
The Irish Economy and the Asian Model

Peter Shirlow and Mark McGovern (eds)
Who are 'the People'?
Unionism, Protestantism and Loyalism in Northern Ireland

Gerry Smyth
Decolonisation and Criticism
The Construction of Irish Literature

Gerry Smyth
The Novel and the Nation
Studies in the New Irish Fiction

REINVENTING IRELAND
Culture, Society and the Global Economy

Edited by
Peadar Kirby, Luke Gibbons
and Michael Cronin

Pluto Press

LONDON • STERLING, VIRGINIA

First published 2002 by Pluto Press
345 Archway Road, London N6 5AA
and 22883 Quicksilver Drive, Sterling, VA 20166–2012, USA

www.plutobooks.com

British Library Cataloguing in Publication Data
A catalogue record for this book is available from the British Library

ISBN 0 7453 1825 8 hardback
ISBN 0 7453 1824 X paperback

Library of Congress Cataloging in Publication Data
Reinventing Ireland : culture, society, and the global economy / edited
by Peadar Kirby, Luke Gibbons and Michael Cronin.
    p. cm. — (Contemporary Irish studies)
    ISBN 0–7453–1825–8 (hardback) — ISBN 0–7453–1824–X (pbk.)
  1. Ireland—Economic conditions—1949– 2. Ireland—Social
conditions. I. Kirby, Peadar. II. Gibbons, Luke. III. Cronin, Michael,
1960– IV. Series.
  HC260.5 .R44 2002
  306'.09417—dc21
                                                          2001008115

Reprints: 10   9   8   7   6   5   4   3   2   1   0

Designed and produced for Pluto Press by
Chase Publishing Services, Fortescue, Sidmouth EX10 9QG
Typeset by Stanford DTP Services, Towcester
Printed in the European Union by Antony Rowe, Chippenham, England

Contents

1 Introduction: The Reinvention of Ireland: A Critical
  Perspective   1
  Peadar Kirby, Luke Gibbons and Michael Cronin

PART I: ECONOMY AND SOCIETY

2 Contested Pedigrees of the Celtic Tiger   21
  Peadar Kirby

3 Culture and State in Ireland's New Economy   38
  Michel Peillon

4 Speed Limits: Ireland, Globalisation and the War
  against Time   54
  Michael Cronin

PART II: PUBLIC SPACES

5 Citizenship and Education: A Crisis of the Republic?   69
  Joseph Dunne

6 The Global Cure? History, Therapy and the Celtic Tiger   89
  Luke Gibbons

PART III: HISTORICAL LEGACIES

7 Colonialism and the Celtic Tiger: Legacies of History
  and the Quest for Vision   109
  Geraldine Moane

8 Religion and the Celtic Tiger: The Cultural Legacies of
  Anti-Catholicism in Ireland   124
  Lionel Pilkington

PART IV: MEDIA

9 The Celtic Tiger's Media Pundits   143
  Barra Ó Séaghdha

10 Broadcasting and the Celtic Tiger: From Promise to
    Practice   160
    Roddy Flynn

11 Screening the Green: Cinema under the Celtic Tiger   177
    Debbie Ging

12 Conclusions and Transformations   196
    Peadar Kirby, Luke Gibbons and Michael Cronin

Bibliography   209
Contributors   222
Index   224

1 Introduction: The Reinvention of Ireland: A Critical Perspective

Peadar Kirby, Luke Gibbons and Michael Cronin

Culture is not some vague fantasy of fulfilment, but a set of potentials bred by history and subversively at work within it.

Terry Eagleton:, *The Idea of Culture* (2000: 23)

'Ireland reinvented itself during the 1990s', boldly proclaimed the 1999 strategy document of the National Economic and Social Council (NESC), a three-year outline of economic and social policy agreed by all the social partners (government, business, farmers' groups, trade unions and the community and voluntary sector) (NESC 1999: 21). Though the NESC makes no reference to the source of the concept, the notion of Ireland reinventing itself is drawn from the work of Professor Rory O'Donnell, whose extensive writings on Ireland's social partnership have invested the concept with major international significance as an innovative model of economic and social governance (see O'Donnell 1999, 2000a; O'Donnell and Thomas 1998). This led O'Donnell to turn his attention to culture. Lamenting what he described as the excessive and unhappy dualism between the economic and the cultural, the material and the moral in contemporary Ireland, he defined a new project 'to reunite our account of the cultural and the economic, the normative and the material, the actual and the ideal' (1999: 34). In offering a cultural reading of Ireland's immediate past, he drew on Kiberd's notion that modern Ireland was invented in the cultural revival of the late nineteenth and early twentieth centuries (Kiberd 1995). O'Donnell co-wrote in 1998 that 'Ireland and the Irish people continue the journey of re-invention at the close of the twentieth century' (Laffan and O'Donnell 1998: 175). In April 1999 he specified further in claiming that 'changes in the public sphere' such as European integration and social partnership can be seen as part of the reinvention of Ireland, a new culture closely related to the successful economy (O'Donnell 1999: 32–3).

This 'new culture' is the subject of this book. The contributors map its contours in different areas of Irish life and from different disciplinary perspectives. While the authors adopt their own stances towards this new culture – stances not always in agreement with one another – what unites them is their critical engagement with their subjects, placing these in an historical context and tracing the forces that have given them their current shape and form, an approach to Ireland's 'new culture' which contrasts with that of its dominant proponents. This is characterised by an adulatory and uncritical tone, and which often fails to trace the new culture's historical development or to identify the forces which have shaped it. Instead, it is seen as marking a break with the past and the coming-of-age of an enlightened, tolerant and liberal Ireland. Furthermore, while this 'new culture' is closely linked by its proponents with Ireland's economic success of the 1990s, widely referred to as 'the Celtic Tiger',[1] the links between economy and culture have been little explored apart from a generalised correlation between economic success and a climate of national self-confidence and creativity. The authors in this book explore the links more closely, illustrating ways in which the precondition of Ireland's economic success, namely subservient integration into a radical free-market or Anglo-American informational capitalism,[2] has itself shaped values, attitudes and forms of cultural expression which function within the contemporary Irish economy. In this manner, then, the book uncovers more fully and analytically the nature and content of this 'reinvented' Ireland and the way in which culture has become the handmaiden of a particular type of economy. Furthermore, some of the authors in these pages go beyond mapping this new culture and illustrating its economic functionality. They explore ways in which culture could inspire political resistance and alternatives, using an engagement with Ireland's past to identify resources for reimagining and reinventing a different Ireland of the future.

Part I, Economy and Society, contains three chapters which examine in different ways the relationship between culture, economy and society under the Celtic Tiger. In Chapter 2 Peadar Kirby examines the nature of the 'reinvented Ireland' of the 1990s, contrasting the bases for this reinvention with those which resulted in the original invention of Ireland over a century ago. In Chapter 3 Michel Peillon argues that the connection between economy and culture has been fundamentally altered in the Ireland of the Celtic Tiger, since culture as social critique has given way to culture as economic commodity, both as a factor of production and a means of consumption. Michael Cronin explores in Chapter 4 what he calls 'the chrono-politicisation of Ireland', the effects of the new time-zones that are shaping Irish culture and society. He finds that 'in consumer societies where mobility has become a supreme virtue, the immobile are the losers'.

The Public Sphere is the theme of Part II. In Chapter 5 Joe Dunne addresses the weakening basis of citizenship as we become more implicated in a consumerist culture and resigned to the inexorable logic of economic growth. He argues for a notion of citizenship anchored in a robust practice of solidarity. In Chapter 6 Luke Gibbons explores the basis for a more multicultural public sphere in Ireland. He questions the assumption that welcoming other cultural influences requires an act of amnesia, or a disavowal of the heterogeneous and often conflicting elements within one's own culture.

Part III examines a number of historical legacies and how they influence Irish society today. In Chapter 7 Ger Moane looks at the psychological legacy of colonialism and identifies ways in which it still manifests itself through various cultural pathologies such as high levels of alcohol and drug consumption, patterns of denial and doublethink, distortions of sexuality and social irresponsibility. In Chapter 8 Lionel Pilkington discusses the relationship between Irish modernity and religious and denominational identity, and surveys some of the historical and political reasons for the assumption that Catholicism is considered to be an impediment to Irish modernisation.

Part IV, Media, contains three chapters which deal with different media through which Celtic Tiger Ireland portrays itself to the world. In Chapter 9 Barra Ó Séaghdha analyses critically the world view of some prominent Irish commentators who have interpreted contemporary Ireland to the outside world. He devotes most attention to the work of journalist Fintan O'Toole, identifying the themes of his work and the limits of his intellectual horizons. The neo-liberalisation of Irish broadcasting is the subject of Chapter 10. Roddy Flynn argues that, far from offering more diversity on the airwaves, the advent of commercial broadcasting has narrowed the range of material available to Irish audiences as commercial criteria assume ever greater dominance. In Chapter 11 Debbie Ging compares the representation of Ireland in the films of the late 1990s and early 2000s with the gritty social realism of the First Wave of Irish film-making from the 1970s and 1980s. She finds that a booming economy has begun to erase self-questioning in favour of a more marketable version of Irishness.

In the final chapter the editors discuss the main conclusions to be drawn from the contributions to the book, and explore ways in which culture offers the basis for forms of political practice which hold the promise of a more radical, egalitarian and multicultural society in Ireland.

Apart from this brief outline of the book's distinctive approach and its contents, this introductory chapter undertakes three tasks. The first examines the dominant understandings of Ireland's economic and cultural success in the 1990s, identifying features of the orthodoxy which are functional to the existence and maintenance of the present social order. These orthodoxies are briefly mapped out and reference made to ways in which they are examined in various of the book's chapters. The second task interrogates the understanding of culture that informs these orthodoxies and contrasts this with understandings which were dominant in previous eras of Irish life. It goes on to flesh out a fuller understanding of culture as the site of struggle over which social meaning achieves hegemony or dominance and illustrates ways in which these struggles are taking place in contemporary Ireland. The final task looks to the future and the role that culture plays in political stances in facing up to the dominant order. It argues that the attitude that culture is simply there to serve the needs of the economy constitutes one of the principal reasons for the failure to construct and articulate more effective, broad-ranging challenges to the dominant social order. The chapter concludes with an argument for an innovative appropriation of culture as a means of developing a new critical political space within contemporary Irish society.

The Celtic Tiger and its Orthodoxy

In the social science literature on the Celtic Tiger, three principal approaches can be identified. Each draws on different theoretical frameworks and, as a result, focuses on distinctive aspects of the phenomenon. The first, drawing on neo-classical economics and on new growth theory, focuses almost exclusively on economic success and the conditions underlying it. In this account, high productivity, cost competitiveness, wage restraint and curbs on public spending are identified as the main contributors to economic success (see, for example, Barry 1999; Leddin and Walsh 1997; Bradley 2000; Fitzgerald 2000). The high levels of economic growth which have resulted are seen as marking a permanent transformation of the Irish economy, holding out the prospect that 'Ireland may achieve a standard of living among the highest within the EU' over the next 15 years (Fitzgerald, 2000: 54). This literature largely neglects the social impact of economic growth, seeing economic growth as an end in itself. It rests on the benign individualist and utilitarian assumptions which inform neo-classical economics and which assume that economic growth results in positive social outcomes (see Kirby 2002, Chapter 4, for a fuller discussion). It is highly influential in economic policy-making and can be regarded as the dominant, hegemonic interpretation of the Celtic Tiger.

A second reading, consistent with the dominant economistic reading but adopting a distinctive focus of its own and drawing on very different theoretical understandings, can be identified in the political economy approaches of O'Donnell (2000b) and Ó Riain

(1997a, 1997b, 2000; Ó Riain and O'Connell 2000). These take the institutions of the Irish state as their focus of analysis, arguing that the success of the Celtic Tiger is largely the result of what O'Donnell calls 'the emerging Irish model of economic and social governance' (in Laffan and O'Donnell 1998: 165). O'Donnell attributes to the institutions of social partnership[3] a central role in mediating Ireland's transformation from economic laggard to economic star through aligning state strategy with economic and social interests (see O'Donnell 2000b). Drawing on the international literature on the developmental state, Ó Riain likens the Irish state's ability to foster more successful connections with global economic forces to the legendary success of the East Asian states of Japan, South Korea and Taiwan in the post-war period. In this reading, then, it is the state rather than the market which plays the crucial role in mediating success. Furthermore, the importance attached by both these theorists to social partnership points up the fact that they devote attention to the mechanisms whereby economic success is translated into social success, though O'Donnell offers a far more optimistic assessment of this than does Ó Riain. Both, however, agree that Ireland has been transformed economically through the agency of the state; it is a reading which exercises some influence, especially among state elites, and may underpin the apparent determination of the state to maintain and further develop the institutions of social partnership.

The final reading draws on more critical currents within social theory, particularly on Marxism, world-systems theory and the new international political economy. Allen's account (1999, 2000) offers a conventional Marxist analysis emphasising how the Celtic Tiger economy has enriched a small elite while leaving the majority, the growth in whose wages has been held in check by national social partnership agreements, relatively worse off. O'Hearn uses world-systems theory to argue that Ireland has 'bought economic tigerhood' (2000: 74) on the basis of its reliance on multinational capital. By contrast, the East Asian tigers succeeded in developing strong indigenous industrial sectors and winning export markets for their products. He links growing social inequality to the nature of the Irish growth model, arguing that employment is concentrated in low-paid service jobs and that the Irish state's fiscal policies favour the rich (1998). A final contributor to this literature is Kirby (2000, 2002). He argues that, under the Celtic Tiger, economic success correlates with social failure and uses a theoretical approach which draws on international political economy to show how the actions of the state have favoured market forces to the detriment of social well being. What these analysts have in common is concern about the inequitable social impact of economic growth. While this approach has little influence among economic or state elites, it exercises more influence among activist sectors of civil society.

Debates on contemporary Ireland are furthermore informed by a powerful orthodoxy relating to a shared understanding of the Irish past. The three components of this understanding might be described as having their origins in an economic, historical and aesthetic presentation of previous Irish experience. In the economic sphere the dominant narrative is one sketched out by Conor McCarthy when he describes the genesis of modernisation in the Irish Republic:

> Up to this time [the late 1950s], a chauvinistic economic nationalism had been pursued, that found its ideological basis in post-Independence isolationism, wartime neutrality and the ambivalence of the political and economic relationship with Britain. This issued in policies based on the development of the agricultural sector, import substitution and protectionism that had been pursued since the Second World War. These policies had now been revealed to be wholly inadequate to the country's needs. (McCarthy 2000: 12–13)

T.K. Whitaker's 1958 White Paper on *Economic Development* is the decisive policy move, backed by Lemass, that marks a break with the previous economic policies of post-independence Ireland and is signalled as the prelude to growth in the 1960s (Brown 1985).

The power of this founding narrative for the architects of Irish modernisation can be seen in the fact that almost 40 years later it is still a virtually unquestioned tenet of political faith that the economic modernisation of the 1960s was a wholly good thing. A second constitutive element of orthodox understandings of the past was the decisive change in perspectives on Irish historiography initiated in the mid-1960s. The main thrust of the writings of O'Brien, Lyons, Foster, McDonagh and others was to challenge the nationalist meta-narratives whether in representations of key historical events (the Famine, 1916 Rising, the Hidden Ireland of the eighteenth century), important historical figures (Patrick Pearse, Oliver Cromwell) or the degree of Irish antipathy to Empire (O'Brien 1972; Lyons 1973; Lyons 1979; MacDonagh 1983; Foster 1989; Wilson Foster 1991; Brady 1994). The shift in historical sympathies was not only inevitable with the arrival of a younger group of scholars on the Irish university scene but also complemented the aggressive commitment of the state to integration into the international neo-liberal system and a desire on the part of the new elites to repudiate a now discredited and devalued nationalist reading of history (Mac Laughlin 1994). The deep hostility to nationalist readings of Irish history was of course also determined by the military conflict in Northern Ireland and the desire of both the

British and Irish States to delegitimise extra-parliamentary Irish nationalism (Lloyd 1999). A third element in the development of consensual representations of the Irish past has been the close correlation between aesthetic representations of Irish 'life and popular ideological commentary. As Conor McCarthy has shown (McCarthy 2000: 135–64), this is most notably at work in the Dermot Bolger/Fintan O'Toole tandem, where dark, dystopian portrayals of a bigoted, ruralist, nationalistic Ireland are contrasted with the (albeit thwarted) liberatory potential of the post-nationalist, secular city. The images and narrative comment in the novels are thus both informed by and corroborate the partial world view of the critic. The economic stagnation of the late 1970s and 1980s, the backlash of the hardline Catholic Right in the 1983 and 1986 referenda and the continued bloody toll of violent conflict in Northern Ireland throughout the same period provided a powerful impetus both for maintaining and for elaborating the different constitutive elements of the modernising, neo-liberal orthodoxy. The combined effect of the economic, historical and aesthetic readings of the Irish past has been to construct a narrative of contemporary Irish society in which the country is presented as a modern, vibrant economy and society which has successfully abandoned its reactionary, nationalist Catholic past (O'Toole 1997). Ireland's contemporary culture is seen as an eloquent expression of new-found confidence where the liberalisation of internal markets is matched by the celebration of individual rights and liberties.

In the version of Irish modernity that emerges from this triple denigration of received understandings of the Irish past, history is now generally admitted into public view in two distinct forms with two separate functions, as distant past and recent past. As distant past (or as a past that has been safely distanced), history can function as a perfectly acceptable and desirable rationale for the development of a heritage industry that massages conflict out of representations (Brett 1996; Sheerin 1998). As recent past, history is used as a bogeyman in a kind of rhetoric of binary terror. Either you accept the deregulated ruthlessness of the market or you will be cast back into the eternal night of emigration and high unemployment. Better dead than Dev. In this either/or scenario, economic destiny is equated with political fate so that oppositional forces who contest the equation are variously presented as naïve, retrograde, irresponsible or ungrateful.

If opposition to neo-liberalism in Ireland has been so weak, it is partly to do with the different versions of the modernisation orthodoxy that have been espoused by the Irish Right and Left. The Right are impatient to move full speed ahead with the modernisation of Irish society so that all the cultural and economic obstacles to the relentless pursuit of profit can be eliminated as rapidly as possible. The Irish Left in the shape of the erstwhile Workers' Party and sections of the

Irish Labour Party embrace a mechanical version of Marxist theory that would see revolutionary forces gradually unleashed by the industrialisation of the society and Ireland's integration into the capitalist world order. In one scenario, modernisation favours the haves, in the other, the have-nots, but both agree modernisation *per se* can only be good for Ireland. A further factor weakening opposition to neoliberalism is the shrinking space for articulating oppositional arguments. In common with many other countries throughout the world, Ireland has experienced a privatisation of the public sphere where both print and broadcast media focus more and more on 'lifestyle' issues and life-politics to the exclusion of larger, political questions. From the prurient focus on celebrities of the scandal sheets to the relentless narcissism of the quality press (my body, my mind, my food, my weekend breaks) and the soap-box quixoticism of talk radio, problems are individualised, de-contextualised and sensationalised. The commitment of one government minister, Charlie McCreevy, to the 'individualisation' of the tax regime was not only a move that predictably made the rich even richer (even if it did indirectly favour some disadvantaged groups in Irish society) but the measure was also eloquent in its expression of the dominant philosophy of the boom. The more 'human interest' in the public mediasphere, the more inhuman indeed the society as a whole becomes. Inequality of earnings has grown continuously through the years of Ireland's economic success. As pointed out in Chapter 2, the proportion of the population on the lowest incomes has continued to grow and Irish spending on welfare and anti-poverty measures has been the lowest of any member state of the European Union.

Pace talk radio and human interest stories in the media, individual tales of woe, no matter how tragic or harrowing, are non-additive. They do not provide an account of structural agency, of how ideological choices have concrete effects, and they offer no hope of overall transformation, only the short-term sop of individual redress. What is offered instead is the illusion of social concern, of taking cognisance of problems and individual instances of suffering, but the only conceivable response in terms of the framing of media representations is either indignant helplessness or individual acts of charity (Devereaux 1997: 239–45). By minimising or eliding larger contextual questions and keeping political critique firmly at a distance, the reader/viewer/listener is left ill-equipped either to fully understand the structural causes behind individual plight or to engage in political action with others to effect profound, long-term change.

A diminished public sphere and a nation of consumers rather than citizens represents a congenial environment for free-market liberalism but the moral coercion of the weekend supplement is rarely enough. A key function of the nation-state in the current global order is to police the local precincts (see Bauman 1998: 65–8). Physical coercion must be present if the lessons of the powerful are to be properly understood. The Irish state is formidably well-equipped in this respect. The Offences Against the State Act is still on the statute books and effectively removes most constitutional rights from a citizen while in police custody. The Public Order Act further restricted the right to public assembly and protest. The Refugee Act includes draconian provisions on fingerprinting, curtailment of appeals procedures and further extends police powers. There are now more people in Irish jails than ever before in the history of the state and the number of prison places has grown throughout the years of economic success. Between 1997 and 2000 alone, 2000 new extra prison places were created. Indeed, the fact that many tigers in the developed world end up in cages is an ironic reminder of the penal realities of contemporary Irish society. Those who end up behind bars are almost invariably the poor and the disadvantaged. A Council of Europe report on the Irish prisoner population showed it to be one of the youngest and poorest in Europe (Council of Europe 2000). Between 1997, the year of the launch of a 'zero tolerance' crime policy, and 2000, four times as many beggars and ten times as many prostitutes were prosecuted by the state (O'Donnell and O'Sullivan 2001). In the period 1995–99, white-collar crime represented just 0.3 per cent of all crime recorded and therefore investigated by the police. While prisons expand to incarcerate and immobilise further the most economically disadvantaged in the society, dominant economic interests are given a clear message that crime pays. Three successive tax amnesties in 1988, 1993 and 2001, each one supposedly final, have rewarded wrongdoers not with one of the new prison places but with amiable discretion and a blanket pardon. Indeed, despite the fact that tax evasion robs the Exchequer of a lot more money than social welfare fraud, in 1999–2000 there were twenty times more checks on social welfare claims than on tax returns (O'Toole 2001). The preoccupation with punishment and social control is an essential feature of the disciplining of populations if they are to be made to live with the economic, social and cultural consequences of aggressive neo-liberalism. As the economic life of the country becomes more and more deregulated, social life becomes consequently more regulated, whether through discriminatory policing and penal practices or through the significant expansion in CCTV and information surveillance technology in Ireland's cities and workplaces.

Interrogating Culture

If there is any insistent refrain in cultural responses to the Celtic Tiger, it is that literature and the arts have thrown off the weight of an encumbered past and have injected a new outward-looking confidence, uncritically associated with entrepreneurship, into Irish society in general. It turns out, however, that there is not just one but rather a number of conflicting versions of the past against which the optimism of the 1990s sets itself:

(i) On the one hand, the target of contemporary writers and artists is taken to be the nostalgia of 'Romantic Ireland', the myth of the west as conjured up by the Literary Revival and commodified for popular consumption in tourism and the Hollywood dream-world of John Ford's *The Quiet Man* (1952). The debunking of romantic Ireland is usually accompanied by demands for more up-to-date representations of Ireland, images of urban life, industrialisation and consumer culture in keeping with the contemporary realities of a modernising society. The difficulty with this call for a shift in emphasis from tradition to modernity, the country to the city, is that it is primarily concerned with content alone, and may often simply transfer the 'forms' and myths of rural romanticism to new urban settings. As several critics have pointed out in relation to Alan Parker's film of Roddy Doyle's *The Commitments* (1991), the emphasis on community, leisure and consumption, vernacular language, music, and – not least – the time-honoured struggles of the Celts against adversity, all but turned the film into a version of urban pastoral, complete with the mandatory 'triumph of failure' theme also found in other wry treatments of modernity in films such as *Eat the Peach* (1987) and *I Went Down* (1998). Much of what passes for the new upbeat confidence in Irish culture – particularly the capacity to turn a blind eye towards the more negative social consequences of the economic boom – draws on the social and political evasions of the romantic idyll, except now it is modern (or post-modern) Ireland which is this side of paradise. As Judith Williamson pointed out in a classic article (Williamson 1986), it is not coincidental that advertising images play endlessly on the allure of desert islands, Nature, or romantic escapism in general, as if the commodity – and the humdrum exoticism of brand names, logos and lifestyles – has become the final outpost of fantasy and consumer gratification. Romantic Ireland may be dead and gone but that has not prevented it re-emerging in commodity form.

(ii) As against the comfort-blanket of Romantic Ireland, critical fire has also been directed at the disillusioned social realism associated with the age of De Valera – ushered in perhaps by Patrick Kavanagh's *The Great Hunger* – and charted with meticulous accuracy in the fiction of John McGahern, Edna O'Brien and William Trevor, or the drama of Brian Friel and Tom Murphy. From the 1980s onwards, these images have received a new lease of life in Irish film and television drama, ranging from *The Ballroom of Romance* (Pat O'Connor 1982) to *Korea* (Cathal Black 1996), *The Butcher Boy*

(Neil Jordan 1998) and the four-part television adaptation of John McGahern's *Amongst Women* (1999). Certainly, the relentless pessimism and quietism of many of these stories in the face of oppression and social paralysis seems out of place in the good times of the Celtic Tiger, leading *Newsweek* magazine to sound off in a recent issue: 'Prosperity has come to the land of Joyce and Yeats, creating a kind of country they could never have imagined: rich and happy.' However, as in the case of the romantic image, one has only to shift the locale for the fatalism of the countryside to re-emerge in the contemporary guise of a gritty, working-class realism. Roddy Doyle's four-part series *Family* (Mike Winterbottom 1994) provides perhaps the emblematic images here, but Charlo, the insensate male protagonist, is in many ways an aggressive urban counterpart of Kavanagh's Paddy Maguire, framed against images of concrete dilapidation rather than the stony grey soil of Monaghan. As in the case of Jim Sheridan's Oscar-winning *My Left Foot* (1989), moreover, not all of the victims accept their fate passively but it is striking that conflict does not always take place along class lines but is cast in terms of the struggle of family and community against patriarchy, privilege and the impersonal forces of the state. At their best, *Family* and related fictions of the 1990s chart new territory, however, in breaking with the reassuring liberal illusion that the ills of contemporary Ireland are simply the residues of the old order – land, religion and nationalism. Social decay, crime, alcoholism, domestic violence, homophobia, racism and alienation are not conveniently backdated to the sins of the fathers but are portrayed as endemic to modernity itself, part of the price of catching up with advanced Anglo-American or European culture. By contrast, one can compare the reverse process in the psychotic parodies of Martin MacDonagh which project onto rural primitivism precisely the kind of anomie and moral disintegration that emanates from the metropolitan centre – albeit in its bleak Thatcherite rather than Celtic Tiger mode.

   (iii) The third set of cultural representations against which the Celtic Tiger defines itself has to do with the Northern conflict, and the unfinished business of the national question. The litmus test of whether a narrative caught the spirit of post-national Ireland thus became its total disregard for the Troubles – which, after all, were supposed to be taking place in a foreign country (even if it was a bit too close for comfort). Depictions of urban violence (themselves spin-offs of the old stereotypes of the 'Fighting Irish') were divested of their more overt political leanings with the emergence of a localised gangster genre focused on the cult of 'The General' – although the best of the bio-pics, the BBC drama *Vicious Circle* (1999), did not flinch from exposing the General's sinister dealings with the Loyalist paramilitary underworld. This version of 'don't mention the war' helps to explain the vitriolic attacks on Neil Jordan's *Michael Collins* (1996), mainly on the grounds that it suggested unresolved tensions and affinities between Collins's guerrilla tactics and both state and IRA violence in the current Troubles. At a less acrimonious level, the eagerness to dispense with – or disavow – the most deeply-rooted conflicts in Irish society, whether to do with the North, sexuality or religion, has led to the search for new post-national narratives in which films, novels or plays are divested of any recognisable Irish traits. Though filmed in Dublin, Gerry Stembridge's *About Adam* (2000) gathered plaudits because it did not look like Dublin, and could in fact have been any hip city, or cosmopolitan setting. More perceptive responses pointed out that the film's mode of story-telling still bore the distinctive stamp of the city that produced Joyce, just at Wim Wender's *Paris, Texas* (1984) carried the signature of New German Cinema as much as its ostensible American subject matter. Not least of the ironies of the new global Irishness is that what could be construed as the erosion of a sense of place, or the most distinctive aspects of a culture, is taken as an assertion of confidence and independence. The profound changes taking place in Irish society undoubtedly call for images and modes of representation that extend beyond the past, but this is only because the past itself is not over, and still awaits its defining moments in the future.

Culture in the Social Sciences

Culture features little in the social science literature on the Celtic Tiger. However, a number of theorists refer to it, usually in passing; these references allow a certain mapping of the role culture is seen to play in Ireland's economic success. Among those who promote the dominant economistic reading, Fitzgerald alone attributes to culture a major role. Referring to 'a new self-confidence' and to what he calls 'a positive, outward-looking attitude that affects business, the educational system, and politics' which he attributes to membership of the European Union, Fitzgerald writes: 'It is this cultural change that is probably the single most important factor underlying the current Irish economic renaissance' since it has led to a spirit of openness and enthusiasm in embracing globalisation and outside influences (Fitzgerald 2000: 55). While he does not specify what he is referring to, he seems to have in mind what O'Donnell calls 'the emergence of an entrepreneurial culture and the adoption of radically new approaches to management and organisation' (2000b: 195). O'Donnell also sees culture, in the sense in which he understands it, as playing a central role in Ireland's economic success:

Without the unleashing of enterprise and improvement in management and organisation, the benign macroeconomic and market access conditions since the mid 1980s could not have produced the commercial breakthrough, so often referred to as the 'Celtic Tiger'. (ibid.)

To the limited extent to which they refer to culture, therefore, the two dominant social scientific approaches to understanding the Celtic Tiger treat it as being equivalent to a successful business culture and they seem to attribute the values informing such a culture to the wider society. Kirby identifies a more critical cultural discourse in the Ireland of the Celtic Tiger through examining some expressions of this in the media. He concludes: 'Values such as individualism, materialism, intolerance of dissent, lack of concern for the environment and a failure to value caring are identified as characterising life under the Celtic Tiger' (2002: 159). This is an attempt to move beyond the elitist and economistic understanding of culture in the work of dominant theorists, to uncover a wider and more demotic meaning of culture, as identified by Tucker: 'From a cultural perspective we must consider people's values, ideas, and beliefs, their identity and feelings, how they view the world and their place in it, and what is meaningful to them' (Tucker 1997: 4).

In this way, then, two opposing understandings of culture can be derived, one an elitist understanding functional and subservient to economic success and the other an expression of people's critique of and dissent from key values and attitudes which characterise the social impact of that success. These two understandings mirror a tension Eagleton found to be at the heart of the meaning of culture since, while it is a critique of social life, it is also complicit with it, 'a secluded form of social critique or a process locked all too deeply into the status quo' (Eagleton 2000: 8). This draws attention to the intersection of meaning and power, to the ways in which culture is mobilised and moulded to serve the needs of a dominant social order. Thus, the emergence of informational capitalism and Ireland's semi-peripheral integration into it bring to the fore a cultural discourse prioritising individualism, entrepreneurship, mobility, flexibility, innovation, competitiveness both as personal attributes to be cultivated by the individual (and which educational institutions are expected to play a central role in facilitating) and as dominant social values. These displace earlier discourses prioritising national development, national identity, family, self-sacrifice, self-sufficiency and nationalism. In both cases, we have examples of how dominant meanings are constructed to legitimise power hierarchies. However, as the quote from Eagleton above indicates, this is not the end of the story: culture also cultivates and gives expression to alternative and more critical meanings fashioned by those marginalised from the status quo. This subversive understanding of culture also finds rich expression in Ireland's history as demonstrated in Chapter 2, but there are also current examples.

In presenting a set of ideas about Irish society that on both the Left and Right have hardened into the political platitudes of Irish modernisation, the architects of the new Ireland studiously ignore cultural movements that would complicate the picture. The last decade of the twentieth century saw a sustained growth in all-Irish schools, the establishment of an Irish-language television station, the creation of third-level degree courses in Irish and the setting-up and the operation of an urban-based Irish-language radio station (see Ó Croidheáin 2001). The Irish language which had been consigned along with Faith and Fatherland to the trash-can of late modernity not only did not do the decent thing and die but actually expanded, developed and was taken over by a new generation of younger, mainly urban speakers. At one level, this can be seen as a classic centrifugal response to globalising forces in a society, local identities being affirmed as local economies become globalised (Castells 1997). At another, however, it is one expression of the need in a society to source elements of a linguistic and cultural past to situate a people in the present, a need that has not disappeared with the radical economic changes in Irish society. Other examples would be the emergence of a radical social discourse in the main churches, a self-aware and proactive movement for rural development in Ireland and the increased interest of young voters in non-establishment movements, politicians and political parties.

One of the difficulties with progressive thinking in Ireland whether dealing with language difference or, say, the persistence of religious belief and practice among the Irish young is what be might be termed *ideological franchising*. Basically, this involves the wholesale import of concepts and analyses from a powerful centre (usually the former colonial power) and their application in Procrustean fashion to the local society. This phenomenon is by no means confined to the long-established tendency of local capitalist elites to borrow dominant paradigms for regional application. Joseph Lee in *Ireland 1912–1985: Politics and Society* concludes that more generally intellectuals have contributed little to Irish public life, which has shown itself to be decidedly uncongenial to intellectual activity (Lee 1989: 638). There are a number of features of the Irish situation which indeed adversely affect the contribution of Irish intellectuals to Irish public life and to the wider international scene.

First, there is the draw of the derivative. Sharing a common language with the British and the Americans, Irish intellectuals borrow heavily from the stock of models and paradigms on offer in the Anglo-American world. There is no translation time-lag and the significant presence of academics in Irish universities educated in other Anglophone traditions means that there is a ready market for intellectual imports. The difficulty lies in their inappropriateness. As Lee observes, Ireland 'has imported much, but it has learned little' (Lee 1989: 627). Ireland is historically, economically, socially, demographically very different from Britain or the United States so that more often than not, the imported models are inappropriate in both nature and scale. Heavy conceptual borrowing often condemns the Irish intellectual to the shadow-play of dependency so that the question of a distinctive Irish contribution to the social and human sciences since independence has always been problematic. Secondly, the development of suitable economic, social and cultural policies is based primarily on self-knowledge, yet the level of funding for fundamental social research in Ireland is extremely low. Only research that has immediately quantifiable economic benefits is favoured and decisions are made with little regard for the long-term consequences for society. This leads to erratic, capricious policy-making whose effectiveness is compromised by a lack of contextual sensitivity and a tendency to embrace the pragmatic fashion of the day.

Paul Bew, Ellen Hazelkorn and Henry Patterson observed more than a decade ago that:

> the present impasse of social democracy [in Ireland] must therefore reside in its dogmatic embrace of modernisation theory which has left it theoretically denuded in a situation in which neither economic growth nor crisis has witnessed the working class embrace the socialist agenda. (Bew et al. 197–8)

In the kind of hand-me-down universalism practised by large sections of the Irish Left attitudes to such phenomena as language revival, agricultural development, non-secular beliefs and so on are preordained and dismissive. The immediate outcome is the persistent marginalisation of the Irish Left which has performed dismally since Irish independence. Its failure to engage with features of Irish society which do not conform to the conceptual grid of more reductive versions of the Enlightenment means that it fails to take advantage of those traditions in Ireland which offer opposition, dissent, resistance, albeit not always in ways sanctioned by the vade-mecums of the metropolitan Left.

Sites of Resistance and Reinvention

In retrieving the notion of culture as utopian critique, 'the very paradigm of a transformed political order' (Eagleton 2000: 16),

Eagleton warns of the dangers of wistful thinking, 'the infantile disorder known as ultra-leftism, which negates the present in the name of some inconceivably alternative future' (ibid.: 22). He states that the desirable future it argues for must be a feasible one, and finding a bridge between present and future is best done by identifying the transformative forces at work in the present social order. By 'judging the present to be lacking by measuring it against norms which it has generated itself' culture 'can unite fact and value, as both an account of the actual and a foretaste of the desirable' (ibid.). In this way, culture has the potential to be a site of resistance to the present social order and, in its own right, a force subverting that order and inventing a new one.

The first obstacle facing such an understanding of culture is the dominant post-modern view that there is no such thing as a common culture any more. In this view, propagated in today's Ireland with an intolerance that would have gladdened the heart of any promoter of a closed, essentialist Irish identity, the attempt to impose a common culture has given way to the celebration of a multiplicity of diverse cultures, from gay culture to pub culture, from Travellers culture to the culture of Dublin 4. What constitutes an Irish culture, in this view, is the rich tapestry of this endless variety. What this view avoids, however, is any attempt to recognise, much less interrogate, the values, beliefs and meanings which lie behind these diverse cultures, and therefore help to constitute the wider society we inhabit beyond the sub-cultures with which we may identify.

Eagleton raises some hard questions for those who see cultural pluralism as a value in itself:

> To pluralize the concept of culture is not easily compatible with retaining its positive charge. It is simple enough to feel enthusiastic about culture as humanistic self-development, or even about, say Bolivian culture, since any such complex formation is bound to include a good many benign features. But once one begins, in a spirit of generous pluralism, to break down the idea of culture to cover, say, 'police canteen culture', 'sexual-psychopath culture' or 'Mafia culture', then it is less evident that these are cultural forms to be approved simply because they are cultural forms (2000: 15).

While inevitably there is a pluralism in all cultures, no society could exist without some common values, beliefs and meanings to hold it together. A concentration on the plurality of cultures can obscure these foundational elements of culture, ensuring the values and meanings promoted by our political and economic elites pass muster for our common values. It also avoids the challenge of constituting an alternative set of common meanings to counter the dominant ones which are often taken for granted. This is where culture and politics meet, where popular mobilisation and organisation give power and voice to the values, beliefs and meanings of those who reject the dominance of an individualist, competitive, acquisitive culture.

In arguing against the wholesale incorporation of culture into the political project of Irish neo-liberalism, the object is not to make piecemeal complaints about physical infrastructure (traffic chaos) or public services (hospital waiting lists). Valid as the criticisms may be, they often give the appearance of dissent while leaving the basic structures of inequality and exploitation in Irish society untouched. Indeed, unless critical thinking has a deep-rooted, clearly articulated basis, what results is either a volatile form of social commentary which is a slave to the gripe of the moment (the opinion piece) or a kind of unhinged moralism which reacts with indignation to specific episodes of injustice but has no overall framework for action (the column). In order for people to act politically, they must be able to operate through time and, in order to operate through time, there be must an element of coherence and consistency in political thinking which allows energies to be maintained. The political and business elites in Irish society, for their part, have not been found wanting in their single-minded pursuit of the deregulation of all areas of Irish economic life (except for wages, of course, which remain highly regulated, particularly for the lower paid) (Green 2001). To this end, there has been a marked integration of the economic and cultural spheres. For the dominant, this integration has brought the benefits of a radically diminished public sphere, a silent and uncritical Academy and a largely docile workforce. However, such proximity brings with it dangers for the dominant classes which became clearly evident in the unprecedented hostility visited on the secondary teachers during their industrial action in 2000 and the outraged hectoring that preceded and followed the Nice Treaty debacle. In both instances, such was the coercive force of consensual thinking that any expression of sympathy for the dissenting position was immediately vilified as an intolerable threat to 'our' hard-won prosperity or the future of Irish civilisation as we knew it. As culture is more closely tied into economic forces, then activating other, alternative traditions in culture has arguably a much greater political effect than hitherto and will meet with a much more aggressive political response as cultural issues are clearly marked as both economic and political.

Notes

1. The term 'Celtic Tiger' was coined by the US investment bankers Morgan Stanley in 1994 but it took a number of years to pass into

popular currency. For an outline of what is seen as constituting the Celtic Tiger, see Kirby (2002).

2. Ireland's economic success in the second half of the 1990s has been dependent on very high levels of US foreign investment to such an extent that one economist has written that, over this period, 'the microeconomic structure of her industrial economy has evolved to more closely resemble a region of the United States' (O'Sullivan 2000: 283).

3. Social partnership refers to the innovative layers of negotiated economic and social policy-making between the social partners (the government, the business sector, the farming sector, the trade unions and the community and voluntary sector) which exist at national, regional and local level in Ireland. See Chapter 2 for a fuller description and discussion.

PART I

ECONOMY AND SOCIETY

2 Contested Pedigrees of the Celtic Tiger

Peadar Kirby

Central to any authentic development is the right of peoples to have a say in shaping their own destiny, in naming the world as they see it.

Vincent Tucker, 'The Myth of Development' (1992: 34)

The claim that Ireland has been reinvented in the 1990s can be seen as an attempt to fashion a history and a legitimacy for the Celtic Tiger. It purports to invest the economic success of *fin de siècle* Ireland and what has caused it with a significance similar to the founding struggles over a hundred years ago which resulted in an independent Irish state, thereby marking a break with that past and the beginning of a new historical period. It therefore offers a cultural reading of economic success, giving deeper historical meaning to the social changes that have occurred since 1987. To this extent it can be seen as creating a pedigree for the Celtic Tiger.

This chapter contests the pedigree offered by O'Donnell as outlined at the beginning of Chapter 1. To do this, it draws on the emerging disciplinary area of cultural political economy which is briefly outlined in the next section. The chapter goes on in its third section to identify in the work of Kiberd (1995) some dimensions of the invention of Ireland a hundred years ago, and to contrast that historical experience with the processes at work in the Ireland of the 1990s. Following this, it identifies in the work of O'Donnell the key roles played by social partnership and the embrace by the state of globalisation in constituting his reinvented Ireland, and it critically discusses the meaning attributed to both. This leads to a comparison of the principles of integration in the nationalist Ireland that grew out of the struggles of the 1890s and in the neo-liberal Ireland of the 1990s, identifying the insider/outside dichotomy in both. The chapter ends by suggesting that an essential starting point for contesting today's dominant social order is to contest the pedigree it fabricates for itself.

Cultural Political Economy

Traditionally, political economy has sought to avoid the tightly focused monodisciplinary approaches towards social analysis characterised by such disciplines as economics, political science and sociology since these have tended to reduce the complexity of social processes to a limited set of variables. Instead, political economy has adopted a multidisciplinary approach to look at the interconnectedness of politics, economics and society. Examples of such approaches for analysing the Celtic Tiger can be found in the work of Ó Riain (1997b, 2000a) and O'Hearn (1998, 2000).

However, political economy approaches have recently been criticised for prioritising the power of institutions and accepting such power as a given (Jessop and Sum 2001: 94). A similar critique has accused classical political economy of assuming that such institutions as states and transnational firms act in a calculated, rationalist way (Palan 2000: 15). This has opened the way to acknowledging the power of culture, and in particular the ways in which meanings are created and struggle for dominance. As Jessop and Sum put it:

> [R]ather than seek objective criteria to identify the necessary boundaries of economic space (on whatever territorial or functional scale), it is more fruitful to pose this issue in terms of an imaginary constitution (and naturalisation) of the economy. This always occurs in and through struggles conducted by specific agents, typically involves the manipulation of power and knowledge and is liable to contestation and resistance. (2001: 96)

This offers a fruitful way to look at the Celtic Tiger since it draws attention away from what we might call the 'objective' features of high economic or employment growth, which are usually offered as its defining elements, to the cultural creation of the term itself and the wider global significance with which it invests recent economic and social change in Ireland. In other words, it focuses analytical attention on the meaning attributed to this change and allows an examination of how a certain meaning achieves dominance despite the fact that other far more critical meanings of the same phenomena also exist (for example, the meanings given by Allen, Mac Laughlin or O'Hearn). This, then, is the approach adopted in this chapter. While its broad focus is on the ways in which economic, political and social power interact to achieve particular outcomes, its particular focus is on the meanings given to these processes, both the dominant meanings which legitimise outcomes and the subversive meanings which contest them. Only in this way can the full import of O'Donnell's concept of a 're-invented Ireland' be properly understood.

Inventing Ireland

An obvious starting point for discussing the concept is to return to what Kiberd meant when he wrote that modern Ireland was invented a century ago, something O'Donnell fails to do. Had he done so, he would have learnt that 'the exponents of the Irish Renaissance shaped and reshaped an ancient past, and duly recalled it, giving rise to an unprecedented surge of creativity and self-confidence among the people' (Kiberd 1995: 641). Kiberd describes the achievements of this creativity:

> That enterprise achieved nothing less than a renovation of Irish consciousness and a new understanding of politics, economics, philosophy, sport, language and culture in its widest sense. It was the great destiny of Yeats's generation to make Ireland once again interesting to the Irish, after centuries of enforced provincialism, following the collapse of the Gaelic order in 1601. No generation before or since lived with such conscious national intensity or left such an inspiring (and, in some ways, intimidating) legacy. (ibid.: 3)

While some of the dominant rhetoric today uses similar language (words such as 'creativity' and 'self-confidence', for example), the similarities are superficial. Fintan O'Toole's description of a dominant strain of consciousness in today's Ireland and of the roots of its seeming self-confidence illustrates the differences:

> Many of us may be glad to see the back of holy Ireland, martyred Ireland and peasant Ireland. Most of us may have wanted nothing so much as to be normal, prosperous Europeans. But what, now that we have arrived, is left to us? What, if anything, is distinctively ours? (*Irish Times*, 28 December 1999)

As so often with this author, the sweeping generalisations are posed in terms of binary and even Manichaean polarities derived from crude forms of modernisation theory and entirely dismissive of any historical complexities that may cloud his clarity of judgement. The irony of his call, later in the same article, that we 'have the creativity and the compassion to invent a notion of Irishness that doesn't depend for its distinctiveness on painting out the bits that don't fit the picture' seems entirely lost on him. Yet O'Toole's status as 'Ireland's foremost political commentator and cultural critic', to use Cronin's description (Cronin 1998: 4), reflects the influence and reception of his views. As such, his writings give voice to, but also help to create, a dominant consciousness in today's Ireland and, as is clear from the extract of his just quoted, this gropes for a sense of confidence by caricaturing and turning its back on the past, rather than by drawing on that past; in place of any 'new understanding of politics, economics, philosophy, sport, language and culture in its widest sense', it offers a conformity to what are regarded as 'normal prosperous European' ways; and instead of offering an inspiring and even intimidating legacy, it leaves us with no vital sense of a future to be striven for.

In marked contrast with this *officialista* view as it might be called, Tucker and Gibbons draw our attention to those sources from which cultural and social vitality and transformation emerge; these can be identified as the roots of the cultural, political and social renaissance of a century ago. Tucker, writing of culture and development, urges the identification of those 'ideas, meanings and ways of seeing' that have been submerged or marginalised (Tucker 1997: 10). This is in tune with Gibbons, who points out that transformation comes about by engaging with the past, 'particularly if it activates muted voices from the historical past, or from marginalised sections of the community' (1996a: 4). Identifying some of the hidden or marginalised dimensions of the Irish Renaissance of a century ago, therefore, is important not just as a way of retrieving a balanced historical memory but as a way of transforming the myopic cultural discourse of today's Ireland.

Five subjects are chosen for examination because they constitute some of the characteristics of today's dominant view of Irish society. It is widely claimed that, in contrast to the past, Ireland has recently become a pluralist society, with more egalitarian values, a more international outlook, a fuller and more complex sense of its own history, and a booming economy which has led to a modern prosperous society. These are certainly some of the elements suggested by O'Donnell in his brief descriptions of a 'reinvented Ireland' (see O'Donnell 2000b: 194–7; O'Donnell 1999: 32–5; Laffan and O'Donnell 1998: 173–7). Each is discussed in turn, contrasting today's Ireland with that of a century ago under each heading.

Pluralism

While we like to think of today's Ireland as more pluralist than in the past, it is largely devoid of the variety of social projects which offered competing visions of Irish society a century ago: parliamentary nationalism, cultural renaissance, Gaelic revival, D.P. Moran's Irish Ireland, a resurgent Catholicism, revolutionary republicanism, working-class militancy, suffragism and the movement for women's rights, agrarian co-operativism, conservatism, unionism. These sometimes overlapping but distinct projects found expression in a rich array of media of communication: the *United Irishman,* the *Leader, An Claidheamh*

Solais, the *New Ireland Review,* the *All Ireland Review,* the *Workers Republic,* the *Irish Homestead,* not to mention the *Freeman's Journal* and the *Irish Times.* Nothing remotely like it exists in any sector of the Irish media today.

Arguably the most audaciously pluralist project of all was the revival of Irish, centred on Conradh na Gaeilge (the Gaelic League), founded in 1893. This urban movement, led by intellectuals and with a well-developed vision of the role of culture in industrialisation and economic progress, grew to be a mass popular national movement. The number of branches increased from 43 in 1897 to 600 in 1904 and the total membership in that latter year was 50,000. Its leader, Douglas Hyde, has been described as anticipating by decades the analyses of Gramsci, Adorno and Leavis (Kiberd 1993: 19). Seán Ó Tuama described this project as 'a new and absolutely audacious human and intellectual venture, the very planning of which and the very execution of which, will of itself help to give our culture a new dimension of experience and a unique quality of its own' (Ó Tuama 1972: 109). It is difficult to identify any project, with strong roots in civil society, which carries such a potential today.

Egalitarianism

In many of these projects a strongly held aspiration was a more egalitarian social order. While this is obviously true of the workers' movement and the writings of James Connolly, it is less recognised that it characterised the co-operative movement also. In recent work, Hilary Tovey has described some key 'value positions' of the movement as 'egalitarianism, communalism, and replacing of relations of competition and exploitation between different economic groups by relations of justice and fairness' (Tovey 1999: 11). Thus, it disliked centralisation and placed an emphasis on participatory structures, its conditions of membership were designed to allow poor farmers and labourers to become members, and it successfully challenged exploitation by local dealers. More fundamentally, as Tovey puts it, the co-operative movement constructed peasant proprietors as 'the bearers of a particular version of or project for modernity' (ibid.: 15) in which the empowerment of the individual and collective association went hand in hand and which had as its aim the creation of a new participative and egalitarian social order. She concludes, however, that this agrarian version of Irish modernity 'was defeated and replaced by an essentially capitalist and urban version' (ibid.: 19).

By contrast, the contemporary form of this capitalist and urban version of modernity lacks any commitment to socio-economic equality, or equality of condition. It has reduced its distributional goals to a relatively minimalist objective, recently reformulated in the National Anti-Poverty Strategy (NAPS) (Inter-Departmental Policy Committee 1999: 3) of reducing the number of what it calls the 'consistently poor',[1] and to a vague aspiration towards social inclusion. The aspiration to equality has been reformulated so that it means anti-discrimination and equal opportunity measures for women and minority groups. While the aspiration towards egalitarianism remains alive in sectors of civil society, notably in the voluntary and community sector, it no longer inspires a distinctive project for Irish society.[2]

International Outlook

Since the widespread opposition to the Boer war which galvanised Irish public opinion around the turn of the twentieth century, Irish civil society has been characterised by a remarkable level of awareness of international issues. At times this found reflection in the state's policy, such as in De Valera's urging of sanctions at the League of Nations against the Italian invasion of Abyssinia in 1935 or the activist phase of Irish foreign policy at the United Nations soon after joining in 1955 (on nuclear disarmament and the admission of China, for example). Waves of emigration and a constant stream of Irish missionaries to Africa and parts of Asia throughout the twentieth century (with the addition of Latin America as a destination since the early 1950s) have ensured that few Irish families have not had some close relative living in a distant country. The resulting international awareness throughout Irish society finds expression in the activism on and expertise about many international issues which is a marked feature of social movements in Ireland. The widespread protests in the mid-1980s against US policy towards and actions in Central America which reached their highpoint during the visit of President Ronald Reagan to Ireland in June 1984 are one prominent example. These turned what was seen as a triumphal visit to his ancestral home into a public relations disaster for the White House. A more recent example is the East Timor Solidarity Group, founded by a Dublin bus driver, which brought a virtually unknown part of the world to public prominence in Ireland and had a major influence on Irish government policy on the issue.

However, this sophisticated critical awareness of the nature of today's international order is in marked contrast to the parochialism which characterises dominant views of Irish society. Thus, the mainstream literature on Ireland's economic success in the 1990s displays little understanding of the larger issues of neo-liberalism and globalisation that are so actively debated outside our shores.[3] Ireland's success is presented as some remarkable achievement of our own doing, rather than as an expression of the highly dependent position of many late industrialising countries on the investment policies of global corporations. Similarly, our historical revisionists rarely advert to international reference points (theoretical or empirical) which might temper their highly dismissive attitudes towards aspects of the Irish experience (this is especially true of their negative judgements on Irish nationalism).[4]

Sense of History

The view that Ireland was more pluralist, egalitarian and inter-national in outlook at the end of the twentieth century than it was earlier in that century thus rests on a particularly self-serving reading of Irish history. That the dominant readings of history in any society often closely coincide with the views of elites in power is nothing new. However, many of today's 'revisionist' scholars of Irish history claim to be providing a more rounded and multifaceted, and therefore more accurate and scientific, version of history. But, as Kiberd points out, the hostility of historians like Roy Foster and F.S.L. Lyons to Irish nationalism and their benign attitude to British colonial rule serves merely to replace an Anglophobic version of Irish history with an Anglocentric one (1995: 641–5). Neither does justice to the aspirations and struggles that have shaped Irish society in the twentieth century.

Moreover, revisionist historiography has had the effect of success-fully redefining national identity in a number of key ways. One is to break up the Irish experience, seeing it as a complex set of fragmented cultures (Lyons 1979: 2); the second is to view the Irish experience through the elitist optic of the Big House or the reception rooms of Dublin Castle or Westminster, as Whelan puts it (1990: 14). The result, as Bradshaw so perceptively notes, is an account of history 'from which the modern Irish community would seem as aliens in their own land' (1989: 349). Contemporary Irish identity has thus been sanitised and made remarkably accommodating to the dominant elitist project of subservient assimilation into multinational capitalism; robbed of reference points from a rich and subversive history, it is characterised, in Jacobsen's words, by 'a high degree of deference' (1994: 95).[5]

Relation of the Economy to Society

The dominant view of the period of Ireland's high economic growth since 1994 is that it has led to a modern prosperous society. However,

gs a fundamental question which has received virtually no
the literature on Ireland's recent development, namely:
'elationship between economic growth and social well-
ᵣ. ᵣ or this literature assumes that economic growth has beneficial
social outcomes; it does not examine whether this is in fact the case.
Some writers have raised this question (Forde 1999; Devlin 1998),
most notably J.J. Lee. He writes that, in the Celtic Tiger, 'people exist
only as producers and consumers ... it is an economy, not a society. It
is therefore virtually the polar opposite to the dream Ireland of De
Valera, which was far more a society than an economy' (Lee 1999: 80).

As this quote suggests, the social projects which were the source
and inspiration of De Valera's 'dream Ireland' devoted much
attention to the conditions for a successful society in contrast to
today's dominant concerns with economic success. Thus, many of the
competing social projects 100 years ago shared the aspiration
expressed by D.P. Moran in the first issue of the *Leader* in September
1900 for

> a self-governing land, living, moving and having its being in its own
> language, self-reliant, intellectually as well as politically independ-
> ent ... developing its own manners and customs, creating its own
> literature out of its own distinctive consciousness, working to their
> fullest capacity the natural resources of the country, inventing, crit-
> icising, attempting and doing. (quoted in Mulhall 1999: 112)

In this view, the roots of economic success, productivity, industrialisation and urbanisation lay in developing the capacity and
inventiveness of Irish people, and the revival of the Irish language was
an essential means to achieve this. Therefore, economic success was
to grow from the development of social capacities rather than, as characterises today's economic model, social capacities being shaped to
serve the needs of a largely imported economic model.

It can be concluded that the thesis of Ireland's reinvention in the
1990s pays scant attention to the actual contours of the period of
national invention a century ago. For, in some crucial ways, the basis
of social and political transformation in both periods is so different
that one is almost the polar opposite of the other. What characterised
Ireland's invention in the period 1890 to 1920 was a strong civil
society, mobilised in a rich variety of social, political, cultural and
economic organisations promoting through vigorous political means
the building of an economy based on native capabilities and resources
to serve the good of society at local, regional and national level and
creating a rich and inclusive 'imagined community' to which the
majority could, with pride, owe allegiance. By contrast, the transformation of Ireland in the 1990s has happened largely through the agency

of foreign capital, attracted by a state which has 'consistently priori-
tised the needs of the economy over social objectives' (Cantillon et
al. 2001: 304) and, through social partnership, co-opted leading
sectors of civil society into a subservient relationship. In seeking an
account of Ireland's present that reunites the cultural and the
economic, the normative and the material, the actual and the ideal,
O'Donnell has made the cultural subservient to the economic, the
normative to the material and the ideal to the actual; he has robbed
social theory of any liberating potential.

The Bases for Ireland's Reinvention

The comparisons of the previous section have highlighted some of the
ideas and meanings being vigorously contested in the 1890s period
which have been submerged, marginalised or, indeed, simply ignored
in the attempt to fashion an historical pedigree for the Celtic Tiger.
This invites closer attention to the bases for Ireland's transformation
in the 1990s so as more clearly to identify the causal mechanisms of
social change in this period, their outcomes and the meanings
attributed to them. In this way, the nature of Ireland's reinvention
can be more sharply delineated.

O'Donnell identifies two major innovations in Irish policy-making
in the 1980s to which he attributes Ireland's transformation since
1987. The first is what he calls a 'significant development in ideas and
policy in the late 1980s [which] involved a new recognition of the link
between domestic action and international context' (1999: 9). As a
result, deeper European integration and internationalisation came to
be seen as a route to success. This is a version of the globalisation
argument advanced by other theorists as a cause of Ireland's high
economic growth rates. John Fitzgerald put it most succinctly when
he wrote that contemporary Irish success 'owes much to the
enthusiasm with which Ireland has ... approached the globalisation
of its economy and the opening up of its society to outside influences'
(Fitzgerald 2000: 55). The second major innovation identified by
O'Donnell is the social partnership approach to economic and social
management, what he calls 'negotiated economic and social
governance' (1999: 12). Obviously, these two innovations are
intimately related to one another as agreement between the social
partners is seen as enabling Ireland to capture the benefits of a
globalised world order (through, for example, maintaining wage competitiveness) and to win wider social support for the efforts to do this
(through, for example, agreement on tax cuts and on social policies).

It is difficult to dispute that these were among the crucial causal
mechanisms of Ireland's economic success in the 1990s. Without an

active embrace of globalisation, the state could never have been as remarkably successful as it was in attracting very high levels of US foreign investment against strong competition from other states; and, though disputed by some economists, social partnership has probably helped to moderate wage rises in key sectors of the economy and to give the trade unions and the community and voluntary sector some limited influence over economic and social policy. What is of interest here, however, is not to repeat the positive account of these efforts but to examine the basis for the wholly positive meaning attributed to them. If they have led to the transformation of Ireland, indeed to its reinvention, we need to examine more critically the nature of this transformation and reinvention.

A good place to start is to look at the darker sides of globalisation, something entirely missing from the accounts of those who see glob-alisation as the key to Ireland's success. Do they assume that Ireland can remain immune from these? If so, they do not tell us how or why. By darker sides here are meant the social inequalities and exclusions which are seen by leading theorists as an essential part of a globalised economy as 'populations and territories [are] deprived of value and interest for the dynamics of global capitalism'. What results is 'the social exclusion and economic irrelevance of segments of societies, of areas of cities, of regions, and of entire countries' (Castells 1998: 337). Even for those who are integrated into the networks of production, 'the new system is characterized by a tendency to increased social inequality and polarization, namely the simultaneous growth of both the top and the bottom of the social scale' (ibid.: 344) while 'com-petitive pressures, flexibility of work, and weakening of organised labour [has] led to the retrenchment of the welfare state, the corner-stone of the social contract in the industrial era' (ibid.: 337).

If Ireland's reinvention is due to the enthusiastic embrace of glob-alisation, has it somehow managed to capture the positive economic dynamic while avoiding the social polarisation and inequality? The answer, of course, is that it has not, as the high economic growth rates of the 1990s have been accompanied by growing relative poverty, inequality and occupational stratification, and by a declining welfare effort. Relative poverty, measured by the percentage of households and of persons whose income falls below poverty lines based on 40 per cent, 50 per cent and 60 per cent of average income have all risen consistently between 1987 and 1997. The distance they fall below the poverty line, while being reduced between 1987 and 1994, increased quite sharply between 1994 and 1997 (Layte, Nolan and Whelan 2000: 165). On inequality in income distribution, after some decades of relative stability in the figures, the period 1994–98 shows a redis-tribution of over 1 per cent of total income away from the bottom 30 per cent of the income distribution. This was described by those who compile the statistics as 'a substantial shift in a short period' (Nolan, Maitre, O'Neill and Sweetman 2000: xix). There is also evidence of growing occupational stratification, both in earnings and in the structure of the labour force. Earnings inequality has grown substantially between 1987 and 1997, though since 1994 the tendency of the lowest earners to fall steadily in relation to those on average earnings has ceased. However, the tendency of the top earnings to increase faster than average earnings has continued so that over the whole ten-year period 'there was a substantial widening in earnings dispersion in terms of hourly wages among all employees' (Barrett et al. 2000: 130). Examining the kinds of jobs created in Ireland's jobs boom of the second half of the 1990s, Kirby concludes that 'rather than occupational up-grading, a more adequate hypothesis to characterise changes in the occupational structure of the Irish workforce under the Celtic Tiger might be occupational polarisation' (Kirby, 2002: 55). In these ways, therefore, Ireland's embrace of globalisation has resulted in a more divided society. Meanwhile, as it became a more prosperous society 'it has made less welfare effort' (Ó Riain and O'Connell 2000: 331): 'By 1997, Irish government spending had fallen to 35 per cent of GDP, marginally higher than the US, and 13 percentage points below the European average' (ibid.: 333). However, for some unexplained reason, these realities are not allowed to colour the positive interpretation given to Ireland's enthusiastic embrace of globalisation. That their reinvented Ireland is one in which some are gaining substantially while others fall further behind seems of little significance to them.

The second key characteristic of this reinvented Ireland identified by its proponents is social partnership. Again this echoes themes found in the writings of Manuel Castells, a leading theorist of globalisation. He writes that power relations are being transformed by the social processes of this new era as the power of the nation-state is undermined. In this situation 'the political system is voided of power' and social actors seek to promote their interests 'by playing out strategies in the networks of relationships between various institutions at various levels of competence' from local, through regional and national, to transnational like the European Union. Thus 'political institutions [become] bargaining agencies rather than sites of power' (Castells 1998: 347). This describes well the impact of social partnership on Irish politics. As Ó Cinnéide has written:

At one time a partnership meant simply a legal or functional entity consisting of two or more parties bound by contract or agreement. Now, because of its 'feel-good' appeal, the term is widely and imprecisely used in Ireland for a wide range of 'participation' and 'consultation' arrangements in public affairs. These arrangements are in fact a version of corporatism, the political system by which policy is made not by elected representatives meeting openly in parliament but by organised interests making agreements among themselves and/or with the government. These agreements, which bind the rest of us, are made around committee tables behind closed doors. (Ó Cinnéide 1998: 46)

This has resulted in 'a major shift in power from elected representatives to full-time officials in the civil service and in the organisations of the major interests' (ibid.: 47) while 'a lot of people now feel more excluded from the political process and are cynical about the whole system' (ibid.: 42). In this way, social partnership marks an emasculation of politics as power is more concentrated in the hands of small elites and it is these who decide who gets a seat at the decision-making table. Those who might espouse a different social project, particularly those groups who decide their interests are not best served by the current model, thus find it more difficult to build alliances and promote an alternative economic and social project. Furthermore, both economic and social policy is effectively ring-fenced from significant influence by such social forces, which is a way of ensuring that it is functional to the needs of capital accumulation by economic elites.[6] This may be one reason why a majority of those who voted in the referendum on the Nice Treaty in June 2001 rejected it against the urgings of all the major political parties, business and farmers' leaders, the Catholic bishops and the trade union movement. For it offered an increasingly rare opportunity to voice an effective protest against the concentration of power and the erosion of the bonds of solidarity which characterise society today. However, as an act of protest it does little more than stop momentarily the political and economic elites in their tracks; a more ongoing challenge to their elitist project of social transformation is necessary. Meanwhile, at election time little real choice is offered to voters who exercise their democratic right in declining numbers to protect their individual interests rather than to promote competing social projects.

In these ways, the bases for Ireland's reinvention are seen as having very ambiguous social and political consequences. They have helped deliver high growth rates, high employment growth and large average increases in income. However, they have also resulted in greater inequality in the distribution of the benefits of this growth, including the distribution of income and earnings. They have accompanied a weakening in the state's welfare effort and have led to a growing concentration of power in the hands of economic and political elites. This, then, is what constitutes Ireland's reinvention. The highly positive reading given these transformations can only be understood as deriving from a fundamental misunderstanding – namely that the interests of the whole of Irish society are equated with the interests of those elites who are benefiting from this newly invented Ireland. But this reading has also taken on a power in its own right, promoting economic growth as an end in itself and equating social success with the enrichment and conspicuous consumption of wealthy elites. This has the effect of dispossessing those who do not share in this success, and who are therefore redefined, not as citizens whose rights and needs can make justifiable claims on society, but as outside observers who can only look on in envy at the growing takeover of society by these elites. The ultimate disempowerment which this myth of a re-invented Ireland imposes on those who are excluded from it is that it is promoted as 'balancing economic revitalisation with social solidarity' (O'Donnell 2000: 202). In this way, the basis for protesting against this social order and making claims on it, namely social solidarity, becomes yet another label attached to the existing social order. Furthermore, the bonds of belonging to this society have been weakened as inequality has grown and politics has been emasculated.

Principles of Integration: Nationalist versus Neo-liberal Ireland

The account thus far has tended to contrast the competing projects of the 1890s with the social outcomes of the Celtic Tiger in the late 1990s. A fuller comparison would need to compare the nationalist Ireland that emerged in the twentieth century with what we can call the neo-liberal Ireland of today.[7] While it is relatively easy to compare economic growth rates, employment and living standards at various periods with those today (see, for example, CSO 2000), it is doubtful that this tells us very much about those elements which make for a successful society. The cultural political economy approach adopted in this chapter therefore goes further and focuses attention on the social meaning and values which predominated in both periods in order to draw some useful conclusions about the quality of life and sense of belonging for members of each of these societies.

In looking back at nationalist Ireland from independence to the 1960s, the litany of economic inefficiencies, cultural narrowness and social stagnation which characterised the Irish state at various times of its existence have become part of the orthodoxy of the so-called new enlightened Ireland of the 1990s. However, it is easy to pass sweeping judgement after the event, to impose on another society the orthodoxies of ours and to dismiss it accordingly. Certainly the deficiencies of that society are all too evident and two in particular stand out: firstly, it never produced an economic base that could help it meet its material aspirations, so that emigration became a defining characteristic of that society; secondly, its very integration around a nationalist principle helped fuel, by way of opposition, a reactionary counter-nationalism (unionism) in Northern Ireland. Yet, to label it as 'a relatively homogeneous, closed, Catholic culture' as against today's 'open, pluralist, culture' (Laffan and O'Donnell 1998: 173) is greatly to oversimplify, missing the currents of dissent that swirled around that society, and to allow caricature to replace informed historical judgement.[8] In particular, it misses what was most successful about that society, namely its ability to offer a sense of belonging, a cohesive identity to which the majority could owe allegiance. Of course, those who dissented from that cohesive identity found themselves outsiders, as happened with a number of celebrated writers. However, the majority of its citizens were insiders, perhaps chaffing a bit at times against some of its wilder rhetoric, but fundamentally at ease with the identity it offered.

Today's neo-liberal Ireland is very much a foreign country. It offers a more solid economic base and its looser sense of identity has opened spaces of accommodation for Northern unionists. These are among its great successes. But, like the Ireland it replaced, it too is characterised by a great gap between rhetoric and reality. Thus, an all-pervasive rhetoric of multiculturalism cloaks the emergence of an ugly racism, a continuing intolerance to the Travelling community and an antipathy in many quarters to the greatest source of multiculturalism in Irish culture, namely the Irish language. Similarly, a rhetoric of social inclusion masks growing relative poverty and economic inequality and the emergence of a new class of wealthy and powerful entrepreneurs associated with economic success. As Ó Riain has written: 'A self-confident professional class has emerged that is deeply integrated into local and global technology and business networks and negotiates individual career paths based on mobility through these networks' (2000a: 183). Increasingly divorced from the national institutions of industrial relations and wage bargaining, this new class is identified as 'the basis of spiralling inequality in market incomes in Ireland' (Ó Riain and O'Connell 2000: 338). However, the values of this new class have become the values of neo-liberal Ireland, an enterprise culture made up of attitudes, values and norms which serve the needs of the market and which are actively promoted by government agencies (Carr 1998). These values offer a far weaker principle of social integration than did those of nationalist Ireland as they are functional to the needs of a far smaller percentage of the population. In this society, it is not the dissenting few who feel outsiders but large groups of workers and citizens who feel disempowered and dispossessed in their own society. The wave of determined strikes by public service workers such as police, nurses, junior doctors, transport workers, airline workers and teachers that marked the years of greatest economic growth under the Celtic Tiger were evidence of this, as was the vote against the Nice Treaty in June 2001.

Economic growth alone does not make a successful society. For that, the alignment of material interests with a secure and cohesive identity, a sense of belonging, is necessary (see Kirby 2001). In the past, the state provided that sense of belonging as it embodied a collective project of social transformation. As Laïdi put it: 'It could be seen as the most complete and most formalized attempt to add meaning to power, to synthesize world order' (Laïdi 1998: 16). The Irish state, founded in 1922, was a very successful example of this merging of meaning and power, emerging as it did out of the re-definition of the 'imagined community' of the nation by civil society. By contrast, the resituating of the state in this era of neo-liberalism so that it becomes subservient to market forces fatally undermines its ability to embody a project of social transformation. This shift is clearly evident in the Irish case as the state is increasingly seen to serve the needs of an economic elite while neglecting the growing inequality that is undermining the cohesion of society. The realities of power in this society are ever more at odds with the meaning it promotes.

Conclusion

Meaning is a central and essential dimension of the stability, cohesion and sustainability of any social order. It is here that culture and politics meet. One expression of this meeting is the fashioning of pedigrees. Just like individuals and families, all social orders depend on furnishing a pedigree that confers historical legitimacy. This pedigree may have a solid foundation in the popular consciousness and its sense of its own history or it may be, as so often it was in Irish history, a bogus genealogy fabricated by usurpers.

Celtic Tiger Ireland is a new social order; to this extent it is true to claim that Ireland has been reinvented in the 1990s. However, this chapter has argued that here the equivalence with the Ireland of the 1890s ends, since the Ireland then invented, and the means used to create it, were the virtual polar opposite of the project of reinvention in the 1990s. Covering the Celtic Tiger with a mantle of popular social and cultural invention is therefore akin to fabricating a false pedigree for it, since today's Ireland has been reinvented through the actions of market-accommodating business and political elites rather than through popular social and cultural contestation of the dominant order. Returning to the quote at the beginning of this chapter, the Celtic Tiger has not emerged from most Irish people having a say in shaping their own destiny and naming the world as they see it. An essential starting point for contesting today's dominant social order is to contest the pedigree it is fabricating for itself.

Notes

1. This refers to the number of those who fall below 40, 50 or 60 per cent of average income and lack a range of basic necessities such as a warm waterproof overcoat; a week's annual holiday away from home; central heating; a car; new, not second-hand, clothes and a dry, damp-free dwelling (see Layte et al. 2000: Chapter 5).

2. It can be argued that the involvement of the community and voluntary sector as a recognised social partner in negotiating the Programme for Prosperity and Fairness, and the commitments given to social inclusion measures within this agreement, reflect moves towards a more egalitarian social project. The test of this will lie in the ability of this programme to reverse the trends towards greater inequality of social condition which characterises the Ireland of the Celtic Tiger. Certainly, none of the four earlier partnership agreements reversed these trends and they may even have exacerbated them (see Kirby 2000: Chapters 1 and 9).

3. See Kirby (2002) for a fuller discussion of this point, together with examples.

4. For example, a leading international scholar of nationalism, Ernest Gellner, has criticised Conor Cruise O'Brien's writings on nationalism. Gellner finds 'a touch of intellectual autism in O'Brien's thoughts' on nationalism and gives a list of leading scholars of nationalism all of whom are ignored by the Irish intellectual (Gellner 1994: 61).

5. The No vote in the Nice Treaty referendum in June 2001 marks a rare exception.

6. Defenders of social partnership argue that it enhances the power of the representatives of various social forces (trade unions, the voluntary and community sector), since it gives them a seat at the table. However, the Irish experience points to at least two consequences of this form of inclusion. Firstly, it is inclusion on the terms of the dominant 'partners' and offers no space for challenging their dominant project of capital accumulation. Secondly, it effectively co-opts in support of this dominant project the sectors which are given a seat at the table, since it greatly weakens their ability to exercise a critical voice and to mobilise citizens around an alternative project.

7. The claim that Ireland today is neo-liberal is a contested one. For example, Nolan, O'Connell and Whelan have argued that the Irish success story of the 1990s 'is not a simple story of globalisation,

forced withdrawal of the state and the promotion of neo-liberalism' (2000: 1). For a critique of this view and an argument that it is difficult to describe the Irish success 'as anything other than an Irish neo-liberalism', see Kirby (2002: 163).

8. For example, the Irish state's ability to preserve a functioning democracy (a rare exception in world terms in the period up to the late 1940s) and its remarkable state-led surge of industrial and social development in the 1930s merit a far more nuanced judgement than that offered by O'Donnell.

3 Culture and State in Ireland's New Economy

Michel Peillon

The breathtaking transformation of Ireland at the turn of the twenty-first century represents only one moment, however dramatic and paradoxical, in the longstanding project of integrating the Irish economy more centrally into world capitalism. Dramatic because, after many years of downturn, the Irish economy has experienced unexpected and sudden growth throughout the 1990s. Paradoxical, as the effort at industrialising generated a fast-growing post-industrial economy. While endeavouring, with rather mixed success, to lay the foundations of industrial development, Ireland ensured some post-industrial prosperity. The new economy constitutes nonetheless the outcome of a deliberate and determined undertaking, which started in the late 1950s. This transformation has been recorded and analysed mainly in terms of economic shifts that have taken place over the years and also by emphasising the metamorphosis of Irish culture.

The accent placed on these two separate registers of change, economy and culture echoes in many ways the formidable intellectual battle which has raged for more than a century now between an account of historical change in terms of material conditions on the one hand, and of the power of ideas on the other. Needless to say this issue has not been solved. Instead, its urgency has faded away and the question is now bypassed rather than confronted. The present chapter addresses this question, but only in an indirect way, by starting with the view that culture constitutes a variable. The position of culture within society (the way it is connected with other sectors of activity such as the economy or the polity) is not fixed. This chapter develops the idea of the variable character of culture in the Irish context. It aims to show not so much that the Irish economy has experienced a deep mutation or that Irish culture has been metamorphosed, but that the connection between economy and culture has been fundamentally altered.

The task of conceptualising the place of culture in society as a variable is not facilitated by the ambiguity that is attached to such a term, and by the use that is made of it. There is really no way of deciding on the appropriate definition of culture, but at least one should clearly state what is meant by culture in the present context. I will eschew the minimalist definition of culture as merely 'representational art', whether in the elitist incarnation of high culture or in its popular form. Such a definition of culture I find too narrow and limiting. The other approach to culture encompasses all practices and all aspects in the life of a group. This anthropological definition of culture, so extended, includes practices and institutions as well as ideas and beliefs, and this equation of culture and society simply renders it impossible to analyse the relationship between culture and other aspects of society. By culture, I will simply refer to the way people represent the world in which they live: the beliefs they embrace, the ideas they hold, the feelings they express, and the meaning according to which they act.

Culture and Economy in Tension

Ireland acquired at an early stage some of the features of an emerging modern society. For instance, universal primary education was established by the British authorities early in the nineteenth century. Deemed a successful experiment, it was soon adopted in other parts of Great Britain. Ireland also participated in the British parliamentary democracy widely presented as an example of political modernity and the nationalist movement saw its task as creating a separate 'nation-state'. In fact, at independence, Ireland quickly established itself as a parliamentary democracy in which citizens enjoyed the whole range of civil and political rights. Relatively modern political institutions were introduced into a society which remained predominantly agricultural and which had undergone little functional differentiation. For instance, the family functioned as a social, economic and political unit. The highly specialised and clearly separated state structure had to operate in a context which had not experienced such a functional specialisation and structural separation. The grafting of relatively modern political institutions onto a largely undifferentiated society generated its own problems, and clientelism functioned as a mechanism for connecting these two facets.

These modern features were introduced from the outside, by a colonial power, even if their introduction triggered internal processes. However, Ireland has, in the second half of the twentieth century, engaged in this transformation in a more deliberate but also a more selective way. It has produced a very uneven pattern of modernisation in different sectors of social life.

Uneven Modernity

The theme of uneven modernity has been mentioned by several commentators. For instance, Luke Gibbons (1988) has argued that public authorities in the 1960s promoted industrial development (economic modernisation) but showed no commitment to social, political or cultural modernisation. This was reflected in the advertising campaigns of the Industrial Development Authority (IDA) that highlighted the advantages of industrial firms settling in Ireland in terms of its cultural backwardness or quaintness. In a rather similar way, Michèle Dillon (1993) has stressed the fact that, until quite recently, Ireland was endowed with a modern economic and social structure, while traditional values continued to dominate the cultural sphere. A traditional culture coexisted with a modern structure. These comments were formulated in the context of her analysis of the 1986 divorce referendum. In a more recent contribution, she has acknowledged that a process of cultural rationalisation was very much in evidence in the 1995 divorce referendum (Dillon 1998).

O'Mahony and Delanty (1998), too, record the gap which has developed in Ireland, during the twentieth century, between socio-economic modernity and cultural traditionalism. This cultural traditionalism, they contend, is well illustrated by the identification of the Irish nation with a particular culture. A nation so defined finds it difficult to accommodate plural identities, simply because one particular tradition provides the basis for the definition and representation of the nation, while all other 'identities' are marginalised and even rejected. The growing cultural differentiation of Ireland makes such a unilateral identification less and less tolerable, and cultural pluralism can no longer be ignored. O'Mahony and Delanty argue that Ireland should respond to this growing cultural differentiation by redefining the Irish nation in terms of citizenship, that is, in terms of rights which protect cultural minorities and organise their coexistence.

Not only was culture lagging behind socio-economic development; culture came to be seen as an obstacle to economic development. A whole literature emerged that sought to identify those factors, mainly of a cultural kind, which hindered modes of behaviour appropriate to industrial development and slowed down a process of modernisation that was, by and large, perceived as inevitable. For instance, Bertram Hutchinson, a professor at the Economic and Social Research Institute in the early 1970s, stressed that some cultural features appeared inimical to economic development (Hutchinson 1969–70). He pointed to the relative disinclination in Ireland to maximise material wealth, which he claimed accounted for the weakness of entrepreneurship at that time. He referred to the rather low importance of work in the life of most people and the emphasis placed on sociability and recreation: this did not facilitate the emergence of the work ethic that is required for industrialisation. He also underlined the fact that a high sense of security, anchored in forms of communal co-operation and strong familial solidarities, sustained established mores and discouraged innovations. In all these respects, the prevalent cultural orientations in Ireland militated against the development of an industrial economy.

A study was also undertaken, at about the same time, which focused on the cultural context of economic development in Gaeltacht (Irish-speaking) areas. The author, Eileen Kane (1977), looked more specially at the cultural factors that seemed to impede the adoption of economic practices favourable to industrial development. She focused, among other things, on the way people experience time. They did not set aside time for an exclusive purpose; time was not specialised, not entirely dedicated to a specific activity. For instance, factory workers in the Gaeltacht areas did not separate their work from other activities on which they embarked. They would take time to visit the local fair or even attend the funeral of neighbours and acquaintances. The industrial requirements of setting time apart for work and, furthermore, of devoting working time to a well-defined and focused purpose, were not easily accepted and adopted by such workers. Men in the Gaeltacht were, and may well still be, engaged in a wide range of employments that included factory work as only one element of their economic pursuits. Diverse activities intermingled and the kind of compartmentalisation which is associated with industrial work was resisted.

Generally speaking, culture is seen as having an impact on the economy in different ways. It constitutes a kind of background that is more or less conducive to the kind of economic practices associated with the development or upholding of the industrial economy. The previous considerations about alleged attitudes of Irish people towards work and recreation clearly fall into this category, as does the porosity of time in rural Ireland in the recent past. Culture also contributes to the economy in a more direct way, by shaping personality and a particular motivational structure that would be reproduced through a process of socialisation. In this context one should take into account the values which are upheld and according to which social honour is allocated. It was widely contended, for instance, that status and deference were granted to clergy and professionals, rather than to entrepreneurs and managers; that making money was not perceived as a valuable activity in itself. The system of honour which operated in Ireland up till the 1970s did not encourage the kind of activity which is required to sustain economic development.

The State between Economy and Culture

Daniel Bell (1979) has contended that advanced societies are differentiated in various sectors of social life, each marked by a distinctive logic. He asserted that the economic, cultural and political spheres are animated by different 'axial principles', and that each pushes society in a different direction. Economic modernity points to systematic wealth creation, with 'economising' constituting its axial principle. Cultural modernity is organised around the development and gratification of the self, while political modernity is identified by representation and participation. The idea that different sectors of social life are animated by different principles can be usefully applied to the Irish situation. The existence of different sectors in Irish society, each characterised by its own dynamic, has been long recognised (Peillon 1982). The main idea of this analysis, which related mainly to Ireland in the 1970s, was that each sector of social life shelters its own configuration of social forces, and the latter generate distinctive dynamics within each sector. A contrast was established between the economic sector and what was called the 'ideological' or 'cultural' sector.

Activity in the socio-economic domain was dominated by a project of economic development in which several forces were involved. This project of capitalist development was endorsed by the representative organisations of the capitalist class, which include both indigenous and international firms. The working class itself, through trade unions, defined its interest in terms of increased employment, and conceded that only successful capitalist growth could realistically deliver that. But they were at the same time qualifying this project by promoting a reformed and benign form of capitalism. The farmers themselves, at least in their dominant organisations, had accepted the project of agricultural commercialisation which was strongly encouraged by the European Community, while a labour-intensive agriculture was by and large marginalised. A complex and conflictual coalition of forces had crystallised around such a socio-economic project and was pushing Ireland in its direction.

The cultural sector was governed by a rather different coalition of forces. The Catholic Church had been allowed to occupy a central position in shaping the ideas and beliefs of Irish people, mainly because it exercised very tight control over schools. A kind of compromise had historically been struck between state and church, in which the Catholic Church occupied a strategic position within the cultural and social spheres. But its influence was in a sense circumscribed, for it carried little weight in the socio-economic sector. The nationalist and Gaelic-revival movement also enjoyed a high profile in this sector. The nationalist movement and the Catholic Church together set most of the cultural agenda.

All this meant that cultural orientations in Ireland did not harmonise with the requirements of industrial development that was pursued by the major economic forces. For instance, education was still dominated by 'humanist' as opposed to technological interests. Dominant values did not favour or encourage entrepreneurship; status was granted to traditional professions rather than to managers. The socio-economic dynamic and the cultural dynamic were pushing Irish society in different directions; they did not coexist harmoniously, but in a state of tension and even contradiction.

The state is endowed with the task of ensuring the continuity and relative coherence of the society over which it has authority. It endeavours to manage the tensions, contradictions and disharmonies that manifest themselves within society, although it does so according to its own agenda and orientations. In this analysis, it was contended that the state apparatus monitored these contradictory dynamics mainly through political fragmentation and a compartmentalisation of diverse kinds of political activity. For instance, the state participates in party politics, which revolved around cultural/ideological orientations. On the other hand, most of the governmental activity was concerned with the promotion of the main socio-economic project, which commanded wide support among the main social forces. However, the state was able to shape this project with a certain amount of autonomy, by playing on the conflicts of interests and tensions within such a wide coalition of forces. By placing itself at the centre of different kinds of political activity or levels (local politics, party politics, governmental politics), each one linked with a particular sector of activity, the state retained its closeness to both the socio-economic and cultural sectors. Although contradictory in their main thrust, these two dynamics did not relate to each other in a direct way – their contradiction remained latent, implicit. It was up to the state to manage the different levels of political activity in a way that ensured their coexistence, and this demanded hard political work. The state had become the linchpin of the whole social edifice. The contradiction between these two dynamics, although not sublimated, was diffused: through the state, they were able to coexist.

The Cultural Basis of Social Criticism

Many thinkers have, in an insight loosely derived from the German philosopher Hegel, pointed to the 'negative dimension' within social life: features and practices contradict established institutions, undermine social order and make it change. It represents the critique of society, not in words but in practice. This practical critique is at work in the recesses of social life, in the shadowy world where the institutionalised order relegates that which does not easily fit. Sometimes, this hidden dimension finds an institutional basis. Some thinkers of the Frankfurt School have pointed to art as a shelter where ideas and practices that undermine the established order and elicit alternatives are generated. They have looked toward a differentiated culture, uncoupled from the socio-economic order and capable of sustaining a critical distance. In Ireland, the cultural field has indeed provided the main basis for a critique of Irish society.

Principles that claim validity and uphold ideal standards carry not only the promise of a better world, but also its moral necessity. Societies fall far short of such standards, and we have to live our daily life with this failure. The strength of the ideal acts as a permanent critique of reality. No embodied situation can quite come up to the standards and expectations set by general rules and principles. Culture also conjures what we should aspire to; it evokes the prospect of a full development of our abilities. Potentiality underlines the fact that 'being' has not been fully realised. It marks the fact that the life people live does not come up to the life they should realistically hope to live. It is to the disenchanted recognition of the historical closure of pos-sibilities that Adorno's complaint that 'what would be different has not begun as yet' is addressed (Adorno 1973: 145). A society that fails to actualise the capacities and abilities of individuals, that does not realise their potentialities, such a society sustains the need for, and the desire for, a different order of things. Who but the creator of culture will give voice or shape to the protest of the repressed, the leanings for otherness which haunt our imagination, to the wants and desires which stir in the midst of positivity? In all these ways, culture feeds the critique of the established social order.

The forces that, in the course of modern Irish history, have worked to limit the horizon of Irish people, the mechanisms through which cultural closure has taken place, are easily identified. One of the most effective ways of reducing the range of possibilities consists in narrowing the cultural horizon of a group: asserting the power of norms over behaviour, leaving little space for quest and experiments, hindering contact with otherness, imposing a fixed concept of self. But we need not exaggerate the effectiveness of this cultural contain-ment. Every day the established ways come face-to-face with refusal and protest. Images of a different way of living are put forward, new experiences and new sensibilities are generated. However deeply buried, what has been rubbed out of existence somehow surfaces again. It does so in ambiguous ways, and rarely as clearly articulated alternatives or explicit blueprints, rarely as culture.

The drive for economic development has in Ireland not responded to any strong ideological orientation, at least not explicitly; it has formed a pragmatic response to a particular situation. This does not mean that such development remained indifferent to the cultural environment. But culture and economy were highly differentiated and they related to each other indirectly, that is in a mediated way and from the outside. This differentiation of economy and culture has, for a very long time, allowed the Catholic Church to occupy a central position within the cultural field while exercising little influence over the socio-economic development of Ireland. The Church's condemnation of creeping materialism functioned as a critique of the way Ireland had been moving towards a fully-fledged capitalist economy. But such denunciations, underpinned by a preference for a society of small-scale property, were largely wasted and the Church was in no position to shape the emerging socio-economic structure in Ireland. Although powerfully anchored in the cultural sphere, its critique of the emerging Irish socio-economic order held little sway. The dominant position of the Catholic Church in the cultural field enabled it to formulate a conservative but strong critique of the kind of society Ireland was becoming. But such a critique, which originated in the cultural sphere, proved itself ineffective, largely because culture had been to a great extent uncoupled from the economy.

A more progressive critical discourse about Ireland has originated in literature, both from writers and critics. Literary journals have contributed in a significant way to the critical discourse on Irish society, and the list of such journals is not confined to *The Bell* (McCormack 1986). Even contemporary engagements with Irish society often come from academics who not only analyse literary texts in their social contexts but treat them as the basis for engaging in a critical discourse about society. Declan Kiberd's *Inventing Ireland* (1995) provides a particularly striking example of such an exercise.

The critical engagement of writers attracted, not that long ago, the wrath of official censors (Carson 1990). Censorship was exercised against such writers not because they expressed criticisms about the established social order in Ireland, but mainly because they were challenging in a rather direct way the dominant position of the Catholic Church within the cultural field. Censorship was part of the struggle over the production and reproduction of culture in Ireland, and was conducted on behalf of a group of people who, as we have noted, eagerly formulated their own critique of the socio-economic order. This critique lost its effectiveness outside the cultural domain. For this reason, the negativity within Irish society did not originate in the cultural field. Cultural critique, either from those in dominant positions within this field or from those who challenged this domination, had little effect on the wider world. In the context of a differentiation between economy and culture, culture both formed the basis of an exemplary critique and proved utterly impotent.

The Implosion of Economy and Culture

The collapsing of culture and society, and particularly of culture and the economy, represents a recurrent theme in the recent social theory literature. The blurring of the boundaries between these two spheres of social life is referred to as de-differentiation or, sometimes, implosion. It signifies the shattering of internal boundaries, and this phenomenon is closely linked with the development of a post-industrial economy and the emergence of a consumer society. Furthermore, it is also contended that culture is moving to the core of social life: that, more than ever before, society revolves around crucial cultural features. We need to ponder on what these two statements mean before we investigate such an idea in the Irish context.

De-differentiation points to the process through which existing boundaries are broken down and areas of social life which were external to each other and clearly separated become closely connected and overlapping. The implosion of economy, culture and society is usually related to the extension of the dynamic of capitalism to culture. The view has long been held that capitalism maintains its growth only to the extent that it absorbs new places or new spheres of activity. It continues to penetrate the most remote areas of the world while intensifying its impact in those places where it is well implanted. Previously recalcitrant spheres of activity are now ingested by the logic of capitalist accumulation. Pockets of cultural production, which had so far been protected or sheltered from the capitalist process, are now assimilated. Cultural practices and production are increasingly com-modified.

The mechanisms through which the economy absorbs cultural activity differ from the mechanisms through which culture occupies a central position in social life. The latter are rooted in the transition which capitalism has effectuated from industrial to post-industrial production. The post-industrial economy relies more and more on cultural products, in the form of information, expert knowledge but also artistic creativity. Culture is also crucially implicated in con-sumption which, more than ever before, sustains the logic of capitalist development.

With the emergence of the new economy, the connection between economy and culture has been radically altered. Notwithstanding its failure to industrialise, the Irish economy is moving in the post-industrial direction, one in which culture is transformed into a strategic means of production. Two main consequences are generated by the implosion of economy and culture in Ireland. Public life and state activity are significantly transformed, while culture no longer provides a basis for the critique of society.

Culture as Factor of Production

In the late 1950s, Ireland adopted an economic policy that endeavoured to attract firms from abroad, promote exports and engage in a process of industrialisation. This policy succeeded in generating significant growth, but was itself followed by a long period of depression. Another dramatic reversal of economic fortunes occured in the 1990s.

Daniel Bell is credited with heralding the coming of the post-industrial economy, that is, the end of the industrial era during which the transformation of nature through technology and intensive labour practices led to a phenomenal creation of wealth. He predicted that wealth creation would, in the emerging economic conditions, depend more and more on the production of services. The shift from the predominance of the industrial sector to that of the service sector would be accompanied, he reckoned, by a significant growth of a labour force commanding high levels of education and expert knowledge. The emerging post-industrial economy would display three basic features: a predominance of services; a highly educated labour force; a reliance on the handling of information associated with a high level of 'theoretical' and scientific knowledge. Is Bell's portrayal of the post-industrial economy recorded in contemporary Ireland?

The characterisation of the Irish economy as post-industrial appears misleading in formal terms, simply because Ireland has never been industrial. It nonetheless points to the shaping of a very specific economic profile. The service sector has experienced quite a regular growth, both in absolute and relative numbers, all through the 1980s and more dramatically so in the 1990s. More crucially, it is contended that the performance of the new economic tasks demands a high level of knowledge and expertise. While the new firms setting up in Ireland mainly required an unskilled labour force, the scene has considerably changed in the very recent past. The financial sector, electronic and computer firms, welfare services, all are based on a highly educated labour force. They participate in what Bell calls the 'knowledge class', to which he assigned so much importance.

The economic sectors most closely associated with an industrial economy (manufacturing, building, transportation) employ a relatively low proportion of third-level graduates. By contrast, those sectors most closely associated with the post-industrial economy (finance, public administration, various services) comprise a number of third-level educated employees which exceeds, and sometimes significantly so, the average for the Irish labour force. But this conclusion needs to be qualified. For instance, the sector of personal services, which is generally included in the post-industrial economy, contains a relatively low number of people with such qualifications.

Finally, the post-industrial economy is said to rely on both 'theoretical' and scientific knowledge. A brief look at occupations of a scientific nature suggests a very significant increase, but from a narrow base. In 1986, 82,230 people possessed a 'scientific or technological qualification', and the figure moved up to 157,940 people in 1996, an increase of 92.07 per cent. This indicates quite a considerable growth (Central Statistics Office 1996: Vol. 8, Table 18A). More revealing perhaps is the relative size of the research and development sector in Ireland. Research and development expenditure remained relatively low in Ireland, compared to most advanced economies. Publicly funded research and development represented only 0.91 per cent of GDP in 1990, well below the level recorded in economically advanced economies (Quinlan 1995: Table 1.2). Nevertheless, the contribution of the business sector has steadily increased; it stood at a low 0.32 per cent of GDP in 1982, rose to 0.82 per cent in 1993 and reached 1.11 per cent in 1997. The ranking of Ireland has considerably improved in this respect.

Colin Crouch (1999) has differentiated between several economic sectors that are usually included under the general heading of the service sector. He points to four different types of economic activity, beside agriculture and industry:

- the tertiary sector (Sector III) contains all distributive activities, meaning transport and the sale of physical goods;
- the quaternary sector (Sector IV) covers mainly business services: the financial sectors of banking, insurance, accountancy, as well as legal, engineering and design services;
- the quinary sector (Sector V) comprises social and community services. It really corresponds to the welfare sector, to which is added public administration;
- the sextenary sector (Sector VI) refers mainly to personal services. These services nowadays take the form of restaurants and hotels, as well as the provision of leisure, recreation, culture, artistic and sports performance.

Theories of post-industrial society focus on Sectors IV, V and VI that are meant to undergo significant growth. Do we observe such a trend in Ireland? The transformation of the labour force since 1986, and particularly of the occupational structure which is registered through the Census of Population, provides some elements of an answer (Table 3.1).

Table 3.1 Numbers of people employed in selected occupational groups 1991–96

	1991	1996	% growth 1991–96
Sales occupations	144,139	156,259	8.40
Communication, transport	80,307	89,229	11.10
Business and commerce	26,814	39,407	46.96
Computer, software	13,958	19,598	40.40
Health	58,483	68,076	16.40
Education	54,419	61,709	13.39
Social workers	5,095	7,081	38.97
Personal services	85,911	126,592	47.35

Source: Central Statistics Office, *Census of Population, 1996* vol. 7, Table 8.

The Irish economy seems to conform perfectly to the expected trend. Table 3.2 displays the information for a more selective definition of the relevant occupational sectors.

Table 3.2 Redefined occupational sectors

	1986	1991	1986–91 % increase	1991	1996	1991–96 % increase
SECTOR IV						
Financial	52,075	58,730	12.77	48,481	62,761	29.45
Computer	7,807	13,059	67.27	13,958	19,598	40.40
Others	2,456	2,797		4,960	6,736	35.80
SECTOR V						
Welfare	110,996	125,740	13.2	125,001	161,797	29.43
SECTOR VI						
Tourism,						
Restaurants	45,000	52,954	7.67	63,146	81,253	28.67
Leisure, Art	8,722	12,550	43.88	10,253	14,996	46.25
Total IV, V, VI	227,056	265,830	17.07	265,684	347,141	30.60

Sources: Central Statistics Office, *Census of Population, 1991* vol. 6, Table 3; *Census of Population, 1996* vol. 7, Table 8.

The three sectors which are expected to enlarge significantly in the transition to a post-industrial economy have indeed sustained a quite phenomenal growth, particularly in the period after 1991, well above the general growth of the labour force itself between 1991 and 1996, at slightly above 10 per cent. The leisure and art sector has nearly doubled its size in these ten years. Overall, those occupations that appear crucial in the transition to a post-industrial economy have increased from 227,056 people in 1986 to 347,141 in 1996. Taken together, they have expanded by close to 50 per cent during this time. Admittedly they constitute a relatively small sector within the labour force, but they nonetheless represented 22.63 per cent of the labour force in 1996 (as opposed to 17.07 per cent in 1986). The trend is clearly marked.

Culture as a Means of Consumption

Culture is implicated in the post-industrial economy not only as a means of production but, more essentially, as a means of consumption. This happens in two main ways. Firstly, cultural products assume the form of a commodity; they are produced from the start as commodities. This process has long dominated the production of books, films, music, newspapers. The capitalisation of culture, although not new, has now intensified. Very few aspects of cultural production escape the commodity form. Information and images are nowadays treated as premium commodities, as are opinions and memories. Even critical discourses have acquired a market value. Only a few pockets of cultural production have managed to remain outside the process of capitalist accumulation and are animated by different dynamics.

Not only does the economy produce more and more cultural commodities, but all kinds of commodities are invested with a cultural content. They are consumed because they function as markers of chosen lifestyles and supports for individual and collective identities. Commodities no longer satisfy needs, but are consumed as images and signs. They belong to a logic of signification, through which cultural differences are marked and claims to social and cultural superiority put forward. The market of honour, through which distinction is claimed and status established, operates increasingly through the consumption of commodities. When this happens, culture is transformed into a means of consumption, it is fully integrated in the dynamic of capitalism and it acts as its driving force.

The Political Construction of Culture as Economy

The state in Ireland has a long history of playing an entrepreneurial role and of animating economic growth. In the absence of an indigenous entrepreneurial class and faced with the inability of the small property class to respond to the emphatic failure of the Irish economy in the 1950s, the initiative came from the state apparatus itself. It instituted semi-state bodies to perform a range of economic functions. More crucially, it actively sought to attract foreign firms that, it anticipated, would spawn indigenous entrepreneurship. It also endeavoured to shape a more favourable environment for industrial development. Education, for instance, was made more responsive to the needs of an industrial economy. In so doing, and as we have already noted, the state was managing the tension between economy and culture.

In the new economy of Ireland, the state remains as proactive as ever. It sees its role as ensuring the best opportunities for Irish business on the world market, and in a sense has become the public face of Irish enterprise, that is enterprise that operates in or from Ireland. At home, it no longer monitors the external relations between economy and culture, but now promotes their implosion. In its effort to create distinctive and thriving economic sectors, it nurtures enterprise. This kind of nurturing has been investigated in relation to the software industry. Séan Ó Riain has stressed the importance of a new relationship between state, which now displays a great deal of flexibility, and various groups in Irish society: small groups of software specialists, some university departments, key individuals in the public sector, industrial associations. He asserts that state agencies 'used the grant-aid mechanism and the relationships developed with firms to build up firms' capabilities – to make "winners"' (Ó Riain 2000b: 242). The successful indigenous software industry has its roots in networks of individuals and institutions; it is embedded in social and cultural practices and can hardly be dissociated from them. The state seems to have been instrumental in ensuring the crystallisation of social practices and cultural orientations into successful economic development.

Culture has become an object of economic government. This political shaping of culture into an ingredient of the economy has also been emphasised by Patricia Carr (1998). She has analysed some mechanisms by which a particular type of individual, of entrepreneur, is moulded through the monitoring of grants to small business. The public authorities are engaged in the production of a 'culture of enterprise'. They exercise their power by advising, monitoring, nurturing: what she refers to as 'shepherding'. The state aims to produce a particular type of individual who should show the appro-priate qualities of a successful entrepreneur in the new economy of Ireland. Applicants for such grants are closely scrutinised to assess personal features such as self-reliance, initiative, dynamism, and so on. She suggests that the state is employing a 'cultural technology', that it is transforming culture into a series of means (of technologies) for economic purposes.

The new economy of Ireland involves two different implosions. The first relates to economy and culture, and we have established that state activity contributes to it. The second implosion dissolves the boundaries between the state and the business class. The demarcation of state apparatus and representative organisations of private interests has already been seriously blurred with the strengthening of what is conventionally called 'neo-corporatism'. This refers to a kind of partnership in which private groups participate in a direct way in public decision-making. Representatives of the state agencies and those of major interest groups sit together and negotiate an encompassing policy which provides the main parameters for setting wages, social welfare, taxation and a wide-ranging set of policy orientations. But the nurturing by the state of Irish enterprise also brings them into close contact. This co-operation turns into collusion when the national interest is defined practically exclusively in terms of promoting Irish firms on the world markets. The state acts in this context as the standard-bearer abroad of national enterprise and sees its tasks as nurturing an indigenous enterprise at home. Most of the activity of the state is meant to be instrumental in the realisation of the project of capitalist development. This double implosion has removed many of the safeguards that, in the past, regulated the alliance between state and enterprise. This kind of collusive collaboration is bound to become prevalent because it is required by the logic of a post-industrial capitalist development at a time when most of the counter-forces have weakened.

Conclusion: The End of Culture as Critique

The implosion of economy and culture eliminates the critical distance between these two spheres of activity. It follows that a critique of the socio-economic order, which in Ireland was largely rooted in the cultural sphere, is losing its institutional basis. Most aspects of cultural activity and production are now so integrated into the post-industrial economy, either as a means of production or as a means of consumption, that the very possibility of a critical stance is suppressed or, more simply, not entertained or even imagined. How, for instance, can artists who design commodities, film-makers who produce video promotions, writers who manipulate the meaning of words for the purpose of advertising, how can the artistic practice of such individuals sustain any kind of critique? The possibility of 'negative practices', that is of practices which undermine or even subvert the established order, are now only upheld in some residual corners of the cultural field.

All this means that the new mode of articulation of culture leaves little room for 'resistance'. On the reverse side, the immediate implication of culture into economy, and vice versa, enhances the effectiveness and potency of a sustained critique, simply because the economy needs a culture which props it up and hardly tolerates a culture which does not play according to its rules. We have seen that the differentiation of culture and economy made it very easy for the cultural sphere to formulate critical discourses. But the same distance considerably reduced the effectiveness of such critiques. The new relationship between economy and culture renders the formulation of a critical discourse far more difficult but, by the same token, makes its impact on the economy potentially far more threatening.

So where in Ireland has the power of negation found refuge? Most collective protests raise material issues that are easily accommodated. Apparently radical social movements have already been institutionalised. Alternative lifestyles and marginal groups in Ireland do not seem to provide the basis for a serious challenge to the established order. Having lost most of its institutional basis in the cultural field, hardly upheld by the collective action of groups, the negative has buried itself deep into the fabric of Irish society.

Protest and resistance are often based on commitment: they derive from adhesion to values enshrined in religion, ethics, ideals. They critically assess the existing society on the basis of general principles. But negation also assumes another form and displays opposite features: subdued, uncommitted and not very systematic. It manifests itself in the form of a sceptical and possibly cynical distance from established reality. It constitutes a refusal to be fully embraced by society, an attempt at 'winning space' for oneself. It does not appeal to values and principles, but to an individualised sense of welfare and, possibly, a pleasure-seeking orientation that introduce a wedge between the individual and society.

Ireland, like all modern societies, needs to mobilise individuals and groups. We may tentatively assert that, in Ireland, the failure to mobilise comes predominantly from the desire to keep a critical distance from society, rather than from commitment to counter-values. This is all the more so in that critical discourses are easily commodified. Even then, the negative potential of these practices is rarely realised. An individualised pleasure orientation is soon transformed into a consumerist hedonism, while withdrawal often leads to isolation within an extravagant and inconsequential world. Negation always risks being negated in the positivity of the world.

4 Speed Limits: Ireland, Globalisation and the War against Time

Michael Cronin

What parallel courses did Bloom and Stephen follow returning? Starting united both at normal walking pace from Beresford place they followed in the order named Lower and Middle Gardiner streets and Mountjoy Square, west: then, at reduced pace, each bearing left, Gardiner's place by an inadvertence as far as the farther corner of Temple street, north: then at reduced pace with interruptions of halt, bearing right, Temple street, north, as far as Hardwicke place.

James Joyce, *Ulysses* (1977: 586)

The appearance of these leisurely, happy-go-lucky people sitting in the middle of the main street of the busiest quarter of the city banishes the tension otherwise inseparable from metropolitan thoroughfares. It is not merely that pedestrians sit or lounge about: the curious fact is that no one appears to walk fast on O'Connell Street. Dublin seems to retain all its eighteenth-century calm and to get along without any of the fuss and bustle characteristic of modern capitals.

Chiang Yee, *The Silent Traveller in Dublin* (1953: 15–16)

In Dublin, there's still an accident on Ratoath Road, near Cappagh. A second has now taken place on the North Quays, at Sarsfield Quay. Overhead wires are hanging down at Beechwood in Ranelagh with delays in the area. More wires are hanging low at Binn's Bridge going outwards and there's a minor accident on Thomas Street but it's not much of a problem. Now with his view of what's happening, it's over to Bob in the AA Sky Patrol. 'So far, it's pretty much business as usual in Dublin. Firhouse very heavy but the real hot spots so far is [sic] the Lucan Road which is extremely heavy inbound. It's also heavy approaching the Newcastle intersection, that's coming in from the west. I'll have more details later from the AA Sky Patrol.' Traffic is also heavy this morning at Newlands Cross on the Naas Road and coming through Clontarf Road into Fairview as well.

Trevor Keegan, RTÉ Radio 1 (23 March 1999)

Joyce is commonly thought of as the mnemonic custodian of Dublin, the architect of the word who would allow the city to be reconstructed sentence by sentence, street by street. He gives place a voice. Chiang Yee's Dubliners, on the other hand, are secure not so much in a sense of place as a sense of pace. They progress in a leisurely fashion through the main thoroughfare of the city, observed by the Silent Traveller in an O'Connell Street with no traffic lights. The city viewed from the Automobile Association's helicopter 50 years later has been emptied of its happy-go-lucky *flâneurs*. Now, there are only vehicles and the obstacles to their progress. Place becomes spectacularly a function of pace and the acceleration of movement means that toponyms are increasingly abstract nodes in the circulatory system of the city.

The French philosopher Paul Virilio has argued that modernity has largely been an affair of the shift from geo-politics to chrono-politics (Virilio 1977). What we wish to explore in this chapter are the consequences of the *chrono-politicisation* of Ireland, the effects of the new time-zones that are shaping Irish culture and society. The iconography of progress in boomtime Ireland has been repeatedly presented in terms of a neo-Futurist celebration of speed (as the advertisement for one Irish telecommunications firm puts it, 'Stand Still and You're History'), yet there has been little in the way of a critique of a chrono-politics which leads to reductive readings of the Irish past and divisive practices in the Irish present.

From Geo-politics to Chrono-politics

Not only Dublin but Ireland as a place has been profoundly affected by the revolution in speed that has seen time take precedence over place in the modern world.[1] Political conquest and military submission for centuries was as much a question of geo-strategic interest as material advantage. From the Spanish in Kinsale (1601) to the French in Killala (1798), Britain felt that geography had done her no favours by placing an island of uncertain political loyalties to her west. It is surely appropriate that *Ulysses* begins on the top of a Martello Tower, a landmark of colonial geo-strategic nervousness, defining Ireland's place in the British military scheme of things, the back door, the exposed flank that must be guarded at all costs. The Treaty negotiations leading to Irish independence in 1922 assuage fears with the cession to Britain of certain ports and, when these ports are handed over to the Irish in 1938, it is in exchange for extensive covert co-operation between the Irish and British armies prior to and during the Second World War. As it turned out, the division of Ireland meant that the Allied forces had bases in the North of Ireland, even if invasion plans were drawn up in case the South were to fall into the wrong hands. When John Major declared in the Downing Street declaration in 1994 that Britain no longer had any strategic interest in Ireland, he was in effect declaring that geography was politically no longer destiny. The Tudor Ghost had been banished from the Feast of Reconciliation.

However, physical location did not only determine the political fortunes of Ireland, it also had far-reaching economic consequences. Physical proximity to a large market meant an over-concentration of activity in that particular market and overreliance on low-value-added exports of agricultural produce. In the 1950s agricultural and food products comprised three-quarters of Irish exports, and almost 90 per cent of Irish exports went to the UK market (Industrial Policy Review Group 1992: 29). In the absence of a large domestic market for goods, Irish export-led manufacturing was seen to be hampered by geographical distance from potential foreign markets. Hence, 'peripherality' would become a key element in Irish applications for EU funding from 1973 onwards. Ireland's position on the edge of Europe was the commanding principle of economic disadvantage and EU structural funds were seen as compensation for distance. Ironically, it is this funding that will contribute to the undermining of the (financial) advantage of (geographical) disadvantage. A significant share of both European and central exchequer funding in the 1980s went towards the digitalisation of the trunk transmission network. A latecomer to technological modernity, Ireland was able to exploit the latest version of telecommunications technology to create the basis of a reticular or network-based economy. In other words, the combination of informatic and telecommunication networks would allow the reticular economy to overcome the obstacle of insularity and peripherality (see Cronin 1993: 16–18). A translator, for example, living at the base of Mount Errigal in County Donegal, using a fax machine or e-mail, could send a translation as quickly to a client in Friedrichstrasse in Berlin as a translator physically located in the same street in the German capital.

Ireland has in fact become the world centre for the translation of computer materials, and over 4000 of the 12,000 people involved in the Irish software industry work in this area. Ireland is the second largest exporter of software in the world after the United States and 60 per cent of PC-based software used in Europe originates in Ireland.[2] The establishment of the International Financial Services Centre, the strong growth in call centres, telesales, telemarketing and other allied services are all predicated on a network-based or reticular model of economic development. The reticular model relies on telecommunications and informatics networks to provide the necessary infrastructure for business growth. The explicit commitment of Irish policy-makers to such development was evident in the establishment by the Minister of Public Enterprise of an Advisory Committee on Telecommunications in June 1998 to advise the Minister on a strategy to position Ireland as a key global centre in advanced telecommunications, the Internet and electronic commerce. The Report of the Advisory Committee in November of the same year sees not absolute, physical, location but relative, technological, location as all-important:

> Electronic commerce will migrate towards those countries which are to the fore in providing low cost, high quality telecommunications and Internet services, supportive legal and business regimes, and a highly entrepreneurial and technically skilled workforce. Given that neither physical size nor location primarily dictate success, Ireland can, with appropriate strategic positioning, sustain its position as Europe's premier knowledge economy.[3]

The Irish economy is thus emerging as a prime example of reflexive accumulation in late modernity where cognitive reflexivity is at a premium in order to sustain the supply of knowledge-intensive goods and services.[4] Peripherality is no longer geographically but chronologically defined. It is defined by the speed with which information-rich (financial products, on-line support, telemarketing of producer and consumer services) and design-rich (popular music, web design, advertising) goods and services can be delivered to potential consumers. The comparative advantage of (small) nations is to take the waiting out of wanting.

In the educational arena, Ireland can only remain in the vanguard of the dromocratic or the speed revolution if the universities become, in Peter Sloterdijk's words, 'prep schools for mobilisation and ... cognitive subcontractors for the "attack of the present on the rest of time"' (Sloterdijk 1998: 51). Hence the general move in Irish universities towards modularisation under the general aegis of the European Credit Transfer System (ECTS). Interchangeable modules with similar numbers of credits mean students may move rapidly from one course, one institution, one country to the next with the minimum resistance from state-specific structures. In the knowledge-intensive economy it is not only bytes and signs that move, people also are mobilised by the nomadic imperatives of the post-Fordist order. Whether prompted by myth or misery, from Brendan to the Liverpool Emigrant, the Irish have a long tradition of travel. However, the mid-1980s saw the start of a dramatic acceleration in the nomadisation of the Irish. Between 1986 and 1994, growth in the number of air passengers on the Dublin–London route was twice that of any other European route from the UK (Barrett 1997: 40). The Dublin–London route is now the busiest in Europe. In 1999, the number of Irish visitors going abroad was 3,576,000 compared with 2,547,000 for 1996, an increase of almost one million in a relatively short three-year period.[5] The island had also become a site of intense nomadic activity with the total number of overseas tourists increasing by 121 per cent between 1986 and 1995. In the period from 1994 to 1999, the total number of overseas visits had, in fact, almost doubled from 3,681,000 to 6,068,000. Movement has most definitely been in the air.

Revolting Farmers

If the Irish pub has become a globalised product, appearing from Tallinn to Tokyo, the tipplers themselves appeared to have followed in their wake, moving backwards and forwards between Ireland and elsewhere. The *peregrinatio* and the Diaspora have variously emerged as metaphors for the nomadic dynamic of Irish globalisation. The Irish pub may have gone global but 'locals' still exist, countless thousands of them who find themselves marginalised by the liberatory euphoria of the technocratic Right and a narrowly modernist Left. Zygmunt Bauman observed in his recent work *Globalization: The Human Consequences* that:

> What appears as globalization for some means localization for others; signalling a new freedom for some, upon many others it descends as uninvited and cruel fate. Mobility climbs to the rank of the uppermost among the coveted values – and the freedom to move, perpetually a scarce and unequally distributed commodity, fast becomes the main stratifying factor of our late-modern or postmodern times. (1998: 2)

The stratification at work in contemporary Irish society is everywhere, but two events in the late 1990s made evident this deeper trend and the particular fallout of the chrono-politicisation of Irish society. The first was a demonstration by 40,000 Irish farmers on the streets of Dublin in October 1998. The second was the publication of a report by Siobhán Airey entitled *Challenging Voices: Pathways to Change*, a study of the effects of poverty and marginalisation on people living in counties Clare, Galway, Mayo, Sligo, Leitrim, Roscommon, Longford and Westmeath (Airey 1999). In 1960, 390,000 people were engaged in agriculture and they accounted for 37 per cent of the workforce. In 1997, the number was down to 134,000 and they accounted for 10 per cent of the workforce. EU and government aid to the farming community has been generous but almost 80 per cent of the subsidies go to the richest 20 per cent, a trend that is set to continue with EU policies favouring large holdings (see Collins 1998). Jim Phelan, Head of the Department of Agribusiness at University College Dublin, found in a study that 70,000 farmers have an income from the land of less than £156 a week. Of these, 37,000 have no other source of support and would in all probability have to join the 3000 farmers leaving the land each year (MacConnell 1998). The collapse of the Russian market, the BSE scare, a fodder problem brought on by a poor summer and the collapse of sheep prices led in October 1998 to the biggest farmers' demonstration in Dublin since the 1960s.

When the Irish Farmers' Association staged a three-week protest outside Government Buildings in 1966 they were brought tea and sandwiches by many Dubliners. Thirty-two years later the *Irish Times*, under the headline '50,000 jobs could be lost within five years – IFA head', had the following underlined sub-head, 'Demonstration disrupts city traffic for six hours'. An inset on the same page was entitled '"All-Ireland day" gives airing to woes overriding traffic chaos'. The Labour Party MEP for Dublin, Bernie Malone, had said earlier in the week of the demonstration that farmers had no business upsetting Dublin commuters and that they should confine their protest to a rally in the Phoenix Park. A rally in a public park would have conveniently immobilised the demonstrators, who only became threatening or objectionable when they themselves embraced mobility and marched to the parliament building which happens to be situated not in the green enclosure of a municipal garden but in the centre of the capital city.

The hostility of politicians and media commentators on the Irish Right and Left to the farmers' demonstration on the grounds of the potential commuter chaos is an emblematic moment in Irish *tachocracy* – the general, headlong embrace of a world of accelerated space-time compression. It is a commonplace of scientific observation that when two objects travelling at different speeds touch, they produce friction. The friction in this instance is of two kinds, *specific friction* and *general friction*. The specific friction is the selective slowness of marching farmers which obstructs the fast track of the commuter. Illicit nomadism (demonstration) is unfavourably contrasted with licit nomadism (commuting). In a similar way, one of Ireland's longest-suffering minorities, the Travelling community, is constantly urged to abandon its nomadic way of living at the same time and often by the same elite groups who are more and more mobile in their own professional and leisure pursuits. The visual translation of this paradox are the numerous encampments of Travellers on the sides of main roads in Ireland, competing forms of illegitimate and legitimate nomadism occupying the same space of circulation. The general friction is the ideological gear-change in Ireland where the pure speed of the knowledge-intensive economy clashes with the different pace and rhythm of groups in the society that cannot delocalise and remain bound to place. Development theorist Susan George, speaks of fast castes, groups of individuals whose power is predicated on their ability to move themselves or their wealth around the world as quickly as possible. She notes:

> Farmers are, of course, the slowest and least prestigious everywhere. They are rooted in a particular place and work with the seasons which are by definition slow. Watching grass or any other plant grow is a metaphor for utter boredom. It makes no difference that none of us could live without the patience and nurturing capacity of the peasantry. (1998: 115)

In the shift from geo-politics to chrono-politics, there is room for a nation that is racy but not of the soil. The peasant must be desacralised, derided as a parasite and a reactionary, a grim relic from the Ireland that ate its farrow. The West is now the rural nightmare from which the young urban modernist seeks to awake. If Charles Haughey during the fiftieth anniversary of the Easter Rising celebrations in 1966 asks rhetorically, 'What finer end could there be for a boy who aspires to become a man according to Pearse's ideal than to follow the calling of the land?', Fintan O'Toole in 1987 in his pamphlet *The Southern Question* denounces 'the great guarantors of Irishness: land, nationality and religion' and makes a ringing call for a 'real and potentially subversive division of urban and rural' (1987: 25).

The call has been answered and the division is there, but it consolidates rather than subverts the position of the politically and financially powerful fast castes in Irish society. The latter are as impatient as the liberal media intellectuals to push forward to a dream of pure mobility, unfettered by the archaic attachments of time and place.

Fixed Margins and Immigration Controls

The French writer Hervé Jaouen in his travel account *Journal d'Irlande* speaks of Irish roads with their endless twists and turns. For Jaouen, this is a non-Cartesian utopia where the classical straight line is banished and the shortest distance between two points is immaterial because, 'dans ce pays, nul n'est pressé' (Jaouen 1990: 68). The tar squiggles on empty West of Ireland landscapes are studies in deceleration. To enter these landscapes is to change time-zone. Ireland means going far (backwards chronologically) without going far (forwards spatially). So what of the inhabitants of the different time-zone? The Western Province of the religious order the Sisters of Mercy at the end of the 1990s commissioned a report on poverty and marginalisation in the West of Ireland, *Challenging Voices*, authored by Siobhán Airey. The specific groups identified as suffering from marginalisation were Travellers, gays and lesbians, people with disabilities and asylum-seekers and refugees. In considering poverty, the report examined the impact of long-term poverty on women and families. A recurrent theme throughout the report is the issue of mobility. Airey notes in the introduction to her report:

> Transport is critical to gaining access to services, and the region is characterised by poorly serviced country roads and an irregular and inadequate public transport service. For the elderly, and for those without a family car, access to essential services may be difficult or prohibitively expensive. The absence of adequate public transport contributes to the exclusion of people in poverty in rural areas. They have few options around transport. Either they pay for it, or they don't travel at all, or they must depend upon the generosity of others. For many of the elderly in rural areas, entitlement to free transport means little. A useable transport service does not exist. (1999: 7–8)

If one-third of the Irish population is at risk of poverty (with 9–15 per cent experiencing persistent poverty), two-thirds of the poor live in rural rather than urban areas. Of those living at or below the poverty line (60 per cent of average income), the position of households headed by women has disimproved continuously during the years of Ireland's speed revolution. In Airey's study, women living in poverty in rural areas experienced persistent difficulties with access to public and private transport. Where private transport was available, women often had great difficulty gaining access to it when they needed it and in the case of public transport, when it actually went to where they wanted to go, it often proved prohibitively expensive and took up 'a considerable amount of time and management to access the service necessary' (ibid.: 132). Distance is less an external, objective given in any society than a social product. As Bauman notes, 'its length varies depending on the speed with which it may be overcome (and, in a monetary economy, on the cost involved in the attainment of that speed)' (1998: 13).

Tourists can now get to the West of Ireland quicker than ever before and the construction of each bypass on the Dublin–Galway road means urban elites can reach their holiday homes in a shorter and shorter period of time. For those living in poverty, however, the distances are still as great as ever. The tourists come and go but the poor remain. The locals, in Seamus Deane's memorable phrase, stay quaint and stay put. The dromocratic deficit in Irish society is articulated at two levels. Firstly, if geography in yuppie parlance is history for the Irish nomadic elite, past and present history for the disadvantaged is still largely a matter of geography. Long, winding, pot-holed roads serving scattered communities are decorative detail on postcards but they do not make for economies of scale for a transport system. The revenue imperative thus curtails services and further isolates the already isolated for whom the shape of the landscape can be cruelly confining. The second level relates not only to access to services and opportunities but also to mental well-being and positive self-image. Coping with permanent indebtedness is extremely stressful, but it is precisely those groups who are continually trying to juggle with money that have no possibility of going on a day trip or a holiday to allow them to relax or switch off for a while. In addition, in consumer societies where mobility has become a supreme virtue, the immobile are the losers. In the absence of properly funded childcare facilities, many women who stay at home to rear their children find themselves doubly penalised. Not only are they often not able to get out of the home to participate in leisure activities but they frequently suffer from a poor self-image linked to their real and perceived lack of mobility. This point was expressed by one of the key persons in Airey's study:

> Women who are not in paid employment are oppressed by the lack of appreciation for their work in the home and family. Society has more regard for people who are 'out of work' – there is some status for work outside the home – none for work in the home. (1999: 126)

Stasis is stigma. Those who are grounded by poverty, disability or prejudice are keenly aware of an isolation that is both social and geographical. They are the Irish locals who can watch the Irish globals riverdancing from Paris to Paraguay but who find themselves trapped in the slow lane of neglect and indifference.

A second feature of the current situation is that while the mobility of one group is celebrated as the outward sign of competitive excellence, the mobility of another fuels fear, paranoia and suspicion. In 1996 the Refugee Act was made law. The purpose was to regulate the procedures by which applications by asylum-seekers who wished to remain in Ireland were processed. The Act provides a statutory basis for deciding on asylum applications and it also provides an appeal machinery, through the appointment of a Refugee Applications Commissioner and the establishment of an independent Appeal Board. When the Fianna Fáil/PD coalition came to power in 1997 they refused to implement most of the provisions of the Act (see Amnesty International 2000). In the first nine months of 1998, 49 deportation orders were signed by the Minister for Justice (compared to 8 in 1997 and 7 in 1996). In 1999, 230 orders were signed and the refusal rate for asylum status was running at 90 per cent. When an

amended version of the Refugee Act 1996 was finally imple
on 17 November 2000, 11,437 persons who had sought prote
the Irish state were still awaiting a decision from the Depart
Justice, Equality and Law Reform on their asylum claim.[6] The
number of asylum-seekers in Ireland as a percentage of the total
population is very small (less than 1 per cent) but the popular press
and national media engaged in a sustained campaign of scare-
mongering that vilified asylum-seekers as dangerous spongers.
Asylum-seekers are on the move, it was argued, so they must be on the
make. As Irish citizens find it easier and easier to travel abroad
through the easing of border controls in Europe and the waiving of
visa restrictions in more and more countries, Ireland itself for non-
nationals proves more and more impenetrable. A further irony of the
asylum application procedure is that the first effect of the system is to
immobilise asylum-seekers. They are not allowed to work. They
cannot study. They cannot travel until a decision has been made on
their fate and they have to live in certain areas. The threat of unsanc-
tioned mobility must be contained at all costs. Again, illicit nomadism
is the bogey of a society that sees movement and speed as precious
constituent elements of the symbolic capital of the new service class.

A Step Forward?

Mary Robinson on her election to the presidency in 1990 asked the
people of Ireland to come dance with her. The call to step forth was
triumphantly answered in Riverdance, a seven-minute Eurovision
intermission that has become a global phenomenon. By the end of
1998 more than 62 million people had seen one of the 2000 plus
shows in over 60 venues. The Riverdance roadshow with three per-
manently touring troupes covering Europe, North America and the
Rest of the World became the world's biggest grossing entertainment
event in 1997 (Mulqueen 1998). For Irish media pundits, Riverdance
was the incontrovertible proof of Ireland's enrolment in the chorus
line of modernity. Fintan O'Toole in 'Unsuitables from a Distance:
The Politics of Riverdance', an essay in his collection *The Ex-Isle of
Erin: Images of Global Ireland*, sees Riverdance as a kind of
post(modern) answer to De Valera's Dancing at the Crossroads. The
stalwart lads and comely maidens in the Riverdance roadshow were
the reality of an Ireland we had only dreamed of: 'What made it
[Riverdance] more than an international business product was the
way it liberated locked-up elements of Irish tradition, the way it
became, quite self-consciously, a parable of the modernisation of Irish
culture' (1997: 153). The parable of modernisation is a hymn to
speed. Michael Flatley, we were told, was the fastest step dancer in the

world. Moya Doherty, in the memo which details her original con-
ceptualisation of the project, describes the mechanics of acceleration:

> From a point of darkness ... enter row upon row of hard-shoe Irish
> dancers as they pound their way downstage towards audience and
> camera. They stream apart to the dramatic entrance of the star
> dancers who perform their energetic routine. Gradually the tempo
> increases, bringing all the ingredients together in an exhilarating
> climax. (quoted in Smyth 1996: 24)

The tempo does increase and Barbara O'Connor notes that '[o]ne of
the most striking characteristics of Riverdance is the fast pace of the
dance which generates a sense of excitement and energy, and points
to the virtuosity and skill of individual performances', but she adds
'the dancing is at a much faster pace than in either local or national
competitive performance situations' (O'Connor 1998: 58). The slow
lane of ornate variations in stepping technique and style is abandoned
for fast-track footwork that maximises rhythmic sound. The
permanent troupes that are named after rivers – the Lagan, Lee and
Liffey – flow unimpeded through global space. Pat Faulkner, Chief
Executive of Tyrone Productions, which has overall control of the
Riverdance organisation, speaks of the giddy pursuit of global profit:

> We are dealing in Australian dollars, New Zealand dollars,
> Canadian dollars, deutschmarks, kroner ... It is just huge. Every
> two weeks we are moving those three shows from venue to venue
> and country to country. (quoted in Mulqueen 1998)

It was therefore highly appropriate that it was one of the Riverdance
dance troupes that performed at the opening of the European Central
Bank in Frankfurt in 1998. The Bank whose explicit aim is to remove
any remaining obstacles to the flow of capital through the European
Union and which has resisted pressures to publicly fund social legislation in member states of the European Union could readily identify
with the profitable velocity of one of Ireland's foremost cultural
industries. Ireland holds almost no senior posts in the European
Central Bank, an organisation that will have a significant influence
over the lives of many ordinary Irish people, but for global cultural
products locality is a design concept not a political constraint.

Frictionless circulation may be the utopia of Mach 3 financial
capital, but on the roads and streets of Irish cities it is a car dealer's
myth. The unprecedented levels of traffic congestion in Irish cities
threaten the fastest-growing economy in Europe almost as if place has
perversely ambushed time. Jim Bourke, manager of the Enterprise
Policy and Planning division of the state industrial agency Forfás,

claimed at a conference on transport planning in 1998 that road congestion was a very serious concern from an Irish industrial development perspective. Skill shortages were exacerbated by potential employees factoring in traffic difficulties when making a decision on job offers (O'Sullivan 1998). Soaring house prices have driven first-time buyers out of cities to distant suburbs with longer and longer commuting times. The young service workers in the knowledge-intensive economy thus spend more and more time immobilised on the irreducibly physical feeder roads to the Information SuperHighway. AA Roadwatch quoted at the outset is the spoken chronicle of this new Pilgrim's Regress.

The chrono-politicisation of Ireland thus engenders its own spatial contradictions, its own categories of exclusion and its own redefinition of mobilising myths in Ireland. There is a further aspect to recent changes in Ireland which is that revolutions famously begin with a repudiation of the past and make loud claims for the future. Dromocratic revolutions are no exception. Milan Kundera once remarked that when people try to remember something, their step falters. They slow down on the street, brow furrowed, trying to tease out information from the grumbling archivist of memory. Conversely, when all hell breaks loose in the home, the man/woman races to the front door, jumps into the coupé (s/he miraculously always finds the keys) and accelerates down the freeway, away from remembrance (Kundera 1996: 34). The faster you go, the quicker you forget. It is in this context of a risk of generalised amnesia that Brian Fallon has argued for a re-evaluation of the cultural and political heritage of the decades following Irish independence in his *An Age of Innocence: Irish Culture 1930–1960* (1998). However, more generally, it is possible to argue for the urgency in cultural debates on contemporary Ireland of what Peter Sloterdijk has called a critique of political kinetics. This is a critique that advances through what Sloterdijk calls 'a pervasive awareness of mobility'. The direction of such a consciousness-raising movement is not, however, 'a forward movement, but a step back, a disconnection that distances us from the process of acceleration' (1998: 49). In other words, the aim of this chapter has been to provide a number of the elements that might feature in a theory of Irish political kinetics, a theory that takes a critical look at the preachers and the consequences of the parables of Irish late modernity. Such a perspective can contribute to a more general strategy of opposition to neo-liberal consensualism which has voided the public sphere in Ireland of dissenting voices. The Welsh psychoanalyst Adam Phillips, in an essay entitled 'Looking at Obstacles', argues that children can find out what an object is only by constructing obstacles to its access or availability. He claims:

The search for obstacles – the need to impose them in their familiar guise of time and space – is part of the endless, baffled inquiry into the nature of the object. I know what something or someone is by finding out what comes between us. (1993: 96)

Remove obstacles and meaninglessness, not insight, ensues. The intuition of romantic fiction is the guarantor of meaning and it is in identifying the obstacles to the onward march of Irish dromocracy that the consequences for Irish democracy become meaningful, consequences that affect Bob on Sky Patrol as much as the silent Travellers on their parallel courses of social and economic exclusion in contemporary Ireland.

Notes

1. The analysis of this shift has been traced in many works. For a recent treatment see Bauman (2000).
2. See Julian Perkin, 'Found in "Translation"', in the *Financial Times* Ireland Survey, 24 June 1996, and Anon., 'Localisation Ireland' in *Localisation Ireland*, Vol. 1, No. 3 (1997: 1).
3. *The Report of the Advisory Committee on Telecommunications*, http://www.irlgov.ie/tec/communications/advsrepo.htm, 3 November 1998, p. 2/22.
4. For a discussion of the issues surrounding cognitive reflexivity in late modernity see Scott Lash and John Urry (1994: 1–11).
5. Central Statistics Office, 'Visits Abroad by Irish Residents', http://www.cso.ie/schools/tourism/tourism.html, page 2 of 3, 6 June 2001.
6. Irish Refugee Council, 'Two years in Limbo – enough is enough!', *Irish Refugee Council News*, 18 January 2001, http://www.irishrefugeecouncil.ie, page 1 of 1.

PART II

PUBLIC SPACES

5 Citizenship and Education: A Crisis of the Republic?

Joseph Dunne

My concern in this chapter arises out of an engagement with education, but it carries me on to address a wider political issue within which the educational one is inevitably framed. The original source of concern is that we may no longer be able to educate for citizenship. The wider issue is a decline in our understanding and practise of citizenship itself that may both reinforce this inability and hide from us the malign consequences it entails. I should first explain, however, why entertaining the thought of such a vicious circle jars with an upbeat story about both education and our wider society that resonates loudly in contemporary Ireland.

In the early decades of the state, the question of citizenship was perhaps assumed to be largely answered by a combination of nationalism and Catholicism. However, the implication of this answer for most schools – that their purpose was to produce good Catholic Irish men and women – no longer carries such force because the wider consensus on which it was based has greatly weakened: we are no longer so sure not only whether it is important but even what it means to be 'Irish' or 'Catholic' (or perhaps even 'men' or 'women', not to speak of 'good'). Since culture no less than nature abhors a vacuum, a manifest crisis for education might have been predicted from the decline of these two hitherto defining, and often closely interlinked, traditions. But this seems to have been averted by another change that has coincided with, and indeed helped to accelerate, that decline: the development since the 1960s of a policy of industrialisation, with concerted economic planning, from which education was to derive a whole new impetus. This development invited schooling into a relationship of apparently virtuous circularity with itself, offering it the new function of promoting the kinds of knowledge and talent that would create a skilled workforce (or more concentrated 'human capital') and rewarding it for the performance of this function by making available to it greatly increased funding, thereby enabling it to cater, at increasing depth, for a widening student population.

The new role of education clearly carries a substantial civic commitment: contributing to national economic prosperity is surely not an unworthy goal and, even if the genealogy of the Celtic Tiger is still a contested issue, no plausible account of our recent economic success can fail to ascribe a very large role to education – the more so when this success is attended by the rhetoric of an 'information society' and a 'knowledge economy'. Moreover, this commitment is enhanced by another recent concern of the education system, distinct from, though not independent of, the economic function – a concern, that is, with *equality*. From ministerial invocations of 'All our Children' in the 1960s to the very substantial profile of 'equity' in the Green and White Papers of the 1990s and the specific provisions for education in areas of disadvantage in recent national partnership agreements, policy has been directed towards improving the retention rates of poorer children in school and addressing the more elusive sociological factors that militate against their scholastic attainment and thus remain as subtle barriers to real 'equality of educational opportunity'. Equality of *educational* opportunity meanwhile has come to be seen as the essential condition of equality *tout court*. For education is now not only the key to national prosperity but also the chief allocator of 'life chances' to individuals – since success in school has become the primary determinant of access to occupational pathways and thereby ultimately to differential levels of income and status. When education is a domain where national interest and individual self-interest can be seen thus to converge, commitment to increasing equality seems to be at the same time a commitment to personal *freedom*. Indeed the interventionism and redistributive effect that it implies might also be claimed as evidence of substantial social *solidarity* – more, for instance, than would be supported by some liberals (with libertarian rather than egalitarian inclinations) who can see no reason why education, beyond provision of certain basic competencies, should not, like other services, be on the market, nor why parents who have the means should not also have the discretion to invest preferentially in their children's education.

Might it not be claimed, then, that schooling testifies to the animation of our society by the three great ideals of the French Revolution – or to our realisation of the best post-war, European form of these ideals in a healthy mix of liberal ('freedom') and social ('solidarity') democracy ('equality')? And should we not be satisfied, then, that we do in fact have a strong notion of citizenship – one shapes, and is at the same time reinforced by, our system of education?

I propose a sceptical answer to these questions. This is partly because of the increasing recourse to private lessons by those who can afford them and because the seamless weave between school life and home and neighbourhood backgrounds in any case makes equality of *educational* opportunity unattainable without other kinds of radical *socio-economic* action. More fundamentally, however, it has to do with inherent limitations in the idea of equality of *opportunity* – even were we to succeed in fully achieving it. For if we a) make schooling the gateway to all life chances (as with the 'points system' we try to do in Ireland with quite ruthless efficiency), b) assume (reasonably, I believe) that 'merit', i.e. 'IQ + effort', is equally distributed across all socio-economic classes, *and* c) effectively neutralise the skewing effects on pupil performance of socio-economic class variables (which we are in fact nowhere near achieving), then the result will be not a more equal society but rather the 'rise of the meritocracy'. Equality of opportunity, in other words, will be a basis on which to build *in*equality of *outcome*. We shall have a kind of equality, but one in which freedom greatly outweighs solidarity.

What kind of freedom is this, and what does it imply about the relationship of individuals to the state and to each other? It is, I suggest, a freedom that is compatible with a purely instrumental attitude to the state and with relations to each other that are based, at bottom, on reciprocal self-interest. The state's role is to provide, on a non-discriminatory basis, a protective and enabling framework through which individuals can pursue purposes and life plans of their own choosing. It can itself be seen as the object of choice – or the outcome of contract – but only while it dispenses services which individuals can recognise as catering to their preferences and imposes no obligations which they cannot similarly recognise as necessary – since, even if restrictive, they have the merit of restraining *others* from interfering with them in the pursuit of their own ends. There is here a priority of the individual over the polity that makes affiliation with the latter extremely thin and provisional. Loyalty to one's polity indeed is hardly distinguishable from the kind of customer 'loyalty' that one might give to a particular store: the kind that quickly runs out when the superior quality of service hitherto delivered is no longer maintained.

The notions of freedom and equality to which the Ireland of the Celtic Tiger is prepared to pay tribute cannot, I suggest, deliver the kind of solidarity required by a healthy conception of citizenship. Not that I want to renounce either equality or freedom. Perhaps it's too much to claim that the versions of these concepts I've just sketched, precisely *because* they exclude solidarity, fail *also* as notions of freedom and of equality. But a defensible political philosophy, I shall argue, must reconcile and integrate all *three* of these basic concepts – as a viable political culture must express and embody them. In the next section of the chapter, then, I search for such a philosophy and culture in a tradition of political thought and practice with an ancient lineage and perhaps some continuing claim on a polity proclaiming itself a Republic. While this tradition can deliver us a strong notion of solidarity, it runs up against difficulties when confronted by the claims for individual freedom developed by liberal modernity; these difficulties I identify and acknowledge in the third section. I go on in the fourth section, however, to identify some deep problems in the project of modernity itself. Ireland is of course now thoroughly caught up in this project and our self-understanding is badly served if its problems are not addressed at the level of philosophical seriousness that they demand.[1] My own effort, here, I confess, is more to take the measure of these problems than to canvass any programmatic solution to them. I do sketch in the fifth section, under the rubric of 'civil society', a perspective which can perhaps help us to find ways of honouring the claims of freedom *and* equality *and* solidarity. But this perspective, even if attractive, will not translate into a realised basis for common citizenship unless very formidable challenges are met. I conclude in the sixth section with a brief indication of these challenges, adverting to the role of the state and also returning to the role of the education system that has served to introduce in this section my critical concern with citizenship.

Patriotism and Civic Virtue: From Nationalism to Republicanism

The stronger notion of solidarity that I have so far introduced only indirectly and negatively, via a critique of prevailing notions of equality and freedom, makes room for *patriotic loyalty*. This differs both from loyalty to family or kin and from the cosmopolitan spirit or sense of universal benevolence that is open to the claims of human beings as such. For 'patriotism' involves a kind of affiliation based neither on primary attachment nor on pure altruism. Rather, patriots understand themselves as shaped by the community or country which is their *patria* – and as claimed by it (not that this claim need in all aspects be exclusive or overriding of other claims but that it is nonetheless real and even in some respects central). But how might sense be made of such a claim?

One way of doing so is in terms of how one understands who one is or, in other words, of what gives one identity. Even if it is a matter of sheer historical contingency that I am an Irishman, that I belong to this particular country and community, I can still acknowledge this fact – unprincipled though it be – as defining in significant respects who I am. What matters to me, what I care about, what brings me joy or sadness, are all bound up with this country and people. My own life story has been shaped through its history, as have the stories of my fellow countrymen and women. Together, then, we have a common stake in this history and it is not an extraneous fact about me, but rather partly constitutive of me, that I-with-these-others form a 'we'. Shared memory, in the form of an understanding of our past and some sense of living continuity with it, is important to us – if only because without it we could not be meaningfully committed to carrying the project of our country into the future. To be sure, since we are an 'imagined community' (Anderson 1991) it is all too likely that large elements of the factitious and the bowdlerised will have entered into our sense of who we are, and so an understanding of the past gives much scope for contests of interpretation and judgement. Our sense of direction for the future is no less exposed to differences and debate, but it is only so long as these debates, however contentious, continue to matter, and to matter precisely to *us*, that patriotism remains possible. It is quite impossible if history has become a debilitating irrelevance or at best an academic preserve, and if debates about 'national' policy are driven on all sides only by self- and group-interest.

'Patriotism' has entered here as part of an attempt to open up the notion of 'citizenship': patriotism is the characteristic quality of the good citizen, what gives meaning to the term 'civic virtue'. Perhaps there will be disquiet, however, that the notion of patriotism that is emerging here is too bound to the doctrine of nationalism (a specifically modern doctrine which emerged in response to the isolation and uprooting of individuals under conditions of early capitalism, developed within the horizon of Romantic thought, and was given political impetus by the French Revolution). The *nation* is a pre-political entity: it is posited, and partly invented, as a social grouping which is in the first instance cultural or ethnic, held together by an amalgam of factors such as shared descent, historical experience and memory, language, custom and belief. The *state*, then, and with it the properly political, arises only on the basis of the nation's prior claim to existence: the state is called into being by the nation and derives legitimacy as the necessary instrument of its self-expression and self-determination. But is this really acceptable as the basis of our politics and in particular of our notion of citizenship? This is a question we can hardly fail to ask not only when we see the excesses to which the cult of 'blood and belonging' can lead in the form of 'ethnic cleansing' in the Balkans but also when we realise that the other black corner on the political map of Europe has been on our own island. And is it not from some of our own greatest writers that we can best learn the sterility of nationalism – so brilliantly lampooned, for instance, by Joyce (in the Cyclops episode of *Ulysses*) in the figure of none other than 'the citizen'?

I believe that a benign form of nationalism can be defended – against both ultra-nationalists and anti-nationalists.[2] But I shall pursue the argument here by appeal to a different discourse, that of classical republicanism. It would be good if this latter term could be rescued from the simple anti-monarchist – if not plain anti-British – reflex to which, in Ireland, it has too often been reduced; and it would be good too if the association could be broken between 'republicanism' and violence ('nationalism' meanwhile being respectably confined to constitutional politics). Republicanism, as I intend it here, has in fact an older ancestry than nationalism, with roots in Aristotle and the Greek *polis*, Cicero and the Roman Republic, in the Italian city-states of the early Renaissance, or later again in a line of political thought running through Machiavelli, Harrington, Rousseau, Madison and Tocqueville.[3]

Already in Aristotle, politics is defined as a realm in which the tribe is being transcended. The clansman, brought into being through blood, is displaced by the citizen who must realise himself through speech and action in a public medium with others. Here the polity (the *polis*) is not an instrument to defend or expand an identity or way of life that is already established pre-politically. Rather, it is precisely through engagement in politics that one achieves identity, not just as an Athenian but as a human being: a point which Aristotle famously makes by saying that 'man is by nature a political animal', and which still echoes in the term 'civic humanism' used to designate the tradition of thought which, in continuity with him, regards citizenship not as an optional status or role but rather as at least partly definitive of our humanity. The proper dignity of a human being resides in a capacity to reason and speak and thereby to direct and give shape to one's life. To deliberate about how to live was inconceivable, however, without others; for to do so was to participate in a reasonableness (*logos*) from which they were not excluded and which, being inextinguishably shared and public, required the give-and-take of open discussion – clarification and amendment through the contributions of plural voices – if matters were to be adequately explored and resolved. Moreover, these matters themselves were overwhelmingly matters of joint concern – they were *politeia* or, later, *res publica* – and to have a share with others in deliberation and decision-making about them was to realise one's dignity simultaneously as a citizen and as a human being. This dignity was essentially related to freedom and the evil to which it was counterposed was that of despotism or tyranny. Freedom, here, however, was not the kind of individual liberty which we moderns tend to define negatively in terms of rights to non-interference by others. Rather, it was freedom to participate in the joint practice of self-rule, which entailed taking one's turn in the active discharge of public offices in the *polis* and also obedience and loyalty to the laws and institutions which were the expression and bulwark of what had already been achieved through this shared participation in citizenship.

A few features of citizenship, in this classical conception, are worth noting. First, it required active engagement on the part of the citizen. It was not a trust that could be devolved onto a cadre of professional politicians – still less of mandarins or bureaucrats – leaving one free to pursue one's private interests. Nor was it reducible to a legal status conferred by a constitution that underwrote the entitlements and immunities attaching to it. Rather, it required active and ongoing commitment on the part of citizens to the pursuit of goods determined through open debate within agreed procedures. The primary good, indeed, resided in the exercise of this very capacity to share in the project of self-rule. Citizenship then was demanding, and to us its most obvious demand lay in the premium it required one to put on the public good even at the expense of one's private interests. A corollary of the curtailment of private ambition was the need for equality between citizens. Equality, however, was not a matter of levelling the playing pitch on which individuals could accumulate differentially (but fairly). It was a matter, rather, of ensuring that citizens had an equal stake and an equal say in determining the decisions that bound them: any appreciable disparity in wealth between them – and therefore extremes either of affluence or of poverty – was undesirable precisely insofar as it might undermine this normative civic equality. Indeed the concept of 'equality' is insufficient on its own to characterise the relation between citizens. Aristotle went so far as to specify the bond between them as one of friendship, a particular form of the latter that he called 'civic friendship'. By this he intended that in a healthy polity citizens will not be mere strangers, nor their relationships to each other ones simply of rivalry or indifference; though in general there cannot of course be intimate knowledge or close emotional ties between them, still, as citizens, they will bear good will towards each other. He can characterise citizens as friends just because the core of friendship for him is reciprocal caring about each other's good and because politics, the arena in which their citizenship is constituted, exists to bring about this good (as well as being in itself, as I have already said, a primary realisation of it).

This good certainly includes material well-being, but the sting for us lies in the fact that it more fully resides in a worthwhile way of life and therefore, unavoidably, in the ethical character of citizens. This ethical dimension is already implicit in the emphasis on citizenship as active exertion rather than assigned status: just to the extent that it is demanding, citizenship requires certain dispositions of mind and character, among which are an ability to deliberate wisely, to moderate one's own desires, and to deal justly with others. Here the educative role of politics comes into focus. For the laws which citizens devise together are not just to deter people from, or to punish them for, vice. They are not there, in other words, just to compensate for a lack of civic virtue; more positively, they are there to cultivate it. In Aristotle's words:

> Any *polis* which is truly so called, and is not merely one in name, must devote itself to the end of encouraging virtue. Otherwise, a political association sinks into a mere alliance ... [and] law becomes a mere covenant or 'a guarantor of men's rights against one another' – instead of being, as it should be, a rule of life such as will make the members of a *polis* good and just. (*Politics*, 3, 9; 1280b, 6–11)

The Classical Ideal in the Passage to Modernity: Liberal Qualms

This classical notion of citizenship is not just a relic from the antique past but an ideal that can still inspire our political imaginations. I have characterised it as republican or civic-humanist, but clearly it also has intimate ties with democracy, both in the latter's ancient roots and in its modern re-emergence in the aftermath of the American and French Revolutions. Still, before one can even broach the question of its contemporary relevance, formidable difficulties have to be acknowledged. The foremost one is its now unconscionable exclusion of all women from citizenship and also of the very large numbers of men who were mere slaves. This drastic disfranchisement on the basis of gender and class was bound up with the strong separations maintained between the public and the private and, correlatively, between the civic-political sphere and the sphere of material production and reproduction. Lofty reserve about matters of wealth was possible only because citizens were ones whose wealth was already secured by the labours of others – who by the very fact of this labour were themselves excluded from citizenship. Freedom was affirmed as self-rule but it also included, as a necessary component, freedom from the meniality of merely productive pursuits and, as a condition of this, pre-political and entirely non-reciprocal rule over all those others who were confined to the domestic sphere – and whose confinement there was the price to be paid for the citizenship of the leisured elite.

Within this perspective, the preoccupation of liberal modernity with *private* rights is altogether understandable; for it was precisely in the private sphere that discrimination and oppression (certainly as we would see it) were entrenched. The liberation that was to come would entail bringing people – in principle all people – over the threshold into the public world, so that their rights could be secured politically through processes in which they themselves could actively participate. But it also involved a reappraisal of the threshold, or a redefinition of the relationship between public and private and especially of the order of priority between them. This involved recoil from some of what had been valorised in public life, especially the heroic ethos derived from the warrior code and dedicated to splendid deeds and the pursuit of immortal glory. It also involved, correlatively, a new prizing of what had been relegated to the private zone. From, say, the Reformation onwards, conjugal marriage and family life appear much more conspicuously as sources of intrinsic satisfaction, and the life of production, business and commerce is invested with new dignity. And both are increasingly seen as sites where a newly valued (and, one might almost say, newly invented) *individuality* can be expressed and asserted (see Taylor 1989).

The inversion of values here clearly lays down the basis for a liberal critique of the ideal of citizenship implicit in the classical notion of politics. From the vantage-point of a newly expanded and newly appreciated privacy, this kind of citizenship is too onerous: as Oscar Wilde said of socialism, it takes too many evenings. But it is also too intrusive, too charged with authoritarian potential. Not only may one not want to participate in endless political debate but, more seriously, one may not want to have to submit to its outcome, especially when it has designs not only on one's behaviour but even on one's character. If total exclusion from public life was the characteristic oppression of the ancient world, perhaps the characteristically modern nightmare is total immersion in it: something that 'the good citizen' has been subjected to from Robespierre to the Red Guards and Pol Pot – and that can all too easily be interpreted from a liberal perspective as only the most extreme realisation of a totalitarian threat already inscribed in the classical ideal. By an ironic self-negation, the best form of politics may now appear as the one that most fully emancipates people from politics – while vindicating of course their newly defined private rights. But what kind of transformation does the notion of citizenship then undergo, and does it survive in a form that bears any continuity at all with the classical ideal?

Citizenship and 'Malaises of Modernity'

The difficulties here bring us back to 'freedom' – or rather to an expanded, and specifically modern, version of this idea that emphasises both a rational capacity to control the natural and social environments and an openness to explore and express our own inner nature (which is found to contain new sources of emotional fulfilment and of moral evaluation). An outlet for the control would be found in productive work; and protection for the openness would be sought in a zone of privacy defined by a new battery of rights. This enlarged notion of freedom (newly charged by cognate notions such as

'autonomy' and 'authenticity')[4] certainly required a reconfiguration of
the classical idea of citizenship – but hardly its abandonment. To the
contrary, the dignity of the modern subject would be undermined if
his or her sense of mastery and active engagement did *not* extend into
the sphere of democratic empowerment. Indeed might it be the case
that freedom cannot survive in the other two spheres (those of work
and of privacy and intimate relationships) if it is not *also* realised in the
political sphere as the practice of self-rule? The crucial modern
challenge, then, would be to find a way of reconciling the three unre-
nounceable roles of the modern subject, as producer or economic
agent, as bearer of rights, and as citizen. So, to understand the
fortunes of citizenship now we need to see how it interacts with and
is conditioned by these other two roles.

Let us consider first its relationship with economic agency and
production. Most workers have little or no say in defining the
purposes or policies of the organisations that employ them; they sell
their labour or skill or time for a price, and work as subordinates
within more or less hierarchical structures. What would be the
analogue or equivalent of citizenship within this sphere, then, i.e.
industrial democracy, is not the operative model. This fact now seems
extraneous in our consideration of citizenship, but it may be instruct-
ive to recall that for the republican tradition in the United States, from
the Revolution through most of the nineteenth century, what might be
called the political economy of citizenship *was* a central concern:
republicans could not be indifferent to the question of what economic
arrangements were most hospitable to self-government. For Thomas
Jefferson, for example, only an agrarian economy was compatible with
the project of self-rule; for only yeoman farmers working their own
land were sufficiently rooted, independent and disciplined to possess
the requisite civic virtue. Although this view very quickly came to
appear quixotic, Jefferson's major premises – that the cultivation of
civic virtue was essential to the political project *and* that the workplace
was a primary site for its acquisition and exercise – continued to
command widespread assent. The constituency of those who, so to
speak, passed the civic test was extended then to include not only
farmers but also independent producers, artisans, craftsmen and
mechanics, who commanded their own tools and workshops, as well
as the disposal of their own product. This position of course was to
prove no more sustainable in the face of the ineluctable development
of large-scale manufacturing under industrial capitalism. Still, a strong
view prevailed – not least within the labour movement itself, right
down to the 1870s – that wage labour could not replace what was
called 'free labour' without disastrous consequences for the commonwealth. To have one's own labour cast as a saleable commodity
was to forfeit independence in a manner that was considered irrec-

oncilable with citizen dignity. Mainstream reform, of course, was to proceed by construing freedom as 'freedom of contract' and – through organised unionisation on the labour side – combating inequalities in bargaining power and then focusing demands on higher wages and improved working conditions. In all this, strict republican principles had already been compromised. But they were to live on in sometimes radical, though nearly always rearguard, campaigns for industrial decentralisation, diffusion of economic power, and various forms of co-operativism in production and distribution. And here it might be added that republican reserve about accumulation and concentration of capital was based not only on its effects on the character of worker-citizens (through the heteronomous nature of the work practices it enforced) but also on its ability to frustrate and even subvert the designs of civic authorities especially at local – but also increasingly at national – level (see Sandel 1998).

This piece of history provides a wider context for policies pursued in the early decades of our own republic and epitomised in a famous but much derided speech by Eamon De Valera in 1943. Recalling it here may seem only to confirm the forlornness to which the republican ideal is now reduced, but retracing abandoned stages of practice and reflection can help to expose assumptions in our present arrangements so that the massiveness of their establishment does not entirely conceal their continuing questionableness. If an aspiration to comprehensive self-rule – which cannot be placed outside the defining terms of the modern identity – was indeed sacrificed to the engine of capitalist expansion, how can this sacrifice be justified relative to this identity itself? The answer must be that it seemed to bring compensations which more than outweighed the losses it entailed. These compensations have required citizens to make a strong demarcation within their economic agency between their roles as producers and as consumers. What has been lost in the sphere of production, then, can be made good in the sphere of consumption. Surrender to the imperatives of growth is the necessary condition of unprecedented levels of consumer affluence that greatly expand the scope for choice and discrimination in one's private life – which is itself more unimpeded and mobile precisely because of the changed nature of one's work. All this can certainly be made congruent with one strand of the characteristically modern definition of freedom – the liberty to build private and intimate spaces within which to fulfil those expressivist needs that arose with the new interiorisation of nature.[5] Still, serious questions surely remain.

One question concerns the relationship between agency or being on the one hand and the modes of having and use which pertain to consumer goods on the other. As commodities become more sophisticated, they become more opaque as well as more disposable (more surpassable by the latest models); and the satisfactions they afford may be liberating but also addictive and even enslaving. Metaphysical issues arise here which tend to be marginalised in political discourse (including political philosophy); for in industrialised countries we are deeply implicated, as individuals, in the consumerist culture and committed, as societies, to the inexorable logic of growth. What is undeniable, though, even within our restricted horizons, is that serious social purpose is not the criterion that governs production. In its early days, to be sure, industrial capitalism could point to the basic material needs it was helping to meet; but the imperatives of profit, competitiveness and endless expansion, by which not only individual firms but whole national economies are now constrained, can no longer claim such unambiguous justification. With the vast bulk of its output designed for those comfortably within the circle of affluence, it is not geared to the needs of those who remain poor. And here a problem arises that bears directly on citizenship. All those poor or otherwise needy people who are invisible to the market must now be catered for by the state, through welfare provision. *Also* the burden on the public sector is greatly increased by the way in which fragmentation and mobility, caused by market mechanisms, undermine alternative sources of caring within families and local communities – as well as by the way in which environmental consequences of growth increase the overhead costs of social living that must be borne by the state. The crisis for citizenship lies not only in the burgeoning of an unwieldy and very costly state bureaucracy. It resides more in the kind of *displacement* that brings this about – and creates an ongoing deficit of responsibility for it. This is most blatantly illustrated by the case of the New Right who aspire to reduce the welfare state – at the same time that their own policies do much to create a need for it. But perhaps we should acknowledge that New Right rhetoric is only a blatant formulation of what is now the default position in our kind of society. Given the nature and the defining power of our roles as producers and consumers we tend to see ourselves as disaffiliated individuals – and *not* to see the link between the hang-loose character of our privacy and the increased overheads and transactional costs to society. So, as our lifestyle increases the burden, it also decreases our willingness to carry it – especially through higher taxes.

We come here to the other component of the modern identity (in addition to economic agency) that we met earlier, the role of rights-bearing subject. There is scope for considerable tension between a strong notion of citizenship and the escalation of 'rights' that tends to occur in contemporary liberal democracies, especially perhaps in the United States (in this, as in so much else, the pace-setter for other societies). Whereas republican citizenship emphasises participation *with* others in political rule, and thus a share in responsibility *for* the polity, rights by contrast are exercised typically *against* the state or other citizens; in Ronald Dworkin's well-known expression, they are what enable one to trump the claims of other players. Such trumping is surely justifiable when basic liberties are thereby protected. When, however, the language of rights is appropriated in pursuit of sectional interests and made into the normal currency of politics, civic bonds are inevitably torn. In single-issue campaigns, all-or-nothing victory is sought through judicial retrieval or constitutional amendment. Even when the constitutional high ground is not at stake, political agency becomes a matter of exerting leverage over the state, which is cast as an external agency on which demands are made rather than an instrument through which common policy is formulated. Deliberation and argumentation between members of the same commonwealth is replaced by bargaining between people who are defined only or primarily in adversarial terms. From a republican perspective, this reduction of civic virtue to competence as a lobbyist or litigant is deeply detrimental to citizenship and to the quality of democratic life. More fundamentally, it faces a crisis even on *its own* terms. For not only can it not support a thriving 'commons'; it is not clear that in the longer run it can even sustain commitment to the basic framework that disaffiliated individuals themselves must rely on to secure their claimed satisfactions. Nor do we lack evidence of this self-defeating character of 'freedom', when private prerogative is unyoked from public concern. Deference to the 'rights' of private motorists, for example, has long conspired with a general inertia on public transport policy; but now private motorists themselves taste the bitter fruits of this paralysis. Or again our freedom to enjoy country hedgerows (and what could be a more quintessentially 'Irish experience' for tourists?) erodes drastically as several hundred miles of them are sacrificed each year to the other freedom to engage in largely unregulated private building.

A Renewal of Civil Society?

The thrust of this chapter, clearly, has been critical. A robust ideal of citizenship has indeed been identified at the core of the republican tradition, but this ideal has been shown both to be fatally compromised in its classical origins and to face very formidable obstacles in contemporary societies shaped by the defining project of modernity. Perhaps no convincing large-scale theory is now on offer about how these obstacles are to be overcome.[6] Still, I shall advert briefly to a perspective in which the genius of republican citizenship is modestly preserved, albeit in a less single-minded form than it once aspired to.

The idea of *civil society* points to a domain of interaction that is neither political in the sense of being coterminous with state action nor private in the sense of being confined to the individual (or even familial) spheres. As a *public* sphere, whose logic is that neither of the state nor of the market, it creates space for free association in which people come together for all kinds of diverse purposes – including the purpose of simply coming together. It is realised in networks of common action, such as credit unions, residents' associations, sporting organisations, youth clubs, trade unions, political parties and churches, as well as in any number of voluntary societies; and it also finds expression in the more informal conviviality supported by parks, playgrounds, town squares, meeting halls, libraries, galleries and other public places. As its name suggests, *civility* is the essential quality which it creates and sustains. This quality gives buoyancy to social life through a kind of trust and civic friendship which cannot be secured by legal entitlement, purchased on the market or enforced by the state.[7]

Civil society is plural and diverse – and thus a bulwark of freedom. This is the case partly because it remains voluntary (no one being conscripted into membership of any of its multiplicity of associations) but also, and more substantially, because it affords scope to people, together, to exercise initiative in the pursuit of common interests and goals. And it is only because the commitment of many people – over several decades or indeed in some cases across generations – has sustained different practices, traditions and communities that other individuals can exercise the thinner freedom of joining or leaving the latter. Moreover, through the openings for participation in diverse enterprises and agencies that it creates, civil society provides the essential complement to representative democracy, the danger of which is that citizens will become 'spectators who vote' – or (as is increasingly the case of the generation of young adults) who do *not* vote. These openings bring people out of a privacy that would leave them isolated, and therefore all the more vulnerable, before state bureaucracy and market automatism. In a modern society, however prized 'autonomy' may be, the forces that affect people's lives are so complex that it is only in concert with others – through channels of communication, organisation and action – that people can hope to get any effective purchase on them. By providing such channels, then, more or less directly, civil society is a kind of proving ground for citizenship and the wider engagement it implies.

The plural aspect of civil society also proves to be a defence of equality – albeit of a more complex kind than the equality of opportunity to whose limitations I have already adverted. Here plurality entails irreducible differentiation. Civil society is constituted by different spheres, each with its own relative autonomy (see Walzer 1984). Foremost of course are the spheres of political power and of organised economic activity; but there are also, for example, the spheres of education, communication through the media, organised sport, health and religion. I speak of the 'relative autonomy' of these spheres because each has its own specific goods, as well as its own specific ways of relating to need, aptitude, competence, interest or faith. It is when these specificities are not respected and advantage in one is translated into and magnified in another that inequalities become intolerable and the civic fabric is threatened – as when those with large business interests come also to control important organs of communication, or when businessmen are favoured by politicians, or politicians become beholden to businessmen. As we should well know, now that tribunals have become a normal feature of our political culture, great damage is done to democracy when the same people come to wield influence in several spheres (corruption and avarice, it may be noted, are the two political vices most consistently targeted in the tradition of republican advocacy). However, the danger lies not only in the fact that the rich may use their wealth to purchase political patronage (irrespective of persuasion), and better health care (irrespective of need), and a better education for their children (irre-spective of need, interest or talent). It lies also in the fact that the goods of other spheres are reduced to economic goods (i.e. com-modities) and their internal logics are reduced to an economic logic (i.e. the 'bottom line'). With respect to education, for example, we have some awareness of the first of these dangers (reflected in measures to offset the effects of parental wealth, or its lack, on the school experiences of children). We seem to have little concern, however, that we are now so heavily exposed to the *second* danger. Integration of the education system into the economy all too easily means its colonisation: the loss of any sense of the intrinsic value or integrity of different subject areas and the triumph of a managerialist ethos which (armed with 'performance indicators', 'unit costs', etc.) reduces accountability to accountancy. This subversion of the proper goods of education can still trade on a rhetoric of freedom for student-consumers, but with the whole system so highly centralised and every content area reduced to a common currency (i.e. 'points'), think how little freedom there is for teachers or schools to experiment with different approaches or for pupils to try a risky subject or indulge a particular interest or passion. The loss of differentiation is not only between education and other spheres but also within education itself.[8]

Civil society is also a focus for solidarity. Given its essential plurality and diversity, however, this solidarity cannot be one of homogeneity or monopoly. This fact implies of course that civil society can be neither theocratic nor ultra-nationalist, but it excludes, no less, the 'liberal' form of orthodoxy that would wash out differences in a reduc-tively secular or putatively 'universalist' bleach. So it is hospitable to the presence, for example, of a strongly Catholic identity (if the latter has not itself become so plural as to make the church into a kind of civil society) or of Irish speakers, enthusiastically promoting the language. If civil society is receptive to such substantive or 'thick' contributions, however, its own essential identity is as an overall ensemble which incorporates many other contributions too, so that all are exposed to and modifiable by each other. If no voice can hope in a civil society to be the only voice, differences may be marked and some conflicts may remain unresolved. Still, the very multiplicity of the sites of possible engagement can bring some hope of mediation. Conflicts are more tolerable when enough overlapping of different groupings ensures that people who are apart or opposed on one front may find common interest or cause on another. A healthy civil society is composed of many densely interwoven strands of association and action; its strength is more like that of a rope than of an iron bar. It is intensely local, though not without regional and national organisation, and it reflects the rich diversity of 'ordinary' life – embracing, for example, the clubs of pigeon-racers, dog-lovers or chess-players as well as amateur-dramatic or local-history societies. It has been realised too in such organisations in Ireland as Muintir na Tíre, the Irish Countrywomen's Association, Macra na Tuaithe (later Foróige, and open to young women as well as young men, in cities well as in the country), the Gaelic Athletic Association, or the co-operative and credit union movements, all of which in their own ways have created and extended existing solidarities, bringing people together across barriers of class or religion. We should, however, also be aware of how the idea of civil society is negated both by deep inequalities between citizens with respect to resources for public participation, and by the power of commercial media to substitute a culture of the spectacle for active civic engagement.

The Role of the State and the Education of Citizens

Here, inevitably, the question arises about the relation of civil society to the state. As an entity that stands apart from the concerted activities of an engaged citizenry, our notion of the 'state' is foreign to ancient republicanism (it does not at all correspond to the Greek *polis*). Because of this very externality, it was natural that in its eighteenth-century origins civil society should see itself as a check on the state – especially through the emerging 'fourth estate', with a proliferation of newspapers and pamphlets giving new meaning to 'public opinion' as an informed and critical tribunal to which the state would now be made answerable. The canonical maxim in this regard was coined by an Irishman, John Curran: 'the condition on which God hath given liberty to man is eternal vigilance'. Now, as in the eighteenth century, however, this 'vigilance' has ambiguous potential. When it is expressed as principled withdrawal from and even hostility to the state, it represents the anti-politics of both early and late economic liberalism. But it can also take the opposite path (which must be that of a reconstructed republicanism) of active, reciprocal engagement with the state. On the one hand, the effectiveness of the state will be seen to depend on the extent to which it latches onto and builds on existing competencies and solidarities (so that the welfare state, for example, will function best as complement to a caring society rather than as attempted compensation for an uncaring one). On the other hand, civil society, for all its vernacular energy and cohesiveness at its best, remains the scene of divisions and conflicts towards which the state, with its command of enormous power and resources, cannot remain neutral.

It is, I think, a positive feature of Irish politics over the past decade that more attention has focused on the contestable interface between the state and civil society and on the fault-lines within civil society itself – especially the growing and many-faceted disparities between the rich and the poor. Crafting institutions and structures that make the exercise of power and decision-making more deliberative and accountable is an essential function of the political imagination, and those who criticise our recent 'partnership' arrangements, on the basis that they circumvent traditional mechanisms of parliamentary democracy, at least have the challenge of showing how the latter can be made a great deal more responsive to the real problems and conflicts of our society.

Whatever the importance of institutions for the mediation of power, I conclude with a core republican intuition that returns me to my own area of immediate concern, education. This is the intuition that structures, procedures and laws will not in themselves give us a healthy polity – nor, for that very reason, reliable conditions for individual flourishing. As sanctioned by the tradition I have been invoking here, power itself is in any case very different from hierarchical control or effective manipulation. Ultimately it resides in the capacity for thought, initiative and concerted action of citizens themselves. For this reason it is fragile, always in danger of being subverted or displaced (see Arendt 1958; Dunne 1997: Chapter 3), but for the same reason, and as the most adequate response to this fragility, it has been thought to require a 'formative project', the active cultivation of those competencies and dispositions characteristic of responsible citizens. The worry that such a project – the incorporation of 'soul-craft' into 'state-craft' – must harbour illiberal intent is perhaps sufficiently allayed by the fact that even some recent liberal writing explicitly advocates it.[9] Our real concern, I believe, should be a rather different one: whether we now have the moral resources, as state or society, to sponsor it. It is of course an *educational* project that is in question, but it would be far too complacent a response simply to consign it to schools as their proper function. The best intentions and abilities of teachers notwithstanding, it defies moral-political gravity to expect schools on their own to counter the deep-lying tendencies of a society – tendencies that bear very heavily on schools themselves. I have already noted the extent to which knowledge is now construed as a commodity, education as a business, students and their parents as customers, and teachers as mere functionaries who must satisfy the demands of their managers and clients. All this is an accurate reflection of what seems to have become the dominant culture in contemporary Ireland; and even our more apparently humane rhetoric in education – such as that of 'independent learning' and 'self-esteem' – comports all too easily with it. As well as autonomy, what students – and all of us – may now most need to learn are the 'virtues of acknowledged dependency' (MacIntyre 1999). Learning them would be an education in truth about ourselves and in justice towards each other. Those of us concerned with such an education in the Ireland of the Celtic Tiger – and that must be all of us concerned about the fate of citizenship too – can be under no illusions about the scale of the challenge that we now face. But perhaps we should not underestimate, either, the residual sources of resistance still widely diffused, even if not always publicly articulate, throughout our wider culture – nor, for all the contrary pressures, the capacity of the young to respond to these sources and indeed to renew them.

Notes

1. It is tempting to suggest that on the back of the Celtic Tiger we have progressed from being almost a pre-modern society to being now almost the paradigm case of a 'post-modern' one. Our achievement then would be to have leap-frogged, as it were, over the stage of modernisation itself and thus to have escaped its besetting problems (those associated for example with the decline of the older heavy industries in countries such as Britain or Belgium). But, quite apart from how we read Ireland's particular trajectory, 'post-modernity' is not, I believe, a rejection of or escape from modernity. Rather, as the socio-cultural correlate of 'late capitalism', it is an intensification of the modern – so that 'hyper-modernity' would be a better term. (Here I refer to post-modern*ity* as a sociological condition; post-modern*ism* as a philosophical style is another matter.)

2. I defend such a nationalism in the particular context of a discussion of European federalism, showing it to be both compatible with the latter and a necessary corrective to some of the tendencies associated with it, in Dunne (2000) and – with more specific attention to the Irish case – in Dunne (1998).

3. Like any substantial political tradition, the republican one is of course internally complex and contested and it is a selective version of it that I shall present here. For an especially influential retrieval of it, see Pocock (1975); and for an illuminating historical account and defence of its contemporary relevance by an Irish political theorist, see Honohan (forthcoming).

4. We owe these concepts to the two main, and in some ways conflicting, strands of modernity: 'autonomy' to the Enlightenment's (and especially Kant's) valorisation of reason and 'authenticity' to Romanticism's (and especially Rousseau's) vindication of feeling.

5. What I refer to here relates to the contemporary quest, greatly intensified in the Ireland of the Celtic Tiger, for self-realisation and self-fulfilment, as well as to the closely linked phenomenon of the 'therapeutic culture'. For incisive analysis, see Taylor (1992).

6. It is this very exhaustion of 'grand theory', or incredulity towards 'grand narratives' (be they of Enlightenment 'Progress', Marxism, socialism – or, melancholy thought, republicanism?) that virtually defines post-modernism as the philosophical style mentioned in an earlier note. It might be claimed of course that the post-cold-war era evidences the knock-out capability of one particular grand theory, that of uninhibited free-market economics. But on my reading it is this would-be post-ideological ideology that is itself a large source of the very *problems* we face.

7. Though it had antecedents in mediaeval social formations, the idea of civil society first crystallised in reaction to eighteenth-century absolutism. It arose with the claim (e.g. *contra* Hobbes) that sovereignty vested in an absolute ruler was not the only source of political authority or of social cohesion. This anti-absolutist impulse, however, was itself to prove only too capable of assuming absolutist forms. For the 'people' whose sovereignty was counter-asserted (most classically in Rousseau's doctrine of the 'general will') would foreshorten to the 'nation' or the 'proletariat' and inspire all the terror and even attempted extermination that defaced the last century. Slowly and painfully learned resistance to all-inclusive designs by *any* kind of state apparatus, then, is internal to the idea of civil society. But this idea *also* entails resistance to another legacy from the eighteenth century, whose absolutist potential we have perhaps been even slower to recognise beneath its original anti-absolutist appearance. When the whole nexus of production and exchange not only expanded to create

new opportunities for wealth – loosened from the old privileges of birth – but came to be seen (in the writings of the Physiocrats and Adam Smith) as having its own laws – that is, as forming an autonomous sphere of eco*nomy* – it could be celebrated as a curb on the ambitions of monarchs and emperors. But if this sphere was linked early on to our idea of civil society, when it itself becomes sovereign – so that no other hand can moderate the invisible hand of the market, and freedom is equated with 'free enterprise' – then the potential of this idea is badly miscarried. So our lesson at the beginning of the twenty-first century is to recognise civil society as the reality which was not only suppressed in the recently collapsed totalitarian regimes of the eastern bloc but is also threatened by neo-liberal policies. (For helpful elucidation of the idea of civil society, see Walzer (1995) and, with particular reference to its historical evolution, Taylor (1997).)

8. For more sustained analysis of what's at issue here, see Dunne (1995); and, for a powerful critique of the newly globalised 'university of excellence', disengaged from any national culture and administered on the basis of 'total quality management', see Readings (1997).

9. For an outstanding example by an Irish philosopher, see Callan (1998).

6 The Global Cure? History, Therapy and the Celtic Tiger

Luke Gibbons

There is no exact line between denying the past and denying the present. At what point does public knowledge of atrocities and suffering become a matter of forgetting, memory, history and commemoration? If we talk about the bloodshed of the Congo, Bangladesh or Biafra as having been 'consigned to memory' or 'belonging to the past', when will these phrases start applying to Chechnya, Angola and Kosovo?

Stanley Cohen, *States of Denial* (2001)

Prosperity has come to the land of Joyce and Yeats, creating a kind of country they could never have imagined: rich and happy.

Newsweek (20 August 2001)

In a recent article by Bernadette Murphy in the *Los Angeles Times*, there is a cautionary tale about the perils of progress in contemporary Ireland. Now that the Celtic Tiger has finally dispelled the lingering gloom cast by the Celtic Twilight, 'Ireland', we are informed, 'is undergoing an identity crisis':

The country known for having raised suffering to an art form is experiencing the unthinkable: good times ... At the same time, the Catholic Church's centuries-long grasp is weakening, freeing many from idiosyncratic Irish guilt, especially regarding sex. (Murphy 2001)

But just in case the Irish might think they never had it so good, there is a sting in the tale in the form of the author's own version of 'idiosyncratic Irish guilt'. For it turns out that there is something to be guilty about after all, and this is the alleged crisis induced in Irish literature by the recent wave of prosperity. 'What's going to happen now', she asks, 'that there is so little to whinge about?' These sentiments (without acknowledgement) were subsequently given the front-cover treatment in an issue of *Newsweek* in August 2001, which asked the leading question: 'Can Ireland Be Happy? If Irish Arts Thrive on Misery, How Are They Doing in Boom Times?' (20 August 2001).

At the most general level, this argument turns on a journalistic version of the romantic agony, the view that writing is essentially about suffering and the tragedy of being human. There is certainly something in this. Asked if he believed in Heaven, John McGahern replied that he didn't know that much about it, except for one thing: there were no writers there. How did he know that, the interviewer asked? 'Because they'd have nothing to complain about', McGahern answered. But if writing is about suffering, then Irish suffering, according to Murphy (and perhaps Frank McCourt), is a class apart. 'Sure, nobody suffers like the Irish', she quotes her father as saying: 'Suffering and Irish writing, he intimates, are hopelessly intertwined.' It is striking that such views are seldom enunciated in recent critical discussions unless by way of deprecation, or as the butt for some ideological target practice – as in Liam Kennedy's mockery of the application of post-colonial paradigms to Irish culture on the grounds that they involve specious claims that the Irish are 'MOPE – the most oppressed people ever'. Or as Fintan O'Toole has put it, somewhat more tactfully:

> In recent years the notion of Ireland as a Third World country has had a certain degree of intellectual currency ... but it is difficult to do this and even more difficult to wallow in post-colonial self-pity, when the ex-colony is wealthier than the old mother country. (O'Toole 1996)[1]

It is not that the 'post-' tag is dispensed with entirely but it is given a new critical valency, shifting the emphasis from a post-colonial to a global, post-national Ireland. If, as Mr Deasy avers in *Ulysses*, it seems history is to blame for our ills, then it is not so much the talking as the global cure that delivers us from our own worst enemy – ourselves.

The issue here is perhaps not one of history at all, but of therapy – the transference of feelgood or therapeutic models from the self-help culture of the United States to the 'abused child' (as Sinead O'Connor described it) of Irish history. In keeping with the original Freudian scenario, moreover, the first step in recovery is to convince the patient that the abuses never happened, but were based on fantasy – in this case, the delusions of nationalist historiography, especially at its 'faith and fatherland' nation-building stage. Revisionism, then, in it first phase, saw itself as introducing 'truth' into these inventions of tradition, though for once the truth is a bearer of good news – it seems history wasn't so bad after all, and all those memories of the dead were greatly exaggerated. With the post-revisionist moment, however – usually associated with Field Day and its fellow travellers – the patient took a turn for the worse again, persisting in attributing to powerful global forces – British colonialism, imperialism, the capitalist world system – discontents that were really of its own making. As if noting with concern the free association of a patient on the couch, Liam Kennedy observes:

> For the Field Day tendency in cultural politics there may be emotional satisfaction, even inspiration, in the exploitation of loose images and metaphors which seem to have some resonance in the context of the continuing agonies of Northern Ireland. (Kennedy 1992–93: 118)

Ironically, the mention of 'loose images' and disconnected metaphors suggests that there may be some basis for the patient's critical condition for, as Marita Sturken notes, 'traumatic memory is often described as "wordless and static" or as a "series of still snapshots", and depicted as an unedited film, without a script, for which ... "the role of therapy is to provide the music and words"' (Sturken 1998: 108).

It is at this point that the need for the global cure becomes manifest, consisting not so much in an abolition of the past but its integration into wider, 'normalising' narratives of the kind found in advanced European or Anglo-American societies. As Heribert Adam describes this process: 'In their eagerness to prevent the gruesome past from haunting the future, well-meaning social engineers seek to create "a common history" between hostile groups. In their most extreme form, they repress past hostilities' (Adam 2000: 95). Hence, for the historian S.J. Connolly, the condition of the Catholic population in Ireland under the Penal Laws lacked any colonial dimension and was no different from that of the peasantry in France under the *ancien regime* (Connolly 1995); for Roy Foster the discrimination against the Irish in Victorian England was indistinguishable from that directed at its own working class (Foster 1993); or again, for Liam Kennedy, the touchstone for the historical treatment of the 'native' Irish is not to be found in affinities with Native Americans, African-Americans or the subaltern classes in Africa or India, but in the civil rivalries of mainland Europe:

> Of the 150 or so officially-designated regions of the European community today, it would be difficult to think of many regions which do not have some experience of colonialism in some sense or other. (Kennedy 1992–93: 115)

Part of Kennedy's rationale for contesting Ireland's colonial (or post-colonial) status is that it 'trivialise[s] the suffering of hundreds of millions of the world's peoples' under 'real' colonialism, but it is difficult to think of a greater trivialisation than that which contends that colonialism was everywhere, and simply par for the course in inter-European conflict. One wonders was Famine also pervasive on a mass scale in the Europe of the 1840s?

Soundtracks for the Soul

If the role of therapy is to provide a soundtrack for the dark night of the soul – 'music and words' for the unedited film of experience – then Roddy Doyle's *The Commitments*, and the endless debates it has engendered, can be said to have set the signature tune for much of Ireland in the 1990s. In the most quoted scene from the film – surely the equivalent for the Celtic Tiger of De Valera's homage to 'comely maidens' speech in the 1940s – Jimmy Rabbitte describes the 'internal colonialism' of Ireland's anomalous relationship to Europe:

> The Irish are the niggers of Europe, lads.
> They nearly gasped; it was so true.
> An' Dubliners are the niggers of Ireland ... An' the northside Dubliners are the niggers o' Dublin. – Say it loud, I'm black an' I'm proud. (Doyle 1988: 9)

Soul music provides the route 'outa' this place, and its affinities with the experience of the black underclass in America furnishes Dublin northsiders with a map to negotiate the economic wastelands of their own city. But what is the precise nature of 'the cure' here, the means whereby the benighted northsiders are delivered from the forces that are oppressing them? For Fintan O'Toole, the solution lies in the global reach of popular culture, enabling the Dublin working class to throw off the oppressive weight of a Catholic rural past – the myths of romantic Ireland – by embracing a new transatlantic freedom:

> These Dublin kids are not romantic Irish exotics. They have grown up with American music. They either know the moves and sounds of Detroit and Philadelphia already or they can learn them. They place themselves, not in relation to the literary landscape of rural Ireland, but in the unbounded domain of popular culture. (O'Toole 1999: 37)[2]

The absence of the Catholic Church, the lack of 'picturesque' local colour and, for Alan Parker, the indifference to the Northern conflict, all add to the universalism of the film, to the likelihood that it could have been set anywhere (the highest form of praise, it would seem, for an Irish film in recent years).

The escape provided by popular culture – whether in the form of Hollywood, Tin Pan Alley, jazz, rock music – from the rigours of 'faith and fatherland' has undoubtedly been a powerful counter-current in Irish culture, and helps to explain why so many of the energies of official censorship were directed primarily at the mass media, and not, as often thought, at 'serious' literature and the work of major writers, both at home and abroad. What I want to question, however, is the assumption that welcoming other cultural influences requires an act of amnesia, or a disavowal of the heterogeneous and often conflicting elements within one's own culture. In Brian Friel's *Dancing at Lughnasa*, for example, radio and the varieties of music it carried in the 1930s offers an emotional release for the restricted inner worlds of the Mundy sisters, an imaginary space in which their bodies achieve a kind of eloquence denied to them in their disillusioned, everyday lives. It is important for the play, however, that this surge of emotion draws not only on the shock of the new but also on dissident, wayward currents within Irish culture itself – in this case, having to do with the banished remnants of a once thriving vernacular culture, and the carnality of the feast of Lughnasa. Friel, moreover, does not confine the outward reach of the local to the metropolitan centre: in the figure of the returned missionary priest, Fr Jack, Ireland's relationship to both modernity and its own subjugated cultures is triangulated through its unresolved relationship with other colonised societies, such as those of Africa. The mediation of music through the radio – both Irish music and Tin Pan Alley – becomes the leitmotif linking the incursions of the First World with the traces of the Third World within, a 'translocal' sense of place that extends to the suburbs of Dublin. While Roddy Doyle's *The Commitments* eschews local colour of the National Geographic variety, the band nonetheless seeks to impress a local stamp of the lyrics of their songs, effecting a true trans-migration of soul. Thus 'What Becomes of the Broken Hearted' carries a line about waiting under Clery's clock:

Wha' was that abou'? Jimmy asked?
A bit o' local flavour, said Deco.
Tha' was deadly, said Derek
Yeh said we were goin' to make the word more Dubliny, said Deco.
(Doyle 1988: 54)

The recourse to American soul music as an appropriate soundtrack for the lives of marginalised Dubliners in *The Commitments* does not simply attest to a new global Ireland, turning its back with carefree abandon on the past: on the contrary, the legitimacy of the claim that the Irish are 'the niggers of Europe', and so on, only makes sense by reconnecting with a colonial legacy in which Ireland was indeed a Third World at the back door of Europe. The jaunty optimism of Alan Parker's movie may emanate from the 1990s, but Doyle's original novel was written against the backdrop of the acute economic depression of the 1980s, in which the meltdown of 'modernisation' – as exemplified by chronic unemployment, 1950s-style emigration, and the crises for both the state and civil society presented by the hunger strikes and the abortion and divorce referenda – was all too apparent. This did not present itself as the new dawn of an period of unprecedented economic growth, but as the twilight of an era of sustained underdevelopment that had blighted successive attempts at modernisation since the founding of the state. The roots of 'Romantic Ireland', then, lie not in the topsoil of the post-independence state (though it certainly nourished them), but in the deeper substratum of a colonial policy that all but converted Ireland into a rural outpost of Great Britain. This was the economy inherited by the new state, and only measures that entailed, in effect, liquidating the kulaks and uprooting the countryside could have succeeded in a policy of enforced industrialisation.

Ghosts of the Recent Past

Notwithstanding the seeming nostalgia for 'Romantic Ireland', it is not as if the legacies of a colonial past are a trip down memory lane, an exotic by-product of the heritage industry. Enough research has been done to date on the psychic or 'social' death experienced by indigenous cultures or native peoples who have lost their land, legal systems and language – not to mention their lives – as a result of the iniquities of colonialism.[3] There are, of course, different modalities here, one of the key features of the Irish situation being the early role assumed by nationalism in arresting, if not entirely reversing, the annexation of a culture – an example followed on a worldwide scale by the wave of decolonisation after the Second World War. But this is more to look at the long-term consequences of conquest and dispossession: my immediate concern here, to return to the original terms of the discussion, is to question the naïve optimism according to which the ghosts of the past, even the recent past, are lifted by the cessation of conflict, or the first upswing in the economy.

As Stanley Cohen remarks, closure here means little more than that the story has moved off the front pages of the newspapers, but it does not follow that it is thereby removed from people's minds: 'The media draw the clearest line: the events disappear from "current" news. Wars end with an official peace; famines are declared to be over' (Cohen 2001: 117). But bringing down a curtain on the past is not as simple as walking out of theatre as soon as the play – or film – is over. Asked why he wanted to make a film about the Vietnam War at the end of the 1970s, Francis Ford Coppola answered that *Apocalypse Now* was not about Vietnam, it was part of it. The body bags might have disappeared from the television screen, and the protests off the streets, but that did not mean that the war was over and done with, and America could now be at peace with itself. In fact, no sooner had the last helicopter left Saigon than the war began to be replayed on the cinema screen in ways that were not possible when it was raging. Only one film was made during the war itself – John Wayne's hapless *The Green Berets* – but the unfolding horrors were broached indirectly, as in renegade westerns such as *Soldier Blue, The Wild Bunch* and *Little Big Man*, all of which dealt with the savagery visited by the white man on Native Americans or Mexicans. The journey into the heart of darkness was still conducted allegorically, however, and at one remove, as if the self-awareness brought about by representation was simply too painful, or too difficult to clarify, while the carnage was going on. Indeed, it may have been the pervasiveness of the western as a deep 'structure of feeling' in American experience, according to which the errand into the wilderness ends with a redemptive triumph over adversity that screened off the full extent of the horror from the popular imagination. Coming to terms, then, with the encroaching disaster involved dismantling these genres, though, of course, as *Star Wars* and *Star Trek* show, there was always the possibility of the western boldly going to new, 'final' frontiers.

It is in this sense, as the expanding literature on trauma, mourning and memory indicates, that the experience of pain and suffering may not coincide with its moment of articulation, often leaving a considerable time-lag before a catastrophe or a shock to the system achieves any kind of symbolic form. The difficulty here is not simply one of vocabulary but precisely that of form: the most readily available genres or narrative structures (for example, the redemptive endings of westerns) may end up doing violence to the experience, sanitising or cauterising it rather than registering the full force of its impact. As a case in point – to cite an American example again – one can cite the early slave narratives of writers such as Frederick Douglass who, though speaking from the harrowing experience of life in the South, nevertheless related their stories along Christian redemptive lines – in the eyes of some, the very narratives that were enslaving them. According to Toni Morrison, it has taken generations for African-Americans to escape from the ignominy of social death, and to regain the cultural confidence to tell their stories in their own vernacular rhythms and styles – which is indeed where jazz, the blues and soul music came into their own. This is not to say that the gap between expression and experience is simply a breathing space, allowing memories to surface in their own good time. The passage of time in between also shapes the telling of a story, and the vantage point from which it is told may determine whether it is opening up, or in fact sealing off, a troubled past.

It is not too difficult to point to Irish equivalents, the most obvious being the contentious debates around the commemoration of the Great Famine, and the related question of its absence from the literature of the period. But silence did not just descend over the Famine – whole fields of experience in nineteenth-century Ireland were effaced from view, unless they lent themselves to melodrama, the Gothic or the Victorian travelogue. It is in this sense that the prose of everyday life had to await the Literary Revival to achieve definition in the writings of Joyce, Synge and others. The twentieth century also had its protracted silences, and if cinema has a special aptitude for engaging with the underlying anxieties or desires of an era – such as Vietnam, or Kennedy's assassination – then much of recent Irish cinema can be seen as attempting to lay the ghosts of the recent, and not so recent, past. Critics keen to celebrate the euphoria of the Celtic Tiger have shown a marked impatience with what they consider the recurrent nostalgia of films set in the 1930s, 1950s or early 1960s, but there is little room for wistfulness or sentiment in the disenchanted worlds of *The Ballroom of Romance* (Pat O'Connor 1982), *The Field* (Jim Sheridan 1990), *Korea* (Cathal Black 1996), *Amongst Women* (RTÉ 1999), *The Butcher Boy* (Neil Jordan 1997), *Angela's Ashes* (Alan Parker 1999) or *This is My Father* (Paul Quinn 1999). What is most notable about these films as popular forms is that, though set in the past, many things they say could only be uttered in the present. This is not to deny that there were artists, writers and political activists who transcended the silence in those decades, or that there were people who thought differently then, even if they could not say it openly. The films in question capture many of these muted voices, but the point is that the cultural spaces from which they are retrieved have as much to do with now as then.

In the *Newsweek* essay that accompanied its cover story 'Can Ireland be Happy?', Carla Power asks: 'Where are today's writers looking for inspiration? So far the answer seems clear: the past':

> The phenomenal success of *Angela's Ashes*, [Frank] McCourt's account of growing up louse-ridden and emaciated in 1940s Limerick, suggests a wealthy culture's fascination with the ghastliness of poverty ... [As the poet Eavan Boland notes:] 'The success of Frank McCourt is about America saying, "This is the peasant hell that we escaped from"' (Power 2001: 44).

The therapeutic assumption here – whether in its original American form, or its 'Celtic Tiger' counterpart – lies in the belief that the telling of a story is sufficient by itself to dispel the ghosts of the past, and this may indeed be the function of the 'rags-to-riches/hell-to-heaven' narrative formulae so beloved of Hollywood. But it by no means follows that all narrative structures provide such consoling fictions. Traumatic memory, as Theodor Adorno emphasised, is not about recovering or indeed banishing previous experiences but rather 'working through' them, and it is this protracted, often painful, process which links the lost voices of the past ineluctably with the present. As he describes it, working through the past, in its 'modish' version, 'does not mean seriously working upon the past ... On the contrary, its intention is to close the books on the past and, if possible, even remove it from memory.' It is no coincidence, he goes on to observe mordantly, that 'the attitude that everything should be forgotten and forgiven, which would be proper to those who suffered injustice, is practised by those party supporters who committed the injustice ... In the house of the hangman one should not speak of the noose' (Adorno 1998: 89).

This theme has surfaced in many recent Irish films, most notably Cathal Black's *Korea* (1996). In Black's film, it is Moran, the comfortable beneficiary of the Civil War, who is most concerned to draw a line over the past, while Doyle, on the losing republican side, is still revisited by traumatic flashbacks from the executions that took place. Yet these flashbacks are not simply throwbacks to the past: they are also prompted by the 'repetition' of the Civil War in the present in that Doyle stands to lose out once more in what is perceived as the civilising process. Though the good times are coming to the rural district in the story – if by that is meant modernisation, rural electrification, the radio – the affluence is not for all as new fishing regulations for tourism deprive Doyle of his livelihood as a fisherman on the lake. Though set in the early 1950s, the fact that modernisation is overlaid by globalisation, in the form of the tremors set off by the distant Korean War in the locality, attests to the film's own moment of production in the emergent 'Tiger' economy of the mid-1990s. Yet there is no sense that global integration is a cure for the memories of the Civil War: rather, in one sequence in the film, images of Luke Moran who dies in the US Army in Korea are intercut with a photograph of John Doyle in his IRA uniform from the Civil War period, as if the killing continues but is now displaced onto an international stage. Though experienced as a personal crisis, the resonances with the wider question of Irish neutrality are unmistakable, for while globalisation is presented as the solution to one kind of (internal) violence, assimilation into the new world order involves participation in the wars and strike forces of the major power blocs, not to mention that other playground of imperial nostalgia, the international arms industry. In Neil Jordan's *The Butcher Boy* (1997), set ten years later than *Korea*, the rural idyll of De Valera's Ireland is truly shattered by the murderous impulses unleashed in small-town Ireland, but it is not at all clear that the newly found prosperity of the 1960s, which has encouraged emigrant families like the Nugents to come home, has the capacity to pick up the pieces. If anything, modernisation even holds out less hope for Francie, the delinquent anti-hero of the story, as the fantasies of American popular culture addle his brain, and the apocalyptic forebodings generated by the Cuban Crisis extend to his own locality as he imagines an atomic explosion blasting open what is left of tranquillity in the Irish countryside.

Korea deals with the traumatic legacy of the Civil War three decades after the event, but the acrimonious controversy which surrounded the release of Neil Jordan's *Michael Collins* in 1996 suggested that, even after 70 years, the war was still not over in Irish popular memory. Jordan himself wrote in his diary of the making of the film that it would not have gone into production had it not been for the IRA ceasefire in 1994, and the ensuing Peace Process (Jordan 1996: 6). By the time the film was released, however, the IRA ceasefire was broken down, and it is difficult not to suspect that as much of the animus directed at the film was motivated by the exigencies of present-day politics as by the historical events themselves. The blurring of the lines between past and present was not helped, moreover, by the inclusion of clearly anachronistic allusions to the contemporary Northern conflict, as in the scene where a car bomb kills an RUC detective squad who arrive in Dublin from Belfast. The most sustained engagement with the Northern conflict took place at the level of form or narrative structure, through the film's complex renegotiation of the gangster genre, and the stereotype of the Godfather. The pervasive influence of such genres, extending beyond the cinema screen to the press and the official criminalisation policies of the British government, shows how much societies can live through an era of upheaval and conflict but still block off an understanding of these events by falling victim to their own myths and propaganda.[4]

With the exception of a few courageous journalists and political activists, one would be hard pressed to find any intimation in the media consensus of the 1970s and 1980s that the Godfathers of one era may be the statesmen of the next, with all the bitter ironies of compromise and betrayal outlined in Jordan's film. The time-lag and political shifts that intervened between the experience and its articulation were not helped either by the rigorous censorship of Section 31 of the Irish Broadcasting Act which sought to further reduce the gangster genre to a silent movie, with inter-titles or voice-dubbing at most to help the uncomprehending. This conspiracy of silence, with different emphases and intensities, ranged across Irish society and instead of drawing a veil over the past, as the *Los Angeles Times* would have it, the public sphere in general has shared with cinema an endless revisiting of the decades following the 1950s. Carla Power, in her *Newsweek* essay cited above, seems closer the mark when she writes, with reference to Joyce's dictum that history is a nightmare from which he was trying to escape, that 'thanks to the boom, Ireland has awoken from its nightmare, and instead of escaping it, the Irish are increasingly willing to explore it' (2001: 45). Whether they have taken the form of revelations of child abuse in orphanages and by the Catholic clergy, scandals within the Catholic Church, high-level corruption in business and in political life, or atrocities in Northern Ireland, these have dominated the headlines in the 1990s and have become the subjects of the numerous legal tribunals presiding over such excavations of the past.

The Owl and the Tiger

In his famous evocation of the end of history, Hegel wrote that the owl of Minerva flies at dusk; wisdom comes after the event, when the distance required for representation has been attained. It is one thing to elicit meaning from the past, however; to expect healing is more than history has to offer. In today's media-saturated world, the gap between an event and its representation has all but disappeared, leaving no gestation period to come to terms with what assails the senses. In one of the more poignant moments during the recent carnival of reaction that attended the execution of Timothy McVeigh, a relative of one of McVeigh's victims expressed dismay that witnessing the execution did not bring the psychological relief and sense of closure that he expected. Justice was not only being done, but seen to be done – but the immediacy of the camera could not compensate for the healing power of time. Perhaps the difficulty here lay in the therapeutic approach to history in the first place, which seeks to effect a premature closure to political crises such as the Oklahoma bombing that admit of no such easy resolutions. Though attributed to the enemy without – Islam, international terrorism – in the initial moral panic, the true horror lay in the fact that McVeigh was the enemy within, re-enacting in real-life the myth of the western hero at the heart of the American dream who operates with lethal force outside the law to save the system from itself.

From a very different perspective, it is difficult not to suspect that the array of state tribunals and public enquiries into the underside of modernity in Ireland is motivated by a similar concern, to pathologise as extrinsic to the system circuits of deceit and power that are in fact part of its inner workings. The necessary fiction here is to present these as aberrations from another era, residues of nationalism and parish-pump politics from the days of bicycle clips, Brylcreem and the Ballroom of Romance. But these local networks are by no means alien to the systemic flows of international finance: they are intrinsic to the growth of the Celtic Tiger, rather than its embarrassing pre-history. Part of the misunderstanding of globalisation here is to construe it as following through the logic of modernisation in its attack on the local, and its annexation of the periphery. But globalisation is not the same as modernisation, and in many ways represents a challenge to First World paradigms of progress and change. While vertical integration into the major concentrations of capital is still the order of the day – the route travelled by the Celtic Tiger – globalisation no longer consists in the undifferentiated hegemony of the centre over the periphery. As Arif Dirlik describes it, the discourse of globalisation

> is rendered plausible by the appearance of new centres of economic and political power, assertions of cultural diversity in the midst of apparent cultural commonality, intensifying motions of people that scramble boundaries, and the emergence of new, global, institutional forms to deal with problems that transcend nations and regions. (Dirlik 2000: 8)

In this configuration, the local is no longer outside but is a point within the system – and, at certain junctures, a stress point that connects new 'Third World' alignments with the memories of one's own 'Third World' past. Thus, while critics denigrate the establishment of historical affinities between Irish society and developing nations, the reality of globalisation is that Ireland is coming into far greater contact with outlying regions of the world economy – and, as immigration shows, with the casualties as well as the beneficiaries of the new world order. The capacity of a society to retrieve the memory of its own unacknowledged others – those who paid the price in different ways for its own rise to prosperity – is a measure of its ability to establish global solidarities with 'the other' without, both at home and abroad.

Cosmopolitanism in a Historical Frame

It is in this sense that a new, historically grounded cosmopolitanism needs to be rescued from the enormous condescension of prosperity. The notion that internationalism or cross-cultural solidarity requires cultural amnesia with regard to one's own past might be contrasted with the humanitarianism of Roger Casement, for whom local and universal attachments were inextricably intertwined. As Angus Mitchel writes, 'whilst his [Casement's] humanitarian work in Africa and South America was seen as the greatest human rights achievement of his age', this universalist ethics was not a product of an abstract or ahistorical conception of human rights but derived from an attachment to the struggle of a resurgent Irish nationalism against the might of the British Empire. Outrage at injustice across the globe did not prevent Casement dying for his own country, stigmatised not only in terms of his nationality but his other 'particularisms': religious persuasion (on account of his eleventh-hour conversion to Catholicism) and sexual orientation (due to the official whispering campaign over his alleged homosexual *Black Diaries*). Instead of jeopardising his fearless humanitarian endeavours in the Belgian Congo and Brazil, Casement looked to his Irishness for the kind of deep sympathetic engagement with suffering that was required to produce what was, in effect, a revolution in the moral sphere: 'In these lonely Congo forests where I found Leopold,' he writes, 'I found also myself, an incorrigible Irishman' (cited in Taussig 1987: 19). As Michael Taussig argues, it was Casement's sensitivity to the colonial condition of his own country that gave him the moral courage to expose the atrocities in the Congo at a time when the imperial ideology of the British Foreign Office had inured them to the terror. As Casement explained in a letter to the historian Alice Stopford Green, a fellow convert to Irish nationalism:

> I knew the Foreign office would not understand the thing, for I realized I was looking at the tragedy with the eyes of another race of people once hunted themselves, whose hearts were based on affection as the root principle of contact with their fellow men, and whose estimate of life was not something to be appraised at its market price. (Taussig 1987: 19)

Instead of narrowing horizons, and closing off sympathies, Casement's re-engagement with the history of oppression in his own country induced a profound sense of human fellowship that enriched his awareness of the sufferings of other peoples. As he described this cross-colonial solidarity: 'the more we love our land and wish to help our people the more keenly we feel we cannot turn a deaf ear to suffering and injustice in any part of the world'. Nor was Casement alone in this. While there was no shortage of Irish people (including nationalist leaders) who identified with empire, or, on the other hand, 'insular Celts' who devoted their energies to Ireland, and Ireland only, many of the Enlightenment currents from the United Irishmen in the late eighteenth century saw Irish freedom as irrevocably committing nationalists to anti-imperialist and progressive causes across the globe.

The great historian of the United Irishmen, R.R. Madden (like Casement, another official in the British colonial service) displayed similar moral courage by campaigning vigorously for the abolition of slavery in the West Indies, as well as for Aboriginal rights in Australia.[5] Later nationalist leaders like Michael Davitt related the defence of Jews against Catholic bigotry to a shared history of persecution: 'Like our own race, they have endured a persecution the records of which will forever remain a reproach to the Christian nations of Europe' (see Keogh 1998). In a similar vein, Davitt, who was the founder of the Land League in Ireland, wrote of the injustices suffered by the dispossessed Aboriginal peoples under British colonialism during his visit to Australia in 1895:

> They are hunted off lands that are still the property of the state and only leased to pastoralists. Thus, with the game they lived upon gone and their hunting grounds fenced in they are forbidden to look for food where once it was found in freedom and abundance. The white man's law justifies him in stealing the black man's country, his wife, and daughters whenever he wants them; but to take a sheep from this moral professor of the ten commandments is to earn the penalty of the bullet. (Reece 1998: 32)

The point of drawing attention to these examples is not to claim that they were representative of Irish people in general or even mainstream Irish nationalism, but rather to contest the common assumption that preoccupation with one's culture and with the past, particularly an oppressive past, militates against international solidarity and an embrace of cultural diversity in a modern social polity.

That this 'rooted cosmopolitanism',[6] deriving from the specificities of one's local or national identity, is not simply a gesture of romantic heroism, or an ideal of solidarity that remains unworkable in practice, is clear from its formative role in Irish foreign policy, particularly during the brief phase of the Cold War in which Ireland, as a non-aligned nation, exerted an influence at the United Nations out of all proportion to its size. This was during a major period of decolonisation in the late 1950s and early 1960s when Western powers, and many of the principles of the Enlightenment which were considered to have legitimised Western expansion, were all but discredited in the eyes of those breaking free from colonial rule. Ireland's pursuit of an independent, activist stance, outside both the Anglo-American and Soviet axes, ensured that it was one of the few Western countries to gain the credibility of the newly emergent nations. To this end, it took the lead among Western opponents of apartheid in South Africa, and was also to the forefront in defending small nations invaded by more powerful neighbours such as Egypt, Hungary, Tibet, Tunisia; in attacking the disastrous recourse to partition in Cyprus, Korea, Vietnam, Germany, West New Guinea, Algeria; and in mediating disputes in Kashmir, Somaliland, South Tyrol and, not least, the Belgian Congo, the site of Casement's first major humanitarian intervention.

The most controversial stand taken by Ireland's foreign policy – at least where American interests were concerned – took place in 1957 when it endorsed an Afro-Asian motion, proposed by India, to lift the embargo on discussing the admittance of China to the UN. This led to a vehement backlash by Cabot Lodge, Foster Dulles and other Cold Warriors at the UN, that extended to approaching the Vatican, and Cardinal Cushing of New York, to twist the arm of the Irish delegation. Had they been more aware of the contingencies of Irish history, they would have realised that Frank Aiken, the Irish Foreign Minister, had been excommunicated by the Catholic Church for IRA activities during the Civil War, and was singularly immune to such blackmail. Moreover, it was precisely such an historical awareness that informed the concept of human rights invoked by Aiken to justify Ireland's stance at the General Assembly. Referring to its 'historical memory' of domination by a foreign power, he explained that this was

> a memory which gives us a sense of brotherhood with the newly emerging peoples of today, a memory which makes it impossible for any representative of Ireland to withhold support for racial, religious, national or economic rights in any part of the world, in South Africa or Tibet, in Algeria or Korea, in [Egypt] or Hungary. We stand unequivocally for the swift and orderly ending of colonial rule and other forms of foreign domination. (cited in Skelly 1997: 22).[7]

Nor was the independent stance of the Irish delegation at the UN blind to the expansionist designs of Soviet and Chinese Communism, particularly as exemplified by the annexation of Tibet. Instead of the Cold War anti-Communist rhetoric that might have been expected, Aiken framed Ireland's response once more in terms of Ireland's colonial past:

> The sympathy of the Irish people with victims of imperialism is nothing new. It goes out to the people of Tibet in their present sufferings as it did in the past. I may recall that in 1904, at the time of the British expedition to Tibet, Michael Davitt, the Irish patriot and social reformer, endeavoured to arouse public opinion in America for the cause of the Tibetan people. Davitt is rightly described in the Soviet Encyclopedia as a 'staunch fighter against colonial oppression'. There can be no doubt that if Davitt were alive today, his voice would be heard in protest against the much more

ruthless and generalized manifestation of imperialism in Tibet. (Aiken 1959: 39)

Aiken added that he was not greatly impressed by Chinese justifications of the invasion of Tibet on the grounds that they were carrying out a civilising mission to a 'savage social system': this was little more than 'the hoary old grounds of nineteenth-century and eighteenth-century imperialism'. Finally, Aiken objected strenuously to implications that the Irish stand on Tibet was not based on Irish neutrality, but was being manipulated by other global powers – as if Irish people needed 'outside suggestions' for the 'feelings which are invariably aroused ... by news of the oppression of a small people' (Aiken 1959: 37–9).

Conclusion

Ireland's independence, at least in relation to American foreign policy, was short-lived, for the opening up of the Irish economy to American multinational investment in 1959, followed by the visit by President Kennedy in 1963, began the erosion of Irish neutrality that has gathered momentum since the end of the Cold War and the advent of the Celtic Tiger in the 1990s. The solidarity extended to decolonising developing nations in the late 1950s, however, demonstrates that, while neutrality in the narrow isolationist sense is indeed an obstacle to global solidarity and to political responsibilities in the wider international arena, this is not necessarily the result of nationalism, at least insofar as it engages with its own subjugated pasts. To reclaim the memory of those who have been forgotten or who have been written out of history in these circumstances is not to indulge in the self-absorption of victim culture but the opposite: to engage in an act of ethical imagination in which one's own uneven development becomes not just a way in, but a way out, a means of empathising with other peoples and societies in similar situations today. Globalisation without this radical memory is indeed a one-way street, cutting off one of the most vital and deeply rooted sources of solidarity with the plight of developing nations and the casualties of the world system. Rather than reverting to the inward gaze of old-fashioned nationalism (itself a caricature of the past), the post-colonial turn in Irish criticism – not least by its questioning of many of the dominant paradigms of post-colonialism itself – represents an attempt to extend the horizons of the local to distant and often very different cultures, beyond the comforting cosmopolitanism of the West.

For many cultural commentators, Ireland's recent economic boom is perceived as bringing Ireland out of an antiquated nationalism inherited from the Cultural Revival and into a new global, cosmo-politan era. As *Newsweek* puts it, recycling this stereotyped view of the past: 'The new found wealth has given Ireland the confidence and the distance to confront its old identity as an isolated, impoverished, superstitious nation.' The dramatic shift from being a country impaired by chronic unemployment and emigration until the 1980s to being a host-culture for immigration in the 1990s is accordingly welcomed as a sign of growing multiculturalism in which Ireland can at last take leave of its troubled past. However, as we have seen, the suffering bound up with historical injustice and sustained cultural loss does not lend itself to overnight cures, and it may well be the process of disavowal, the surface optimism of a culture in self-denial, which poses the greatest problem to a genuine engagement with cultural difference. The ability to look outward, and particularly to identify with the plight of refugees and asylum-seekers, may be best served by reclaiming those lost narratives of the past which generate new soli-darities in the present. In the *Newsweek* cover story, Anne Marie Hourihane is quoted as stating: 'Irish people have no reverence for the past at all, because it was so poor and unhappy. They can't get to the future fast enough.' But if Irish people find it difficult to identify with those parts of their own history that carry the stigma of poverty, there is little likelihood that they will be able to relate to those who come to the Ireland of the Celtic Tiger reminding them of their own unrequited pasts.

Notes

1. It is noticeable that at this late date, the phrase 'Celtic Tiger' had still not gained general prominence. Coined in 1994 by the American investment bankers Morgan Stanley, it passed into popular currency in 1997.

2. Or as he describes the impact of popular culture elsewhere, sex, drugs and rock and roll have come to replace 'the old Irish totems of Land, Nationalism and Catholicism' (see his 'Introduction: On the Frontier' to Bolger (1992: 1)).

3. See Patterson (1982). For a valuable account of the crippling psy-chological consequences of colonialism, see Moane (1996).

4. As in the case of the American western in the 1970s, the advent of the Celtic Tiger allowed the gangster genre to shift locale, receiving a new lease of life in the exploits of 'the General' and other not so amusing figures in the Dublin underworld.

5. Though there is no trace of this in Steven Spielberg's recent film, Madden was the key defence witness in the trial which followed the seizure of the *Amistad* by slaves in 1839, travelling over 1000

miles at his own expense to give crucial, damning evidence about slave conditions in Cuba. See Jones (1987: 99ff.).

6. For the concept of 'rooted cosmopolitanism', see Brennan (2001). In his *Feeling Global: Internationalism in Distress* (1999), Bruce Robbins reworks cosmopolitanism in cultural terms, relating universal principles to affective commitments and allegiances.

7. Skelly also cites Patrick Keatinge: 'An instinctive sympathy for other "small states" – occasionally amounting to a belief that "smallness" (usually undefined) is a guarantee of virtue – can be found in many public policy debates through the history of the state' (Keatinge 1978).

PART III

HISTORICAL LEGACIES

7 Colonialism and the Celtic Tiger: Legacies of History and the Quest for Vision

Geraldine Moane

The Celtic Tiger obviously presents enormous challenges to Irish society. It is a phrase which captures an important moment in history, in which economic, social and cultural structures are undergoing profound transformation. This period of major transformation has naturally and rightfully provoked much discussion of the impact of the change on values, culture and psychological patterns. Much of this discussion has been framed in economic terms, as representing a choice between Boston or Berlin, surely a rather narrow choice to be offered. Indeed, that this is represented as a choice at all is indicative of the paucity of vision at the present moment, all the more surprising as we are placed at the dawning not only of a new century but of a new millennium. The poverty of outlook is in contrast to the richness of competing historical visions over the centuries in Ireland.

Perhaps the narrowness of the Boston or Berlin vision is related to the relatively narrow versions of history which have dominated debates in the past few decades, where a false polarisation has been offered between the Irish as passive victims of colonisation on the one hand and as colluders and agents in the imperial enterprise on the other. Both of these examples of false polarisation with their inevitable simplifications may themselves be seen as legacies of our history, for one of the most enduring themes in writings on colonisation is the creation of false polarities, the division of the world into two opposing categories of 'us' and 'them', of 'good' and 'bad', of 'black' and 'white', of 'rich' and 'poor', referred to by Fanon as a 'Manichean' world view (Fanon 1952).

As we live through a period of significant change, it would appear that we are poised to repeat the patterns of history as we embrace the benefits of economic growth while ignoring the evidence that the pursuit of economic growth at all costs leads to predictable social

..ۡlems of alienation, fragmentation, high levels of drug and alcohol use and increasing levels of violence (Greene and Moane 2000). It is clear from extensive social research both nationally and internationally (Cantillon et al. 2001; United Nations Development Programme 2001; World Health Organisation 2001a, 2001b) that not only are we failing to attain even minimum standards of equality, health and education, but that:

- Ireland rates the highest in the European Union (EU) after Britain in the levels of income inequality;
- Ireland has among the highest rates of alcohol consumption and drug abuse in the EU;
- life expectancy is one of the lowest in the EU, with large inequalities in access to health services;
- levels of literacy in Ireland are among the lowest in the EU.

Many of these problems were present prior to the Celtic Tiger, and indeed some may be seen as legacies of economic underdevelopment. However, it must surely be a cause for alarm that we are showing no improvements in these basic indicators, and that at least in political discourse there is little evidence of major concern about the failures of the Celtic Tiger, and little new thinking about the shape of Irish society into the twenty-first century and beyond.

The perspective from which I wish to discuss these social changes draws on research in colonial and post-colonial psychology, feminist psychology, and the emerging field of liberation psychology (Nandy 1983; Martín-Baró 1994; Wilkinson 1996). What these areas of social psychology (spanning sociology and psychology) have in common is a focus on power differentials, domination, oppression and liberation. They share the assumption that power differentials in society shape psychological patterns, and that the interlinkage of social and psychological patterns plays an essential role in social and cultural change. Given the limitations of space, this chapter will necessarily make more general statements than some of the complexities of these issues (which I have explored in detail elsewhere (Moane 1999)) require, and will confine itself to a discussion of the Republic of Ireland.

In this chapter my focus is on the psychological legacies of history and their role in shaping the transformation which we are now undergoing, with particular reference to how we may better take advantage of this period of transformation to create a better society. If psyche and society are interlinked, however, it follows that an understanding of psychological patterns requires a social analysis, and vice versa. I will therefore begin with preliminary comments on colo-

nialism and systems of domination before proceeding to a discussion
of the historical and psychological legacies of colonialism.

Colonialism and the Celtic Tiger

Elsewhere I have described colonialism as a system of domination
and, along with other writers, have suggested that colonialism is a
well-developed system of domination, with clear mechanisms of
control which maintain the status quo (Moane 1999). The post-
colonial state itself is thus a system of domination in which positions
of power vacated by colonisers are occupied by the native elites. It is
thus predictable that a post-colonial state would perpetuate patterns
of inequality and marginalisation, and it is likely that a post-colonial
state would also be vulnerable to domination by outside forces.
However, it is also the case that a colonised country has developed
patterns of resistance and subversion which mitigate against complete
domination. These patterns of resistance and subversion may be
important sources of innovation and offer a ground for resisting new
hegemonic structures and ideologies such as that of global capitalism.

The changes that Irish society is undergoing in the late twentieth
and early twenty-first centuries involve much more than economic
development; they also include profound transformations in the
power differentials which have characterised the post-colonial state. A
reminder of some of major developments in the last decade of the
twentieth century will illustrate this point. These include:

• the Peace Process which reshaped the political and constitutional relations between the Republic of Ireland, Northern
  Ireland and Britain; the undermining of the power of the
  Catholic Church;
• a shift from mass emigration to immigration; the emergence of
  a multi-ethnic immigrant community;
• official Famine commemorations from 1994 to 1997 which
  involved state, community and individual projects nationally
  and internationally and generated major debates about colonialism;
• major shifts in gender relations, including two women presidents
  and increasing participation of women in political and economic
  spheres;
• the continuing development of European integration marked by
  two major treaties, and, in 2002, a common currency;

- unprecedented success for Irish artists internationally, ranging from literary prizes to superstar status.

These developments involve major shifts in power relations both on the island of Ireland and between Ireland, Britain and Europe. These power relations involve not only pre-existing colonial links between Britain and Ireland but also new configurations of race and ethnicity. They are evolving in the context of increasing globalisation, where world political economic developments are dominated by the interests of global capitalism. This form of global domination is linked to the colonial domination of previous centuries, where domination was maintained through economic and cultural mechanisms, with military force also playing a role.

The Celtic Tiger thus offers an opportunity for a renegotiation of the legacies of history, offering a way out of perpetuating a top-down system of domination and the opportunity for developing a more egalitarian society. In this chapter I will suggest that the pressures to re-enact dominator patterns of history come both from our own historical legacy and from contemporary global forces which combine to push us toward a path in which we recreate the patterns of domination reminiscent of colonial domination. However, such a path is not inevitable, and indeed legacies of history may also provide the very resources needed to create a society characterised by greater equality, vision and social justice. Such a society is surely possible for a small, relatively wealthy country, a society where basic needs would be met, where there would be equality of opportunity, where diversity and creativity would be encouraged, a society which would nourish our potential for compassion, co-operation, generosity, support and solidarity.

The development of a more egalitarian society obviously goes against the pressures created by national and international patterns of domination, and thus requires both commitment and vision. Legacies of colonialism present a challenge here, for one of the most enduring themes in writings on colonialism, domination and oppression, already alluded to, concerns the dualistic or Manichean nature of systems of domination. In such a world view the possible positionings are either dominant or subordinate, oppressor or oppressed, inferior or superior. Fanon (1967) and Memmi (1967), who wrote extensively about psychological aspects of colonisation, both warned of this dualism, arguing that the narrow world view of colonisation meant that culturally and politically this was the only option available to the colonised. Psychologically also, the only models, scripts or discourses available are those of domination or subordination. Psychological legacies of colonialism, I will argue below, also present a challenge to the vigorous pursuit of policies and visions which run counter to prevailing patterns of domination. Before discussing these psychological legacies, I will first consider the historical context in which psychological patterns may have arisen, and describe some insights into how it is that psychological pattern may be maintained across time.

Psychology and the Legacies of History

When viewed through the lenses of post-colonial and feminist psychology, with their focus on power differentials and experiences of oppression, it is clear that Irish history is marked by the repeated occurrence of trauma, dispossession, loss and defeat, whether their causes are seen as colonisation, natural disaster, capitalist expansion or other factors. Important features of Irish historical experience such as major land dispossession and plantation, continuous military occupation of the country from the seventeenth century onwards and the calamitous Famine of the nineteenth century have shaped a history of trauma (Curtis 1994; Ó Gráda 1998). Such a view of history will also highlight a long history of resistance ranging from armed uprising through political mass movements to parliamentary strategies, as well as collusion, betrayal, apathy and self-interest.

This is not to suggest that everyone was totally oppressed or suffered oppression in the same way. There was considerable variation in the positionings available in Irish society, ranging from the colonial administrator through to the priest, the rent collector, the peasant, the merchant, the spinner, the gentry, the rebel, the musician, the servant. To speak of 'the Irish people' as one category then is clearly to ignore the complexity of social stratification and positionings within Irish society. It overlooks the massive differences in the experiences of even such a large-scale calamity as the Famine of 1845–48. It denies the capacity of individuals and groups to transform and transcend their life circumstances, to be agents of change, to create niches in their lives where they can be proud, happy, creative and loving. Yet, to focus completely on the specificities and variations within the Irish context is to ignore the overarching patterns of domination which endured for hundreds of years and which clearly have left economic, political, cultural, social and psychological legacies.

The year 1921 is generally accepted as a watershed in Irish history, marking a radical transformation in political and economic structures. It is hardly plausible, however, that a decade of transformation could undo the legacy of hundreds of years. Indeed this is precisely the argument I wish to apply to the Celtic Tiger – that now, as then, a decade of transformation cannot undo historical legacies. Legacies of history continued to play themselves out in the twentieth century – from a Civil War about which there is still relatively little discussion, decades of poverty, disease (TB in particular), emigration, through to the 1950s, and continuing conflicts over partition. Other twentieth-century themes which have obvious historical roots include the domination of the Catholic Church and the continuing maintenance of a highly unequal and patriarchal society. Indeed I have argued elsewhere that a legacy of colonialism in the Irish context is a well-established system of male domination with a centralised authoritarian power structure (Moane 1994, 1996).

It is surely obvious that there will be distinctive psychological legacies of such a history which will be quite different from those of countries with a history of domination such as Britain, the US and many European countries. Before discussing the nature of these psychological legacies, I will first explore how it might be that psychological patterns may be maintained across time. An obvious place to start with this exploration of the legacies of history is with the Famine of 1845–48, although Peck (2000) suggests that the preceding century of military, political and cultural domination itself created patterns of helplessness and passivity which influenced the responses, particularly of peasants, to the events of the Famine years. It is indisputable that the Famine had a profound and devastating effect on those who suffered it. Over a million peasants died during the Famine, itself an experience almost unimaginable if it were not for modern television scenes of starvation from around the world. The suffering associated with starvation and malnutrition, the horror of witnessing people die, the fierce and desperate struggle for survival, the grief and isolation as families and communities disintegrated, the despair as efforts to sustain life proved fruitless, the anger at the sight of food being withheld and other obvious social injustices are among the psychological reactions to such an event.

What is striking from a historical and psychological perspective is the relative absence of sustained analysis or commemoration for over 100 years following the Famine. Silence is recognised as one of the most immediate reactions to severe trauma (Herman 1992). The expression 'unspeakable' literally captures this aspect of severe trauma. There had been little cultural or artistic expression in relation to the Famine in Ireland until the commemorations of the 1990s. Folklore accounts are notable for the lack of accounts of direct experience of famine; both in Ireland and the US, famine impacted on 'others', those in the next parish, not in the immediate family. Many

Irish-American families who emigrated during the Famine continue to maintain silence about when and why their ancestors arrived in the US (Ó Gráda 1998; Peck 2000).

Peck has argued that the Irish-American context not only failed to provide a safe context for recovery from the trauma of Famine, but was in fact a context where recovery could not happen and where indeed retraumatisation occurred. She reports high levels of admission of Irish immigrants to mental institutions in the Boston and New York areas in the post-Famine years, and suggests that factors such as the loss of the native language and the experiences of poverty and anti-Irish racism both compounded the traumas of famine and prevented survivors from healing or expressing their grief and other emotions. Withdrawal, shame, guilt, unresolved anger and conflict over nurturance needs are among the patterns she and others identify in Irish-American families (McGoldrick 1996). Similar arguments can be applied to other contexts of emigration. Certainly in the British context, contemporary research on Irish communities continues to show higher levels of admission to mental hospitals and of scores on indicators of mental illness (Bracken et al. 1998).

The concept of transgenerational transmission of trauma can help to understand how psychological patterns can be transmitted across generations (Danieli 1998). This concept has been explored in many contexts of historical trauma, most thoroughly in the case of Holocaust survivors, where studies have focused on families as the locus of transmission, although recent developments have begun to theorise how culture can be involved in the transmission of trauma (Antze and Lambek 1996). Holocaust research has shown that the actual sufferers of trauma, i.e. survivors of the Holocaust, tended to retreat into silence and withdrawal, which was challenged by their own offspring, the first post-trauma generation. This generation tended to be asymptomatic, yet their offspring, the second generation post-trauma, have been found to have symptoms such as excess guilt, obsessive compulsive patterns, and addictions. The third generation continued to show these symptoms, albeit in diluted form, and there is emerging evidence of symptoms in fourth-generation survivors.

The concept of survivor guilt is also one which has been explored in the context of Holocaust survivors. Psychological patterns associated with survivor guilt show remarkable similarities to patterns associated with alcoholism, although this connection has not been explored empirically. Obviously high levels of guilt are one element in survivor guilt. Other elements include confusion and emotional volatility, shame, and an unbearable sense of double bind where to survive or to perish are both unattractive options, the former because of its aftermath. Shutting down, impatience with the past and will-ingness to turn a blind eye are the follow-on psychological reactions to such an unpleasant psychological state which have been linked with the silence and withdrawal characteristic of Holocaust survivors.

Retraumatisation plays an important role in transgenerational trans-mission of trauma. It is intuitively obvious, and has been supported by research, that recovery is more difficult where there is further trauma, and that retraumatisation in a context where recovery is incomplete would be experienced as more traumatic, bringing to the surface again patterns of guilt, anger, shame and grief that are among the reactions to trauma. The continuing silence about the Famine (until the official commemorations that took place between 1995 and 1998) is a testimony to enduring conflict about the Famine and its aftermath which, in a psychological context, can act as a barrier to recovery. The 1916 Rising, the War of Independence and the Civil War may be seen as markers of another period of trauma and transformation in Irish society, and again the continuing silence about the Civil War in particular may be seen as indicators of continuing conflict about these events. The generation born at the turn of the century in Ireland would have been the fourth generation post-Famine. They faced into a century of considerable upheaval and lived most of their adult years during the 1930s–1950s, a period already referred to as one marked by high levels of poverty, disease and emigration, with echoes of the Famine years.

I would like to argue that the unusually harsh regime of Irish society from the 1930s through the 1950s was related not just to economic hardships characteristic of the time but also to the psy-chological legacies of the famine and of our colonial history more generally. The high levels of violence and brutality characteristic both of civil society and of institutional life which have only recently been acknowledged were both tolerated and ignored (Ferguson 2000), illustrating capacities for denial which themselves are legacies of a traumatic history. The extent of denial and of doublethink in relation to levels of abuse in institutions has now been well documented (Raftery and O'Sullivan 1999). Many official reports expressed horror and concern at the abuse in institutions, yet officials turned a blind eye and accepted the denials and excuses offered by the religious who ran the institutions. These patterns of denial in relation to abuse, particularly sexual abuse, continue up to the late twentieth century and into the present time, as numerous cases, including the Kilkenny case of the 1970s and the McColgan case of the 1990s, demonstrate (ibid.).

Psychosocial Legacies of History I: Cultural Pathologies

Turning to contemporary Irish society, a number of patterns can be identified which may be more accurately labelled 'psychosocial', since they are a combination of social and psychological patterns. A complete discussion of Irish psychological and psychosocial patterns is not only beyond the scope of the present chapter, but would require comprehensive and innovative research programmes for which resources are not yet available. Both Irish and international writers on colonialism have highlighted numerous patterns which may be seen as legacies of colonialism; two of the most common in the Irish context are a weak sense of identity and a strong sense of inferiority (Moane 1994). On the other hand, an enduring legacy of colonialism in the Irish context which has received little attention in the psychological literature is the loss of the native language, with implications for consciousness, creativity and identity.

My aim in the present discussion is to focus on a limited number of patterns which seem to be clearly characteristic of Irish society, either because they have been demonstrated to be so by research or because there is general consensus about them. Some of the patterns discussed below are recurring themes in the literature on psychological aspects of colonisation and oppression generally, where these patterns are contextualised as responses to colonial or other forms of domination. In that context, while they are hardly functional, they are understandable reactions to domination. Their manifestations in the present Irish context, on the other hand, can be seen as creating serious psychological and social problems, and may be deemed to be cultural pathologies.

The first and most obvious pattern, already alluded to, is very high levels of *alcohol and drug consumption*, patterns which we are only now fully acknowledging. Stereotypes of the Irish have always included drinking and alcoholism, which may in part account for the vigorous denial over decades of the extent of problem drinking in Irish society. Certain statistics were cited to challenge the view that there were problems with alcohol, including ones which showed that Ireland has the highest rates of teetotallers, that the Irish consume less beer or wine per head than those in continental countries, that they did most of their drinking in public which created a false impression of the quantities they consumed. What these figures obscured was that the pattern of Irish alcohol consumption was exceptional. The most distinctive pattern is public consumption of very large amounts of alcohol (bingeing) and public tolerance of drunkenness. The view that the Irish are not exceptional in our alcohol use has finally been discredited by recent comprehensive national research which shows that they are among the highest consumers of alcohol in Europe, and that Irish students are among the highest consumers of drugs in Europe (World Health Organisation 2001a).

This exposure of high rates of alcohol consumption has been facilitated by the Celtic Tiger, since rates of alcohol consumption have increased considerably over the years of economic growth. It is perhaps typical of the more punitive and authoritarian approach to social problems characteristic of systems of domination that the solution to this is seen as regulation and control. This does not recognise that alcohol consumption permeates Irish culture and is offered to young people as a necessary vehicle for fun and status. A full examination of the role of alcohol in Irish culture, and a commitment to alternatives such as sport, leisure and creativity, must be minimum elements in a programme to tackle alcohol problems. Of great concern in this context is the high rates of alcohol consumption among the current youth generation, the generation most likely to have transcended the traumas of history both because of their distance intergenerationally from the traumas associated with history and because of the social transformations occuring during their development. In this instance the combination of vulnerability to alcohol abuse as a legacy of colonialism and the international trend for increased consumption of alcohol to accompany economic growth may be taking its toll of the current young generation to a dangerous degree.

Alcohol and substance abuse are related to patterns of *denial and doublethink*, which are seen by many writers as a central legacy of colonialism, related to the dualistic or Manichean world view discussed at the beginning of this chapter. Ironically, the Celtic Tiger has also helped to expose this pattern through the example of different tribunals in which politicians deny outright facts which are known in the public realm, the most obvious example of denial. At its most simplistic, denial involves a refusal to acknowledge a reality that is plainly obvious to other observers. Other examples of thought patterns associated with denial are minimisation and blaming the victim. Doublethink involves a capacity to entertain two conflicting thoughts simultaneously. Examples of denial and doublethink are widespread in Irish society. The phrase 'Irish solution to an Irish problem' refers precisely to policies which incorporate doublethink, a combination of 'this is not happening here' and 'we'll make provision for it anyway'. Hypocrisy is a pattern clearly associated with denial and doublethink. The Irish psychologist Vincent Kenny has provided a detailed exploration of thought patterns associated with subordination which may be linked to denial and doublethink (Kenny 1985).

The phrase *distortions of sexuality* (MacCurtain 1987) may best describe a third set of psychosocial patterns in the area of sexuality which can be seen as legacies of colonialism and also of the dominance of the Catholic Church. Narrow definitions of sexuality as involving only procreation, and of womanhood as involving only motherhood, have been given legal and constitutional status. Laws on contraception and Article 44 of the Constitution are obvious examples of this pattern, but ongoing debates over contraception, divorce and abortion which, in the year 2001, included a proposed constitutional referendum to eliminate suicide as a grounds for abortion are indicative of a deeply obsessive and distorted view of sexuality and of women. Meaney (1991) has linked such obsessive concerns with controlling women's bodies to the colonial struggle to control the national territory (Mother Ireland). This has certainly had an impact on women's and men's experiences of sexuality which has yet to be researched. Absence of proper sex education even in the face of rises in sexually transmitted diseases and teenage pregnancies are further manifestations of a failure to adopt a realistic and holistic approach to sexuality.

The emergence of racism (MacLachlin and O'Connell 2000) may be seen as a manifestation of a fourth pattern much discussed in the literature on colonialism, which has been labelled 'displacement of anger' or *horizontal hostility*. In the colonial context it refers to a pattern whereby anger which is rightly felt towards the coloniser is displaced onto peers, i.e. the colonised, or onto groups who are more subordinate. This has been used to explain the remarkably high levels of racism exhibited by Irish Americans. Racism may also be linked to experiences of anti-Irish racism and to revulsion at the sight of scenes of destitution and poverty being re-enacted. Horizontal hostility can also take the form of passive aggression, non-co-operation, backbiting, begrudgery and other indirect expressions of anger. If, as seems likely, the Celtic Tiger shifts the emphasis away from the collective to the individual, thus reducing inhibitions against the expression of anger, and as immigration provides obvious targets for anger, it may be expected that racism will continue to be expressed in virulent and hostile terms as well as in the more established institutional and everyday forms.

A fifth pattern is a syndrome which for the present I will label *social irresponsibility*. This is manifest most obviously in disregard and disrespect for laws, rules and regulations. It includes an attitude of carelessness which applies not just to rules and regulations, but also the environment (obviously manifested by littering). Again the roots of this patterns may be traced to hostility towards the colonial regime, combined with the need to survive at all cost. Fintan O'Toole has

written of this as a sense of alienation from the state, a difficulty
accepting that 'the system' is now our system, rather than one to be
subverted and undermined (O'Toole 1996). However, it is a pattern
which is again taking a higher toll in the context of economic development, with rises in road deaths and disregard for planning
regulations being obvious manifestations.

These five psychosocial patterns have been discussed because they
are notable features of Irish society which may be linked to legacies of
history and which are recurring themes in writings on colonisation.
They are patterns which, I have suggested, render us vulnerable to
the social and economic forces operating on Irish culture at the
present time, in which the domination of colonial times threatens to
be replaced by the domination of global capitalism with its emphasis
on consumerism and its disregard for social concerns. Each of these
patterns is associated with obvious social problems which in many
ways seem to be exacerbated by the changes associated with the Celtic
Tiger. It is all the more important that we find the strength and vision
to resist these forces and forge our own path. In order for this to
happen, I suggest that it is important to first acknowledge positive
aspects of the legacies of history.

Psychosocial Legacies of History II: Cultural Strengths

While early writings on colonisation and patriarchy tended to view
both systems as involving unmitigated domination, more contemporary views acknowledge diversity and contextualisation, struggling to
find a balance between the extremes of modernist universalism and
post-modernist specificity. One of the outcomes of this dialogue has
been a recognition of agency, of resistance and of possibilities for
transformation among those who have been oppressed. This has
created another dialectic between the desire to acknowledge fully the
creativity, courage, vision and determination of movements of
resistance and of cultural renaissance while also recognising the
oppressive context in which these movements developed. Thus,
throughout Irish history, there has been resistance to colonisation
which has taken a wide variety of forms including armed resistance,
mass political movements, boycotts and sabotage, and cultural
resistance. The psychological concomitant of this is a recognition that
these experiences of individual and collective agency and resistance
may be sources of psychological strengths.

Theorising about resistance, about psychological strengths, and
indeed about the psychology of liberation is not as well developed as

are analyses of oppression and of domination. There are a number of positive aspects of Irish culture which could be considered strengths. Here I will confine myself to three themes which are chosen, as above, because there is good evidence that they are indeed characteristic of Irish society and because they are recurring themes in writings on oppression and liberation.

The first, *creativity and imagination,* is apparent at a number of levels in Irish society. This involves not just the capacity to produce what are appreciated as works of art, literature, drama, music and so forth. The spectrum of creativity runs from large-scale artistic productions through community arts to creativity in everyday life. In systems of domination such as colonialism, where there are so few opportunities in political and economic spheres, creativity offers a vehicle for self-expression and advancement. It plays an essential role in resistance, with examples ranging from carnival to coded ballads (Scott 1990). It allows for subversion, it offers an escape, it provides a focal point for identity and community, it is a source of hope and vision, it binds communities together. Currently, although material support for creativity in the Irish context may continue to be inadequate, there is still widespread appreciation and admiration for creativity and imagination.

Like creativity, *spirituality* has been of vital importance in sustaining individuals and communities in the face of oppression, as the examples of African-American and Native-American cultures show. In the Irish context the dominance of the Catholic Church has meant that institutionalised religion has been the primary focus for spirituality. The emphasis on conformity to Catholic values and practices and the lack of alternative spiritualities has made it difficult to untangle spirituality, a sense of harmony with a greater force along with spiritual and ethical practices, from religiosity, an adherence to the observance of institutionalised religious practices. This has made an exploration of spirituality problematic in the Irish context. However, there can be little doubt that spirituality has played a pervasive role in Irish culture.

The third pattern, *solidarity and support,* can be seen as an outcome of histories of resistance – which involve sustained, mutual co-operation and loyalty – and indeed of experiences of oppression generally, where individuals, groups and communities survive by pulling together, presenting a united front, offering support and sustenance, and encouraging each other in everyday life as well as in resistance. Experiences of trauma also call for solidarity and support, and many documentations of catastrophe, including famine, highlight the mutual aid, sharing of resources and generosity of spirit which exist alongside more competitive and self-interested behaviour. These patterns continue to manifest themselves in Irish society in the sense of social cohesion and community solidarity and support, especially notable in impoverished communities (O'Neill 1992). Solidarity and support can coexist with the patterns of social irresponsiblity discussed earlier – the former is more likely to be manifest at community and interpersonal levels, while the latter is manifest in the relatively more abstract political and legal spheres.

A point that may be obvious here is that these are qualities which are rarely given prominence in systems of domination and indeed may be seen as subverting the enterprise of global capitalism, which emphasises conformity, individualism and materialism. From the viewpoint of writings on decolonisation and on the more recently emerging liberation psychology they may be seen as psychosocial resources which may be drawn on to sustain liberation from patterns of domination and oppression. That they are particularly strong features of Irish society may be seen as a positive legacy of colonialism. The danger is that if contemporary Irish society positions itself into an increasingly dominator mode, these patterns will become muted if not undermined.

The Importance of Vision

I have cast the present historical period as a moment of major realignment of power differentials in Irish society. While the prevailing pattern is one of a continuing enactment of domination and a narrowing of vision to include economic growth alone, there is also the potentiality for new power relations, new gender relations, new cultural forms, new spiritual forms. One of the challenges to those who resist continuing domination is not just the effort to influence change through traditional political and cultural outlets, but to develop new visions which can open the imagination to new forms of social relations which are not based on domination and subordination. Ireland's historical legacy can be seen as double-edged in this context, since, as I have argued, it both renders us vulnerable to internal and external pressures towards domination, and it has also provided us with experiences of oppression and resistance which provide a basis for forging links with global movements that resist the domination of global (Western) capitalism.

Our historical legacies also provide a rich source of culture and imagination which may be mined for the task of forging new visions more relevant to the twenty-first century. Global changes in the late twentieth century have undermined the (Western-based) radical movements which inspired egalitarian political activism, and contemporary global culture also tends to be ahistorical. One implication of this is generational differences both in views of history and in access to radical and visionary ideas. Along with the radical transformations in Irish society, there is a danger of the 'generation gap' becoming ever wider as older generations remain rooted in twentieth-century history and politics while younger generations look to the present and future. It is unlikely that younger generations will identify with narratives of trauma, oppression and dispossession (when indeed they themselves are being deprived of access to housing), while, as resistance to global capitalism increases, they may more readily identify with narratives of resistance and of liberation.

It is also the case that contemporary Irish society contains many examples of resistance and of vision, most of which occur on the margins of mainstream society and are ignored by mass media. Marginalised groups such as Travellers (Sheehan et al. 2000) and gays and lesbians (O'Carroll and Collins 1995) have struggled to maintain and develop their cultures and resist assimilation by the mainstream. Working-class and impoverished communities continue to undertake political organising around ideals of empowerment and equality. The feminist movement perseveres in asserting a radical and vibrant politics and world view. These movements share a common cause with global radical movements such as those of indigenous people or of anti-capitalist protestors which can help to offer an alternative global vision to the one prevailing in Western media.

The strategies for liberating ourselves from the Manichean world view of domination and subordination suggested by writings on decolonisation and liberation involve a continuing engagement with history, the cultivation of vision and the further development of solidarity and support with post-colonial and other marginalised groups. These strategies may be contrasted with the current tendency in Ireland to jettison the past as if it were no longer relevant, thus leaving us to repeat patterns of history, to embrace utilitarian economic ideologies and to ignore the obvious social costs of prioritising economic growth, and to view Ireland's successes as somehow isolated from broader global trends. The psychological and cultural weaknesses which I have argued are legacies of history both predispose us to these latter social patterns, and these social patterns in turn maintain and may even develop further these weaknesses. It is thus all the more important that there be sustained commitment to liberating strategies, and to the enhancement of our psychological and cultural strengths.

8 Religion and the Celtic Tiger: The Cultural Legacies of Anti-Catholicism in Ireland[1]

Lionel Pilkington

A recent article in Britain's main liberal newspaper, the *Guardian*, writes despairingly of what it terms the resurgence of religious 'fundamentalism' in Ireland. Arts Correspondent Fiachra Gibbons argues that just at the point when Ireland's tiger economy is beginning to weaken, the Irish are returning to religion.

> Could it be that with the Celtic Tiger showing the first signs of mange, and an unprecedented 10-year property boom evaporating as fast as the profits of the IT multinationals in which the Irish had put their faith, a chastened nation is once again on its knees? (28 July 2001: 13)

As evidence of fundamentalism, Gibbons cites the scenes of mass devotion during this year's visit to Ireland of the relics of Saint Thérèse of Lisieux ('Nothing like it has been seen since the hysteria of the Pope's visit') and the current best-selling status of *The Glenstal Book of Common Prayer* with 9500 copies sold in two weeks. The religiosity that the article describes and laments is, therefore, unambiguously Roman Catholic and, in this respect, Gibbons's piece is just one in a long history of liberal critical argument which holds that Ireland's full development as a modern nation-state has been and continues to be impeded by the country's dominant religion.

Commenting retrospectively on objections to the breaking of an icon of the Virgin Mary in his 1899 play *The Countess Cathleen*, for example, the poet W.B. Yeats described the play's Catholic protesters as 'medieval believers' and remarked, 'I had not known that to many simple Catholics such an impiety, whatever the motive, was as shameful as a naked man' (Yeats 1972: 121). For Yeats and Lady Gregory, 'cultivating the people' (a phrase that Yeats borrowed from

Wagner so as to describe the ideological work of the Abbey Theatre) was about preparing Ireland for statehood by means of a literary education and this, in turn, was linked to the view that Ireland needed to be educated away from the 'superstitious' and 'medieval' nature of Catholic religious belief (see Pilkington 2001: 6–63). Even Plunkett, a liberal reformer and the enlightened founder of the Irish Cooperative movement (the Irish Agricultural Organisation Society), frequently expressed the view that advancing away from Catholic religious practices is synonymous with a movement toward social and political maturity. In his important work *Ireland in the New Century* (1905), Plunkett describes what he considers is a fundamental anti-economic feature in the Irish character fostered by the majority religion: 'a defect in the industrial character of Roman Catholics which, however caused, seems to me to have been intensified by their religion' (Plunkett 1905: 101–2). Ideas such as these – for years commonplace amongst unionist politicians in Northern Ireland (see Brewer and Higgins 1998: 100–5) – often resurface in contemporary liberal critiques of Irish culture such as that offered by Fiachra Gibbons's recent article in the *Guardian*.

In the context of Ireland's Celtic Tiger prosperity – where in 1999 the gap between rich and poor was second only to the United States (Conference of Religious in Ireland 1999: 8) – what, if any, is the role of religious belief? In particular, is the expression of Catholic religious devotion in Ireland a distorting form of recidivism or the potential basis of a radical political critique? This chapter offers a tentative starting point for addressing these questions. Beginning with the Drumcree crisis in Northern Ireland, the chapter discusses the relationship between Irish modernity and religious and denominational identity and surveys some of the historical and political reasons for the assumption that Catholicism is an impediment to Irish modernisation. In addition to examining its tenacious hold on Irish cultural discourse and critical commentary, the chapter also investigates the debilitating implications of this assumption for Church of Ireland Protestants.

Drumcree

Around about the same time that the term 'Celtic Tiger' emerged as a media byword for Ireland's current phase of capitalist success (O'Hearn 1998: 1–3), the first of a series of annual confrontations took place at the Church of Ireland parish church of Drumcree near Portadown in Northern Ireland. On each first Sunday in July, after the conclusion of the morning Eucharist, the members of Portadown

District of the Orange Order file out of church and, having marched in military formation to a security barrier, demand to parade back to the town centre by its 'traditional' route: that is, through the mainly Catholic and nationalist Garvaghy Road and against the expressed wishes of its residents.

The crisis at Drumcree began in earnest in 1995 when the Garvaghy Road residents agreed to allow an Orange parade to proceed through their area on the understanding that no future marches would occur. Once this parade had taken place, however, the agreement was denied by the Orange Order, and the 1995 march concluded with a triumphant victory dance involving Ian Paisley and David Trimble (Garvaghy Residents 1999: 146–7). In 1996 and 1997, the Garvaghy Road residents again objected to the planned Orange Order march and the Royal Ulster Constabulary authorities agreed, at least initially, that the march would have to be rerouted. The Orange Order responded with protests across Northern Ireland involving the extensive use of roadblocks, intimidation and harassment. As a result of this widespread disruption, the RUC Chief Constable changed his earlier ruling and a large force of baton-wielding riot police forced a path for the Orange marchers through the protesting residents. In 1998 the situation altered again as the newly-elected British Labour government under Tony Blair insisted that it would adhere to a ruling by the Parades Commission that the march through the Garvaghy Road should not be allowed. To date, the confrontation at Drumcree remains at a stalemate. The Portadown District of the Orange Order considers the Garvaghy Road route to be its inviolable and non-negotiable right and on this basis it has refused to enter into any direct dialogue or exchange with the nationalist residents of the Garvaghy Road. The Church of Ireland authorities have decried the association of Orange Order protests with violence, but have refused to cancel or postpone the church service. For the Catholic residents of the Garvaghy Road, on the other hand, for whom Orange marches evoke decades of systematic discrimination, painful memories of political subordination and inequality and the local ongoing reality of anti-Catholic harassment, Drumcree is synonymous with extraordinary tension and the constant threat of extreme violence. It is within this context that the Garvaghy Road residents demand the right to be consulted as equals in relation to any future proposed march and insist on the need for face-to-face negotiations. Although the Drumcree crisis, now in its seventh year, varies in intensity it has also become a focus for horrific sectarian attacks on Catholics. In the Portadown area alone there have been numerous Drumcree-related violent incidents since 1995 including the 1996 murder of Michael McGoldrick, the kicking to death of nationalist resident Robert Hamill in front of an RUC Land Rover in 1997 and the 1999 murder of Rosemary Nelson, a lawyer acting on behalf of the Garvaghy Road Residents' Association. The crisis at Drumcree appears a million miles away from the apparent social consensus and cultural sophistication of the Celtic Tiger. Media reports tend to present Drumcree as unrelated to the economic success story of the Tiger except as an anomaly and an embarrassment. Whereas the Celtic Tiger denotes Ireland's rapid growth within a global, high-speed and predominantly service-based capitalist economy, Drumcree appears time-bound and fixed obsessively to a specific locality; here, the characteristic experience is not speed, but an obdurate, slow-motion choreography of waiting. Whereas in cultural terms the Celtic Tiger suggests a secular Anglo-American, post-nationalist utopia, Drumcree is regarded as an outpouring of atavism. Indeed, the yearly confrontation at Drumcree in which the Orange Order and the Garvaghy Road residents wait to see whether the British government will facilitate or prevent the march taking place, performs that which Celtic Tiger Ireland most wants to suppress: a recrudescence of Ireland's colonial history in the form of the still-unresolved political conflict in Northern Ireland.

It is also possible, however, to regard Drumcree as an embarrassment to the Celtic Tiger, not because the former illustrates a cultural phenomenon that is the opposite of the modern, but because it exposes features that are endemic to Ireland's current modernity. By drawing attention to anti-Catholicism as an ongoing physical reality in Ireland and by underlining its close relationship to mainstream Irish Protestant identity, Drumcree forces a reconsideration of the cultural and denominational basis of that process of modernisation of which the Celtic Tiger is seen as the natural and triumphant culmination. This confrontation in which the Orange Order members emerge from a Church of Ireland religious service and then spend days engaged in protests against not being allowed to walk offensively through a Catholic residential area has, in other words, directed a new and unusual attention on the nature and political significance of Protestant self-identity in Ireland. In so doing, it inverts (albeit temporarily) a fundamental and longstanding cultural assumption of Irish modernisation. Instead of the view that Ireland's economic, cultural and political progress depends on an accelerated movement away from a benighted Catholic past, Drumcree suggests that it is the unyielding nature of mainstream (Church of Ireland) Irish Protestantism and its informal links to the anti-Catholic practices of the Orange Order that exists as one of the principal obstacles to political change and accommodation. At the

Union Jack-bedecked Church of Ireland church tower of Drumcree, it is as if the fast-track, forward-moving logic of the Celtic Tiger is thrown, temporarily and violently, into reverse gear.

This post-Drumcree public questioning of the relationship between the Church of Ireland, the Orange Order and loyalist political violence and intimidation is quite unprecedented. In the past, with the dominant view of the crisis in Northern Ireland as a conflict between law and order supported by a predominantly Protestant population and a militant republican movement steeped in Catholicism, attempts by political commentators to ask searching questions of Irish Protestantism or of Irish unionism, let alone attempts to portray Irish republicanism as a heterogeneous movement that also includes Protestants, were often dismissed as giving succour to republican paramilitary violence. Thus, in a paralysing circular movement, just as the war in Northern Ireland increased and exaggerated Ireland's denominational asymmetry, it also made it particularly difficult to discuss. But there is an additional and more extensive reason for the marked reluctance to criticise the traditions and practices of Irish Protestantism, the view that Irish Protestantism is, simply, more liberal and more progressive than its Catholic equivalents.

Yet, far from being in the vanguard of the campaign for political change or liberal reform in Ireland, the Church of Ireland in the twentieth century has on the whole been strikingly conservative. The Censorship of Films Act of 1923, for example, was strongly supported by Archbishop Bernard, a senior member of the Church of Ireland and a celebrated Provost of Trinity College, Dublin. As for the Censorship of Publications Act of 1929, Archbishop Gregg's mild censure was accompanied by the wish that the government should display similar fervour in prohibiting gambling. In contrast to the Church of Ireland's strenuous objections to compulsory Irish in 1926, for example, its criticism of repressive political, social and cultural legislation was pusillanimous. Yeats's celebrated speech on divorce in the Irish Senate in which he referred to southern Protestants as 'no petty people' was a masterpiece of rhetoric, but as far as the Church of Ireland's position on divorce and other social legislation was concerned, it was also inaccurate. Yeats himself was well aware of the distance that existed between his view of Irish Protestants as radical critics of mass democracy and the actual position taken by the Church of Ireland. A year earlier in 1924, Lennox Robinson's controversial removal from his position as treasurer on the Carnegie Library Committee because of the alleged indecency of his story, 'The Madonna of Slieve Dun', was precipitated by the objections of *both* the Catholic *and* the Church of Ireland representatives on the

Committee. Even in the case of De Valera's 1937 constitution, now a virtual synonym for Catholic intolerance, the articles in question (44.1.2 and 44.1.3) were drafted after consultation with the Church of Ireland's senior conservative prelate, Archbishop Gregg. Not until the 1969 appointment of George Otto Simms as Archbishop of Armagh and the establishment of the Church of Ireland periodical *Focus* (1958–66) did liberalism become a definite feature of the Church of Ireland as an institution (see Acheson 1997: 230).

Despite its tenacious hold on Irish cultural and political discourse, then, the view that Irish Protestantism is more liberal than Irish Catholicism is based less on fact than on widely-held cultural assumptions. Whereas in Irish literature and cultural narratives Catholicism is most usually taken as benighted, authoritarian and atavistic, Irish Protestantism tends to be conveyed as misunderstood and beleaguered, the victim of a bloody-minded nationalist history, and a beacon of liberal progressiveness. If Irish Catholicism seems to require rigorous interrogation and sceptical analysis, it is assumed that Irish Protestantism requires merely sympathy, nostalgia, accommodation and respect. It is impossible to imagine, for example, a Methodist, Presbyterian or Church of Ireland version of the TV comedy *Father Ted*, a Martin McDonagh play about Portadown loyalists, a Paul Durcan satire on Ulster Unionism, or the lyrical, haunting dramaturgy of Frank McGuinness's *Observe the Sons of Ulster Marching Towards the Somme* turned to a narrative of the Irish volunteers in 1916. In relation to Ireland's dominant cultural paradigm in the twentieth century – the anxious drive to modernisation – Roman Catholic Ireland appears always in need of a much higher level of cultural refinement, of questioning, parody and subversion, than its Protestant equivalents. A line from Thomas McCarthy's poem, 'The Lost Province of Alsace' puts the matter succinctly: 'Thinking / finds a Protestant in me.'

More worrying than such patronising sentimentality is the fact that this point of view seems to have been absorbed into the matrices of Irish Protestant self-representation. When attending a 1995 ecumenical service in St Mary's Cathedral, Tuam, which had been organised by the Church of Ireland to commemorate the 150th anniversary of the Famine, I was surprised to discover that one of the readings chosen for the service was an extract from Patrick Kavanagh's poem 'The Great Hunger'. Certainly, the poem was broadly appropriate to the service's concern with the spiritual and material dimensions of hunger, but it also seemed quite extraordinary that a selection from one of Ireland's most famous literary tirades against twentieth-century Catholic authoritarianism should have been chosen as a reading for a national ecumenical service. If the title of

Kavanagh's poem is itself an act of shocking facetiousness, implying an analogy between male sexual repression in the 1940s and the starving to death of almost a million people a century earlier, here, in the context of a Church of Ireland commemoration of the Famine, the poem seemed arrogant and insensitive. It was as if the Church of Ireland as an institution could not bring itself to express regret for its role in the Famine without simultaneously implying that, while its involvement in the injustices of this period may well have taken place, they had occurred in the historical past, and that as such they had long since been outstripped by the psychological damage inflicted by Irish Catholicism on present-day Ireland. The opening stricture of Archbishop Robin Eames's sermon at the service – 'objectivity in the interpretation of history is not always an attribute when we Irish look into the past' (Eames 1995) – was now far from clear-cut. At what point exactly does the Irish past cease to be history, and to what extent was Eames's phrase 'We Irish' intended as sincerely inclusive?

As a Church of Ireland member I was disappointed and embarrassed at this awkward lack of generosity towards the painful history of my predominantly Catholic friends, colleagues and neighbours. But perhaps I need not have been. There was no word of criticism in the report of the service in the *Irish Times* and the local papers (the *Tuam Herald* and the *Connaught Tribune*) were both unanimous in their enthusiastic welcome for Dr Eames's address. Indeed, if the service was a disappointment it was also, unfortunately, predictable. As journalist Carol Coulter has argued, Dr Eames's public utterances on Irish political conflict tend to dovetail almost exactly with the responses of the Ulster Unionist Party (Coulter 1998: 8). Less than a year later, for example, in the summer of 1996, Archbishop Eames was carefully circumspect in his comments about the extensive Orange Order protests in the build-up to that year's Drumcree crisis, understanding and condoning of the actions of the RUC in their batoning of nationalist protesters from the Garvaghy Road, but then sharply and robustly critical of the subsequent nationalist boycotts of Protestant businesses associated with the Orange protest.

The notion that the Church of Ireland is more liberal than its Catholic counterpart is based, therefore, on widely-accepted ideological assumptions. As a result, the culture of nationalist, Catholic Ireland is subjected to regular and often salutary revisionist interrogation, whereas the same cannot even begin to be said of the culture of Irish Protestantism. Also, while De Valera's Ireland is now popularly understood as a synonym for Catholic autocracy and a level of intolerance that has come to be regarded as almost pre-modern, the persistent anti-Catholic discrimination, political gerrymandering and RUC repression that characterised the Stormont period remains relatively unexplored as does Protestant anti-Catholicism in pre-independence Ireland. True, scholars such as Kurt Bowen, Terence Brown, Andrew Gailey, Vivian Mercier and Trevor West offer meticulous studies of aspects of Irish Protestant history and culture, but no systematic analysis exists of the relationship between Protestantism, anti-Catholicism and political authority. Even Hubert Butler – an Irish Protestant intellectual who was regularly courageous in speaking out against injustice in the 1950s and 1960s – is strangely silent when it comes to Stormont and the RUC. In contemporary historiography and cultural criticism the relationship between Irish Protestantism and sectarianism tends to be vigorously avoided.

The idea that the Church of Ireland is necessarily liberal is tenacious because of the relationship of this assumption to bourgeois modernisation and its insistence on the primacy of the state as the pinnacle of political achievement. In this context, the Church of Ireland's nineteenth-century role as Ireland's 'established' church (until 1869), and the necessarily clandestine and extra-constitutional nature of much nationalist resistance to the British state in Ireland offer some historical explanation for Ireland's denominational asymmetry. The persistence of this ideology *after* Irish independence, however, when it was the Catholic Church that was so closely identified with the state, must be traced to at least two additional factors: first, the manner in which the Church of Ireland community in the Republic of Ireland constituted itself as a minority and the way in which this minority community was recognised as such by the emergent Irish state and, secondly, to an ongoing anxiety concerning the potential of Catholic religious practices to challenge the ethical basis of state authority.

Ireland's Privileged Minority

It is widely acknowledged that the Irish Protestant community was treated generously not only by the Cumann na nGaedheal government of the 1920s, but also (although to a somewhat lesser extent) by subsequent Fianna Fáil and coalition administrations. In late 1922 over one-third of the 60 Senate seats were allocated by the government to ex-unionists and Irish Protestants (Whyte 1971: 145). The majority of this group consisted of members of the former ascendancy or public figures like W.B. Yeats who were prominently aligned to it. While the government's offer of Senate seats did not nearly meet earlier southern unionist demands as articulated in the

Irish Convention of 1918–19 and the Anglo-Irish peace negotiations of 1921, the public stature as senators of people like Sir Thomas Grattan Esmonde, Sir John Keane, Andrew Jameson, the Countess of Desart and Sir Horace Plunkett (not all of whom were in fact Protestants) did offer the Church of Ireland population a considerable level of symbolic reassurance. They did so not because they were Protestants (Esmonde, for example, was a Catholic and Desart was Jewish) but because they belonged to an Ascendancy élite and so were perceived by southern Irish Protestants as the natural representatives of their interests. For Jack White in his book *Minority Report: The Anatomy of an Southern Irish Protestant,* the over-representation of the gentry in the Senate was understandable because 'these were the people on whom the Protestants themselves had depended as their spokesmen' (1975: 93). Nor was the disproportionate political representation of Irish Protestant gentry in the Senate simply symbolic since to some extent it matched the continuing relative economic advantage of Protestants within the state. As R.F. Foster points out in relation to the occupational proportions of southern Irish Protestants in general, 'a modest, unofficial form of "Ascendancy" lingered on' until well into the 1930s (Foster 1988: 534). Separated from their co-religionists in Northern Ireland because of the Ulster Unionist insistence on the permanence and inviolability of partition, southern Irish Protestantism constituted itself as a discrete minority within the Irish Free State by aligning itself to the culture of the dwindling Anglo-Irish Ascendancy. As far as the Irish government in the 1920s was concerned, this privileged treatment of Irish Protestantism afforded the useful political expedient of underlining the tolerance and inclusiveness of the Irish state, thus serving as a reassurance to nervous English investors. Like the post-independence playing of 'God Save the King' at the Royal Dublin Horse Show and at Trinity College commencements, the public face of Church of Ireland society – a world of cricket, garden fêtes, Christmas bazaars and badminton clubs – bestowed the dubious advantage of prestige by association. Brendan Behan's description of an Anglo-Irishman as 'a Protestant with a horse' conveys the nuance exactly: even without the horse – and even if in many cases the association of wealth, education and leisure was often grotesquely inappropriate and misplaced – Protestant self-identity in Ireland conveyed an aura of privilege.

For the southern Protestant population itself, thinking of its social identity in terms of an élite served as a psychologically attractive salve to the extensive damage inflicted on it by the Catholic *Ne Temere* decree (that insisted that the children of mixed Catholic/Protestant parents be brought up as Catholics) and to the serious isolation that it experienced within a state that was increasingly associated with the social and moral teachings of the Catholic Church. De Valera's welcome to the Papal legate at the Eucharistic Congress in 1932 in which he spoke of 'our people, ever firm in their allegiance to our ancestral faith' (quoted in Whyte 1971: 146) encapsulated this bleak new dispensation. Nevertheless, thinking of Irish Protestant social identity in terms of the Ascendancy has had some profoundly damaging consequences. It flatly contradicts the lived experiences of the majority of Irish Protestants (for whom contact with the Big House was often non-existent) and, ironically, it confirms and exacerbates their impression of social and cultural alienation. It also, needless to say, relegated to an historical limbo the work of Church of Ireland socialist republicans such as Maud Eden, those belonging to the Church of Ireland anti-conscription group of 1918, or Protestant Irish-language activists such as Seán Nelson Beaumont who wrote for the socialist, Irish-language periodical, *An t-Éireannach.* Sentimentalisation and a diminution of political options, then, was the Irish state's dubious gift to what Kurt Bowen has termed 'Ireland's privileged minority'. By 1929 mystifying the Ascendancy and lamenting the loss of the Big House had achieved the status of a literary sub-genre explored with prolixity in Edith Somerville's *The Big House of Inver* (1925), poignantly evoked in Elizabeth Bowen's *The Last September* (1929), and sentimentally indulged in Lennox Robinson's popular Abbey Theatre play, *The Big House* (1926). If in post-independence Ireland, the Church of Ireland community in the 26 counties was represented, and represented itself, primarily in terms of the dying world of the Anglo-Irish ascendancy, this was a representation that was also enthusiastically embraced by the new Catholic middle class for whom the notion of an élite was in itself profoundly agreeable. The state's generous treatment of its tiny Protestant minority, then, had more to do with the social and economic calculations of its Catholic bourgeoisie than it did with any radical desire to rethink democracy in terms of the needs and experiences of minorities.

In short, for the emerging Irish state the long-term advantage of this idea of a privileged Protestant identity was that it helped to naturalise the idea of a native social élite as such and thus accorded well with the growing élitist position of the Cumann na nGaedheal administration in the late 1920s (see Regan 1999: 246ff). The Church of Ireland's particular view of itself as a minority, then, was (and arguably still is) crucially related to important features in the self-representation of the Irish state: its mystification of an élitist, class-based society as a natural or 'traditional' characteristic of Irish society, and its promotion of the partitioned Irish state as the natural, tolerant and inclusive expression of Irish nationhood.

The Irish state's sentimentalisation of the lot of the Catholic minority in Northern Ireland, on the other hand, on whom the Northern Ireland state conferred no privilege whatsoever, was no more than political betrayal. If in 1926, as Terence Brown rightly points out, the 7.4 per cent Irish Protestant population of the 26 counties felt a 'sense of isolation and of political impotence' (Brown 1985: 109), this was surely nothing compared to the utter despair experienced by Catholics in Northern Ireland when, in November 1925, a leaked report of the Irish Boundary Commission made it clear that partition and Stormont were there to stay. The contrast between Ireland's two minorities is certainly stark. The Irish Free State's generous allocation of senate places to ex-unionists and southern Protestants could not have been more different to the treatment meted out to Northern Ireland's Catholic minority by the Ulster unionists who, as Eamon Phoenix points out, had successfully pressurised the British government *not* to provide any such weighted representation for nationalists in the Northern Ireland Senate (Phoenix 1994: 393). The experiences of the Northern Ireland Catholic minority under a 'Protestant government for a Protestant people' – a story of wholesale expulsions from employment at times of sectarian tension, of systematic discrimination in housing and employment, and of the multiple and continuing injustices inflicted by the aggressively sectarian Ulster Special Constabulary in the 1920s and the still overwhelmingly Protestant RUC – bears no comparison to the distress of southern Irish Protestants.

There are some hopeful signs of change. One of the outstanding contributions of the recently established Church of Ireland group Catalyst, for example, is that it sets out to address directly the relationship between the Church of Ireland and anti-Catholic sectarianism. Catalyst is a small body of clergy and lay-people that argues that the controversial Drumcree service should be cancelled or postponed until an accommodation with the local nationalist residents has been agreed. It also believes that the Church of Ireland should disassociate itself from divisive political practices such as the flying of the Union Jack from church towers, the playing of the British national anthem and the facilitation of Orange Order ceremonial events. The group has been a major contributor to the Sub-Committee on Anti-Sectarianism of the Church of Ireland General Synod and is highly critical of the inaction on this issue of the Church of Ireland hierarchy. Most importantly, for Catalyst the potential of the Church of Ireland as a radical ethical and theological force lies in its willingness and ability to challenge first of all the Church of Ireland's historical allegiance to the British state and its traditional support for unionism (see Catalyst 1999).

Catholicism and the Irish State

Unlike the Church of Ireland in the 26 counties, the history of the Catholic Church since Irish independence is one of an increasing association with the trappings and execution of state power. The panoply of state ceremony during the 1929 centenary of the Act of Emancipation and during the Eucharistic Congress of 1932 are graphic illustrations of what appears in this period as the Catholic Church's close and seamless bond with the Irish state. As Tony Fahey points out, until recently the Catholic Church in Ireland has been involved in a high level of partnership with the state, so much so that by the mid-1960s it had the highest proportion of clergy and religious to laity as any country in the Catholic world and was the country's main provider of social services (Fahey 1998: 414). Nonetheless, although the bond between church and state exercised a very powerful influence on the formulation, implementation and delivery of Ireland's social policy agenda for many decades, the Catholic Church's relationship to the Irish state was never harmonious or consistent. As well as a history of mutual co-operation and support, there is another, less documented history of tension and disagreement. Catholic vocationalism or social Catholicism in the 1930s and 1940s, for example, was an attempt by the Catholic Church not just to influence specific policy decisions, but to advance ideas for an alternative political order. Inspired by Pope Pius XI's encyclical *Quadragesimo Anno*, vocationalism argued for a reduction of the power of the state so as to usher in a new form of social harmony based on the co-operative interests of the various professional and vocational groups (see O'Leary 2000: 39). The encyclical advocated a more participative form of democracy, that is, with members of each industry and profession – workers and employers – uniting together to 'strive according to the talent, powers, and position of each to contribute something to the Christian reconstruction of human society' (quoted in Mullarkey 1999: 98). Opposed to socialism and class warfare and in favour of private property and social hierarchy, vocationalism was by no means a revolutionary creed. Its radicalism lay in its conception of national politics not in terms of the supremacy of the state, but in terms of a corporation that could function successfully only if the component parts of society worked actively to the common good. To this extent, Catholic vocationalism gave a new emphasis to the agency of the individual. In particular, it challenged the emphasis of representative democracy on passive delegation: the idea that the political agency of the individual may best be served through the mediation of elected political representatives. Unsurprisingly, the Irish government of the day – the Fianna Fáil administration of Eamon De Valera – responded coldly to the proposals of the Catholic vocational movement and, when two critical reports advocating elements of vocationalism were submitted to the government in 1943, their conclusions were quickly dismissed.

Although the Catholic Action movement in Ireland certainly contributed to legitimate southern Protestant fears concerning social exclusion, the militancy of Catholic vocationalism and its robust critique of representative democracy does also contribute to a number of radical political initiatives (O'Leary 2000: 52–5). Recent scholarship has shown that much of the history of rural collective action and of community politics in Ireland is partly indebted to a philosophy of Catholic social action and vocationalism (O'Leary 2000: 42–4). Groups such as Muintir na Tíre (founded in 1931 by Fr John Hayes), Clann na Talmhan (founded in 1938–9), and the Save the West campaign (established around the efforts of the County Donegal priest, Fr James McDyer in 1963) saw themselves in direct opposition to Ireland's political and cultural establishment (salaried state politicians were sometimes referred to as 'pocket nationalists' (quoted in Varley and Curtin 1999: 66)) and held a shared concern with evolving a more participative form of democracy. 'Building a capacity for collective action among those victimised by the *status quo*', Tony Varley and Chris Curtin remark, 'was ... taken to be the *sine qua non* of progressive social, economic and political change' (Varley and Curtin 1999: 74). Although the energy and politics of Muintir na Tíre and the Save the West Campaign was partly indebted to the involvement of parish priests (Varley and Curtin 1999: 72) and to the inspiration of the Catholic vocational movement (O'Leary 2000: 42–4), their relationship with the Catholic hierarchy was often fraught and adversarial. In the case of Muintir na Tíre, for example, Fr Hayes's preference for a non-sectarian community politics was vigorously opposed by influential senior Catholic ecclesiastics such as Archbishop John Charles McQuaid and Bishop Michael Fogarty (Varley and Curtin 1999: 64). The importance of these groups for Irish cultural history lies in their agreed assumption about the failure of state politics to respond to the needs and freedoms of the people and the extent to which they helped articulate an 'ideology of the subordinate' (see Varley and Curtin 1999 and Varley and Curtin forthcoming).

In more recent times, various elements within the Catholic Church in Ireland such as the Catholic bishops' overseas development agency Trócaire (established in 1973), the Justice Commission of the Conference of Religious in Ireland or CORI (formerly the Conference of Major Religious Superiors established in 1960) and the Irish Catholic Bishops' Conference (in its 1999 Pastoral Letter *Prosperity with a Purpose: Christian Faith and Values in a Time of Rapid Economic Growth*) have highlighted issues such as poverty, debt and colonialism in a manner that is often highly critical of the Irish state. The strategy of the of the CORI Justice Commission and of *Prosperity with a Purpose* is to acknowledge the advantages of the Celtic Tiger's economic achievements, but to argue that this success is precisely the reason why more attention must be paid to the issue of poverty, to the growing disparity between rich and poor (CORI 1999: 1) and to the careful regulation of market forces (Irish Catholic Bishops' Conference 1999: 23–4). The Justice Commission of CORI has been especially trenchant in arguing for a more participative and interventionist form of politics in Ireland and in warning that Celtic Tiger wealth generation has involved a decline in egalitarianism and a diminution of political rights and responsibilities. As Brigid Reynolds and Seán Healy (two of the core members of CORI's Justice Commission) have argued, what is needed in Ireland is not a rejection of modernisation, but an alternative philosophy of modernity based on social inclusion and on a dynamic system of participative democracy (Healy and Reynolds 1998: 1–20). Within the context of these developments, any blanket portrayal of Irish Catholicism as a negative force in Irish society or as necessarily antithetical to Irish modernisation is just as distorting and as unhelpful to the growth of progressive politics on the island of Ireland, as is the view that Irish Protestantism is necessarily and inextricably wedded to political unionism and to support for the British state.

Conclusion

The view that Catholicism impedes modernisation is closely connected to the idea that the material practices of Catholic religious belief (its strong sacramentalising of the Eucharist, for example, or the use of statues and icons and the worship of saints and relics) conveys a threat to the full and proper working of the state. For many liberal commentators, Catholicism is regarded as an obstacle to Ireland's full modernisation not only because of specific doctrinal beliefs (such as the Church's strong opposition to divorce, contraception or abortion), nor because of recent evidence of institutional corruption or hierarchical complacency in relation to paedophiliac priests and religious, but because of the physicality of its liturgical and devotional practices. As in the case of Fiachra Gibbons's article in the *Guardian* or Yeats's and Plunkett's remarks about the 'medieval' and 'superstitious' character of Roman Catholicism, such practices are often viewed as serious impediments to the development of a sophisticated contemporary society. It is not just Catholic religious beliefs that are the problem, therefore, but also the network of liturgical and devotional practices that bring these beliefs into being. However, it is also possible that these practices are deemed inappropriate to modern Irish society because they exist so entirely outside the state and the norms of marketplace Celtic Tiger capitalism as to seem utterly incomprehensible. As the material expression of a utopian and alternative ethical sphere, expressions of popular religious devotion (such as the recent extraordinary spectacle of devotion to the relics of St Thérèse or the phenomenon of 'moving statues' in the 1980s) trouble the intellectual and ethical authority of the state because they testify to a disjunction between the state and the people, and in so doing, confirm the existence of an intense utopian hunger. The fact that an estimated 2 million people paid homage to the relics of St Thérèse during their short visit to Ireland this year is evidence not of 'hysteria' (as was claimed by Fiachra Gibbons in the *Guardian*) but of a widespread ethical desire which is also transparently not fulfilled either by the workings of representative democracy or by a substantially discredited European and Irish political élite.

Within this context, it may well be that the ethical strength of both the Church of Ireland and Roman Catholic Church in Ireland will lie increasingly not in any nostalgic clinging to the dubious prestige of British or Irish state power, but in their deliberate and critical separation from it. While there can be no doubt that railing against the hypocrisy and institutional corruption of the Catholic Church in Ireland or against the moral cowardice and tiresomely predictable pro-unionist positions of the current Church of Ireland leadership will remain for many years a necessary and important activity, it also true that attacking either church in the name of a liberal or left-oriented politics by focusing on devotional and sacramental practices is gravely mistaken. Not only are the signs and practices of religious worship nothing to do with institutional corruption, but they can and do exist as enduring physical manifestations of hope and renewal and as the potential foundation for an alternative public sphere. The consumerist utopia of Celtic Tiger Ireland considers the idea of an ethical society of justice and equality as increasingly irrelevant to Celtic Tiger success (almost to the same extent as the state's new-found appetite to purge and punish individual corruption) and it discourages any criticism of the idea that the country is best served by unrestrained market-force capitalism. Within this context, the recent resurgence of religious belief in Ireland may well be a 'fundamentalism' of sorts, but it is fundamentalism only in the sense that it suggests an enduring and utopian determination for the building of a just society.

Note

1. In memory of Kevin Esmonde (1948–2001).

PART IV

MEDIA

9 The Celtic Tiger's Media Pundits

Barra Ó Séaghdha

In recent years Ireland has impinged on the consciousness of the world in two principal areas: the conflict in Northern Ireland and the attempts to resolve it, and the remarkable performance of the Republic's economy in the 1990s. A peaceful Northern Ireland might emulate the performance of its southern neighbour, thus ridding Britain of an international embarrassment and reducing its financial burden. Ireland could then return to where it properly belongs in most British eyes – at the periphery of attention. With the evidence of the past 30 years before us, only those suffering from national megalomania would expect the world, even the British political world, to have a detailed knowledge and understanding of Ireland, a country of a few million people. This is where what can be called the 'gateway pundit' – one who acts as interpreter between a peripheral, relatively unknown country and a larger centre of power – can reasonably expect to have a shaping influence on the framework within which Ireland is viewed by the political/intellectual world, including policy-makers.

In the case of Ireland as seen from Britain, the story that seems to make sense is a simple one: secular reason, liberalism, modernisation, anti-nationalism, the big picture, the future, on the one hand; nationalism, Catholicism, conservatism, narrowness, the past, on the other. There is even a happy ending in prospect: the Celtic Tiger victorious over the ancestral voices. The story is so clear, obvious and easy to assimilate that there seems no need to question it, especially as decent, liberal and presumably perceptive Irish sources seem to confirm it. But is the story really so simple? How have the preconceptions of the most sought-after Irish pundits meshed with those of the audience they are invited to address? Has the political/intellectual world, primarily in Britain but also in the United States, been treated to a comfort blanket of reinforced preconception or to the oting of real questions by these pundits? Before examining the record of some key pundits, it may be useful to sketch in the broad background against which they have operated.

In recent decades, certain sectors in the Republic have evolved with disconcerting speed. The older generations grew up in a society heavily influenced by the Catholic Church, with a near-unanimous belief in a united Ireland (aspired to but not effectively pursued), with a rather static economy and high levels of emigration. The generation that reached adulthood in the mid-1960s or later witnessed economic growth, an interest in economic Europe as a route out of stagnation, the increasing influence of international mass media, and relatively small but lively feminist and radical movements.

In Northern Ireland (where an inturned and reactionary establishment had failed to give even symbolic recognition to its large nationalist minority), this period witnessed the break-up of the political order. After the brutal repression and political incompetence which met the first wave of street protest within Northern Ireland in the late 1960s, fateful errors of judgement, understanding and policy at both regional and UK level created the conditions for a military–political movement so determined not to return to the old order that it paid little heed to the effect of its shootings and bombings on the unionist population who would have to be part of any future united Ireland. On the other side, frustration at the failure of the minority to return to its subordinate role found expression in the random killing of Catholics.

In the Republic, reaction to the ongoing conflict varied: some turned away in exasperation from the call of a past they were hoping to put behind them; some overtly or covertly supported militant nationalism; some sought a flexible, non-violent, nationalist position in the hope that a relationship of trust could be developed with unionism; some reacted to militant nationalism by embracing its political opposite (as if it, too, did not need to acknowledge its responsibility for the situation and to challenge its own foundations). For the liberal intelligentsia, using the term at its loosest, the dream of the 1960s was a painless, speedy process of modernisation. The Troubles in Northern Ireland put an end to the dream. Modernisation proceeded, accelerated by entry into the EEC, but under perpetual threat.

In the late 1970s the second international oil crisis and internal economic mismanagement led to a decade of economic depression, dramatic levels of unemployment and large-scale emigration, accompanied by a right-wing Catholic backlash against modernisation and secularisation. Crucially, this was the formative context for many of those who came to prominence in the dramatically different conditions of Irish political and cultural life in the 1990s.

Setting the Pattern: Conor Cruise O'Brien

Through several of these phases, over the best part of three decades, the outstanding gateway pundit was Conor Cruise O'Brien, whose intellectual distinction, range and combative style opened doors in both Britain and the United States. As those who have followed him in interpreting Ireland to the world have largely accepted his framework of understanding, it is important to look back at the intellectual trajectory of Conor Cruise O'Brien in relation to what used to be called 'the Irish question' over the last quarter of a century and more. Our concern here is not with the civil servant, international diplomat, essayist, author and Labour Party politician, but with the journalist and lecturer who has worked untiringly to advance a particular understanding of the Troubles and, more generally, of political conflict in Ireland.

At the end of *States of Ireland* (O'Brien 1972), a ground-breaking book which fascinatingly combined national and family history, personal experience, political reflection and polemic, O'Brien made a crucial choice. He had personally witnessed some of the less pleasant aspects of the Stormont regime in its last years, had been physically attacked at an Apprentice Boys gathering, and had seen the brutal killing of uninvolved civilians become the loyalist tactic of choice. In the light of these, he decided that pursuing nationalist goals and threatening the foundations of unionism would provoke a violent backlash. If the Provisional IRA did not end its campaign, the resulting intercommunal strife – in effect, a civil war – would completely dwarf any alienation or unpleasantness suffered by the nationalist minority in Northern Ireland under continued unionist rule. In other words, and no matter how much of an unexamined reflex this has since become, O'Brien initially moved towards supporting unionists, not out of respect for or appreciation of the rightness of their arguments, but out of fear of the havoc they would wreak if aroused. Clearly, his expectations of unionism were very low. It can therefore be assumed that he regarded nationalists as more flexible, more malleable or simply weaker than unionists. Otherwise, his support for unionists would have been tantamount to incitement – setting one unyielding block against another. O'Brien set himself the task of isolating militant nationalism in Northern Ireland, of reducing any possible Southern support for the IRA by accusing all Irish nationalism, and all nationalist history, of conscious or unconscious complicity in the violence of the IRA. To ensure his goal of securing Northern Ireland's position within the UK and preventing large-scale and uncontrollable loyalist terror, it was necessary to work towards the creation of a chastened and apologetic Southern state, without fellow-feeling for the Northern minority (no longer to be seen as a separated part of the Irish majority), without legal claim to the territory of Northern Ireland, and shorn of any rhetoric or symbolism that might be construed as threatening by unionists.

The last three decades have indeed seen many historians, commentators, politicians and ordinary people in the Republic significantly re-evaluate their own history and their sense of the national future. It was thus possible for O'Brien to believe that nationalist convictions in the Republic could be diluted, that American support for the IRA could be radically reduced, and that a beleaguered SDLP would have to accept an internal UK settlement. The most efficient way of ending the Troubles would be the isolation of Sinn Féin and IRA members and supporters, whose opposition could then be dealt with through the security apparatus. Even if, after his experience as a government Minister in the mid-1970s, an increasingly conservative O'Brien genuinely saw militaristic republicanism as a threat to the stability and the very existence of the Republic's political order, it needs to be remembered that it was *realpolitik* – brutal political calculation – and not a constructive political programme that underlay his support for unionist positions. In a sense, nationalism had to be destroyed in order to save nationalists, especially Northern nationalists, from the nightmare they risked bringing on themselves and on the country as a whole.

The Anglo-Irish Agreement of 1987, signed by the same Margaret Thatcher who had faced down the H-Block hunger strikers of 1981, was the first major blow to O'Brien's hopes for this strategy: it gave constitutional nationalism in the Republic an official right to express itself on Northern Ireland. It also bypassed unionist opinion. O'Brien sympathised with the explosion of unionist anger that followed.

Suspending Analysis

It is important to note that O'Brien was not actually engaging intellectually with unionism. Any seeming analysis of unionism tended to boil down to the basic form: 'How will such-and-such an action/initiative/reform be interpreted by unionists?' The underlying assumption since the mid-1970s had been that unionism was an immovable mass, incapable of change, growth or flexibility. In one sense, this could be described as a kind of historical despair: nothing positive could come of shaking unionism to the foundations. In another sense, and one that has not been properly acknowledged, it was a form of condescension. What did it say of O'Brien's fundamental appreciation of unionists that they were to be spared the ordeal of articulating, constructively developing and cogently defending their world view, their sense of themselves and their history as they saw it? It could only mean that unionism was to be defended rather than analysed, that the simulacrum of a political culture that had held sway in Northern Ireland for half a century had to be preserved. By implication, the formation of a self-questioning critical unionist political culture would only confuse matters and speed the collapse of unionist positions. Hence, the suspension of rigorous analysis where the words and deeds of most loyalists and unionists were concerned. The focus had always to be outward, towards the enemies of unionism. As the British were the guarantors of unionism, it followed that they too had to be discouraged from re-evaluating the past and reconceiving the future.

A word of caution is necessary at this point. It is normal for intellectuals to exaggerate their own importance. When O'Brien came back to Ireland in the late 1960s and became active in the political and intellectual world, the new middle classes had already begun their rise. The Troubles were a major threat to that rise, one that necessitated a reinforcement of the Border, both economically and ideologically. O'Brien dramatically embodied the changes involved. It may be that his arrogance alienated as many as his intelligence and eloquence convinced. Nonetheless, as the most internationally prestigious Irish public intellectual of his generation, Conor Cruise O'Brien was a hero to many younger intellectuals who saw themselves as modernisers and who wished to escape from the constraints of Irish nationalism and of the Catholic Church.

What was the nature of the example he set? He showed that intellectual life mattered. He demonstrated intellectual freedom by ruthlessly attacking orthodox opinion. He involved himself deeply in matters both Irish and international He was able to gain prestigious platforms for his opinions in the British media and he was acclaimed as the finest analyst of Irish nationalism and of the Northern Ireland question. He presented Irish nationalist/republican history in almost entirely negative terms and relished every chance to expose ambivalence, self-contradiction, selective memory, inadequacy, evil and failure. He did not apply his analytical and polemical skills to unionist politics, behaviour, selective memory and failure. Nor did he apply his analytical and polemical skills to British history, politics, decision-making or failure.

In the Master's Footsteps

Among those commentators from the Republic who have easy access to mainstream or prestigious British media today are Fintan O'Toole, Kevin Myers, Ruth Dudley Edwards, Roy Foster and Colm Toíbín. All have broadly respected the intellectual exclusion zone established by Conor Cruise O'Brien. Myers dwells on every nationalist misdeed, past and present, expects little of unionism but says nothing whatever to distress the historical memory of his *Telegraph* readers; Ruth Dudley Edwards has tended to excoriate nationalists and to dwell on, rather than to analyse, the image of decent, law-abiding, inarticulate, misunderstood unionists; Roy Foster, sometimes spoken of as the leading Irish historian of today, has summarised recent historical research in accordance with the principles of an earlier revisionist generation and has added a few elegant footnotes to British/Irish relations; Colm Toíbín has recently shown signs of moving beyond the naïve polarities by which he has operated since rebelling against his political upbringing as a student in the 1970s.

There is particular reason to single out Fintan O'Toole for closer attention here. With his professionalism and appetite for work, his ability to grasp and analyse masses of detail, his clarity of style and his versatility, O'Toole is a formidable presence. On individual issues – standards in public healthcare, social services, social justice, administration, fund-raising, government/business relations and so on – he is an extremely impressive and perceptive commentator. Nothing in what follows is intended to detract from his genuine achievements in these areas. Indeed, it is because he is not writing to some tortuous personal agenda, because his writings touch on so many aspects of Irish life, and because he is patently committed to understanding Ireland and making it a better place for all who live there, that his case is especially illuminating. In addition, his particular left-liberal position is the quarter from which interested British opinion, for example, would tend to expect enlightenment. He has become the prime critical interpreter of Celtic Tiger Ireland to itself and increasingly – on TV and radio as well in the print media – to the English-speaking world. Our concern here is with the overall historical, social and political framework within which he operates, and with the way his analysis of the Republic conforms to stereotypical expectation. It is also with his debt to his illustrious predecessor, and with the degree to which he establishes a ground from which to present a counterview and, more importantly, a counterforce to the orthodoxy of Celtic Tiger Ireland.

Before the Tiger

Having, like Colm Toíbín, learnt his trade with the magazines *In Dublin* and *Magill* in the early 1980s, O'Toole quickly rose to prominence. The highlights of his journalism of that period are presented in *A Mass for Jesse James* (O'Toole 1990). Articles on popular piety, emigration and social injustice capture the flavour of vital aspects of the period very well, but the overall perspective is also interesting. In his forays into rural Ireland and into popular piety, O'Toole can be seen as an anthropologist of the old school reporting home, as conscientiously and as objectively as possible, to his secular, urban public on life 'out there'. The understanding offered is essentially bipolar: rural/urban, quaint/normal, Catholic/secular, nationalist/internationalist, traditional/modernising, uncritical/critical, immobile/mobile, Ireland/America, past/future.

Fixated on the suffocating orthodoxies that dominated the first half-century of independent Ireland, O'Toole is unable to recognise any progressive forces in Irish life or history that might connect with his own aspirations for the country. There is no historical perspective on either Catholicism or nationalism within the broader context of religion, identity and power in Britain and Ireland over the centuries. Looking at the contemporary political scene, O'Toole is rightly angry about hypocrisy, emigration, hopelessness and injustice. However, there is no sense of active politics, of energies that can be harnessed, of social or political movements that can be galvanised into action. There is a vocabulary, but there is no grammar that might connect and move the forces of progress. The conclusion of a 1989 article on emigration to the US helps to pinpoint the problem:

> Thirty years of being an offshore economic dependency of the United States have left us with a society that is seen by an increasing number of its young people as a pale imitation of the Real Thing across the Atlantic ... That isn't a tragedy, but it is part of the script that was written when we decided that other countries would have to do our developing for us. If we're serious about wanting the emigration to stop – and I'm not at all sure that we are – then we're going to have to write a whole new script (1990: 130–1).

O'Toole is grateful for the modernisation brought about by inviting in, welcoming and minimally taxing foreign capital because it began the process of freeing Ireland from ruralism, nationalism and Catholicism. But he is also aware that it is turning us into a cultural and political colony of the United States. He is right to deplore the

failure to do our own developing, but this is where he finishes –
exhorting us to find a new script but offering none.

It is striking too that Ireland's principal journalistic analyst, when
he chooses from a decade's production to give his picture of the
1980s, has almost nothing to say about Northern Ireland. Only in the
introduction is the question analysed in any fashion. His contribution
to *The Southern Question* (O'Toole 1987), a polemical pamphlet,
shows that this is no accident. Freed from the constraints and commissions of workaday journalism, O'Toole is in a position to present
his ideas as he pleases. With a TV film about the then Taoiseach
Charles Haughey and the same politician's collected speeches as his
raw material, O'Toole denounces the Fianna Fáil party's record,
highlights the systematic substitution of rhetoric for understanding,
and paints independent Ireland as a failed entity which has used a
nineteenth-century romantic dream of unity as an excuse for not
dealing with its own realities. He conjures away the realities of power
within and between Ireland and Britain, conjures away the specifics
of political, social and cultural activity and organisation, conjures away
competing and sometimes irreconcilable senses of order, allegiance,
democracy and justice (as expressed not only in public discourse but
in the texture of day-to-day life), and conjures away both unionism
and British imperial ideologies as needing analysis or mention.
O'Toole sees the century before independence, a period of vast
political and social change and conflict, as bequeathing to independent Ireland only a cloud of romantic nationalist rhetoric. He does not
comment on the balance of forces that found form in the political
settlement of 1920–21 or on the structure of power in Northern
Ireland before and after the current Troubles. In this failure to deal
with those aspects of history that might trouble either his own rigid
framework of understanding or the artificial clarity of the message he
wishes to deliver, O'Toole appears to have modelled himself on the
tendentious post-*States of Ireland* Cruise O'Brien rather than on the
searching thinker of earlier years.

Breaking the Rules

With due acknowledgement of the fact that *The Southern Question* is
a pamphlet rather than an extended political study and that O'Toole
scores some palpable hits, there are a number of observations to be
made which bear significantly on O'Toole's reading of Celtic Tiger
Ireland a few years later. First of all, O'Toole seems shocked that a
politician like Haughey should have adapted the rhetoric of a self-

sufficient Ireland to the new Ireland of multinational investment and EEC membership. However, adapting rhetoric to suit changed circumstances has always been the stuff of politics. Secondly, O'Toole seems to want all political rhetoric to be banished from the field of politics. This is itself a dream and a denial of the unavoidable role of imagination (visions of a transformed future, shared symbols and so on) in harnessing political energy to particular goals (whether these be constructive or destructive). It also sits oddly with the consciously deployed rhetoric of O'Toole's own prose. Thirdly, O'Toole is particularly distressed by the ruling Fianna Fáil party's tendency to present itself more as a national movement than as a political party. Instead of engaging critically with the specific history and core values of Irish populism, he uses one less than convincing quotation from a political scientist – who very tidily contrasts populist clientelism with the 'values of universalism, achievement, and collectivism generally associated with modernity' (1987: 23) – to identify the Irish experience as entirely anomalous in international terms. Showing a schematic understanding of political life around the world that verges on the naïve, O'Toole expatiates: 'Irish politics are the great exception to all of the worldwide rules because they have managed to preserve peasant forms long after the disappearance of a peasant society' (ibid.). Not only that but, 'in Ireland, the inevitable has not happened' (ibid.: 24). For O'Toole, the textbook cannot be wrong: it is the country that is at fault in not conforming to the rules. O'Toole's ideological affinities have always been implicit, not explicit, in his writings. By resisting ideological labelling, he has in fact been a more effective promoter of his own beliefs and has had easier access to major organs of opinion, from the *Irish Times* to the *New Yorker*. There are moments, however, when a rather naïve, neo-Marxist, mechanistic model of economic and political development surfaces.

Preparing to Meet the Tiger

It should now be possible to see how the different strands of O'Toole's thinking intertwine. In global terms, Ireland is an anomaly, stuck in pre-modern, populist politics. The Republic has refused to accept its own limits and has wasted its energy on a nineteenth-century romantic dream of unity. What modernisation has occurred since the 1960s has put the country in the position of a powerless satellite of largely American capital. To deal with the history and grievances of the Northern minority (which should concern us as much or as little as those of any other foreign minority) would be to risk reinforcing

nationalist feeling in the Republic; to open up either the unionist or
the British dimension of the Irish question would be to risk the same
thing. Far better, then, to ignore these issues completely. To ignore
the Northern Irish and British dimensions while opening up the
European would be too blatant an absurdity; Europe is therefore to
be ignored also, except for unspecific references to its non-anomalous
conformity to worldwide political rules. This leaves O'Toole with two
countries to talk about: Ireland and the United States.

How, then, is Ireland to transform itself? How is the reign of empty
rhetoric and disastrous economic management to be brought to an
end? An active politics would be the standard left-wing answer, but –
unhappily – O'Toole does not live in a standard country. Life outside
urban Dublin is alien to him. Entirely secular in his own beliefs, and
with no bridge over to progressive forces among the believers, he is
disconnected from another large swath of the population. With anti-
nationalism as an *a priori* position, he cannot connect with or seek to
activate traditions of resistance or progressive thinking within Irish
history and experience: the language of civic republicanism, which
overlaps with the more constructive elements in both Catholic and
Protestant traditions of the last two centuries; the European revolutionary traditions that fed into the militant nationalist movements of
the United Irishmen in 1798, Young Ireland in 1848 and the Fenians
in 1867; the language of rural resistance, before and after
Independence; the struggle for political self-respect; active feminism
from the Ladies Land League onwards; the progressive, internationalist Irish-language activists of *An tÉireannach* newspaper in the 1930s;
Ireland's constructive record in the League of Nations (1930s) and
the United Nations (1950s) – these and others are contaminated by
contact with the bugbears of land, nationality and religion. A people
that let itself be blinded for so long cannot be trusted. From a knowl-
edgeable distance, one must wait for the people to catch on and catch
up. In the meantime, one can only moralise.

Conscience of the Middle Class

In the end, O'Toole is not a political commentator at all, but a moral
commentator on politics. His history is a matter of – often brilliantly
selected – emblematic moments and statements. The lines of political
and historical energy that run through surface events either escape
him or are avoided as too dangerous to handle. The compromises and
forced improvisations of day-to-day politics never cease to outrage
him. That is why he can be brilliant on particular scandals, moments

and failures of political language, but banal, overwrought or simply wrong on the larger picture. This is also why someone from a dog-matically left-wing political background can become institutionalised as the conscience of the *Irish Times*-reading middle class. As many churchgoers will attest, a weekly exhortation to behave can easily be accommodated. A brief spasm of penitence is sufficient: one doesn't have to question or transform one's behaviour. Besides, there is some common ground. There is a confluence between O'Toole's anti-nationalist internationalism and the short-term economic self-interest of many business and professional people in the Republic who do not wish to be bothered by Northern Ireland. On issues of personal morality (contraception, divorce, abortion, homosexual rights, and so on), left and right liberals are in general agreement. And no one is, publicly at least, in favour of special interests and corruption in high places. An undefined internationalist politics is acceptable in a com-mentator, but it is not organisable on the ground and is therefore unthreatening.

Meeting the Tiger

By 1990, when O'Toole collects his 1980s journalism, the Celtic Tiger-cub is, perhaps providentially, padding into view. In *The Southern Question*, O'Toole had this to say: 'Unable to conceive of itself as an entity, Ireland has failed to act as an entity. It is this which has rendered genuine politics impossible' (1987: 20). Since the 1960s, 'the state itself has been transformed into a local co-ordinator of inter-national investment. There is no economic entity and hence there is no real political entity' (ibid.: 19). Up to now, there has been an ambivalence in O'Toole towards the modernisation of the 1960s. On the one hand, modernisation is necessary as a way of urbanising, mod-ernising, de-nationalising and secularising Irish people. On the other hand, modernisation is carried out by low-tax, multinational-friendly investment policies and, what's more, it is the new generation of Fianna Fáil who, without admitting their past errors, claim credit for and benefit from the social revolution. Now, as the 1980s come to an end, a second wave of economic confidence is rising, investment is again flooding in (with huge growth and opportunity, this time in the IT sector above all others), unemployment is dropping rapidly and everywhere money is talking. In keeping with his previous writings and opinions, O'Toole will continue to denounce corruption, the neglect of the health system, the failure to tackle the heroin problem in the inner city and other deprived areas, and so on. In addition, there will be no shortage of opportunities to deplore any sign that the

Irish money-making classes are behaving in the inelegant, self-serving, greedy style of any capitalist economy in formation. For the secular cleric of today, as for the clergy of the previous dispensation, Irish exceptionalism is to be the rule: the newly rich Irish will be expected to show shiningly clean hands to the world, as their grandparents amid their poverty were to show pure souls. But there is another side to the matter, one that will give O'Toole a role as celebrant as well as critic of this new Ireland.

Let the Celebrations Begin

Even as he sums up the 1980s in the introduction to *A Mass for Jessie James*, O'Toole discovers a new dizzy style in keeping with the 1990s:

> In the public language of Ireland in the eighties, the country was a dream, reality was incomplete, events were unbelievable even though they had happened, anything could mean everything, and everything was unprecedented ... Since the world itself was so fantastic, so fictional, then to reflect it was to invent it. (O'Toole 1990: 13)

On the same page, he goes on to say this:

> There is a radical openness about Irish culture after the eighties. Modern Ireland is permeable, economically, culturally, and in terms of population. It lets in the great tide of international blandness and it lets out much of the life blood of the country. But when the identity that is thus undermined is as rigid and narrow and illusory as the Irish one was, then a loss of identity is not necessarily a bad thing. (ibid.)

Already he is changing his 1980s spots for 1990s stripes. What was seen as a disaster, Ireland's failure to define itself as a political and economic entity, can be reinterpreted as a blessing. The recalcitrant realities of land, nationality and religion can be dispelled by the new globalised economy and a wave of the post-modern wand. With the Republic busy internationalising itself, 'tribal' politics will be consigned to the benighted North, the Catholic Church (undermined by scandal and internal questioning) will continue to weaken its hold on the country, while new technology – both in the form of factories and as a feature of almost every family home – will dissolve the rural/urban divide in favour of the urban; and to fill the space vacated by the old dissolving certainties, to discharge harmlessly the kind of national self-assertion that found expression in dangerous political dreams, there will be culture.

O'Toole's journalism of the early to mid-1990s focuses on and works to accelerate this broad process. The first collection is titled *Black Hole, Green Card: The Disappearance of Ireland* (1994). The second is called *The Ex-Isle of Ireland: Images of a Global Ireland* (1996). In broad terms, *Black Hole, Green Card* celebrates three deaths: in 'The Lie of the Land', that of the mystique of a single, stable, island unit; in 'Scenes from the Death of the National Movement', that of Fianna Fáil – riven by conflict and entering coalition government for the first time – as something more than an ordinary political party; in the section titled 'Religion', that of the authority of the Catholic Church. In the *Ex-Isle of Erin*, the celebration continues, but now emigration is also reinterpreted: what had been a disaster for family and individual, an indictment of a state that failed its citizens, becomes a dizzy adventure across time, space and identities. O'Toole, still showing no interest in any European culture, continues to read extraordinary, uniquely Irish significance into entirely unexceptional aspects of emigration and globalisation (the fact that emigrants in their letters use the word 'home' far more often than those who still live there, for example). Though showing more interest in historical detail than before, he continues to write of emblematic moments rather than patterns of power and resistance. He has a tendency to leap from the particular into the most emphatic and unsustainable generalisation: 'Emigration undercut the very notion that an Irish theatre could safely reflect Irish reality'; 'There is a connection between the contempt for ordinary urban buildings expressed by Michael Collins and the IRA's subsequent willingness to destroy Irish cities'; 'The difference between home and abroad has shrunk to virtually nothing' (O'Toole 1996: 163, 167, 173).

One of the finest pieces in *The Ex-Isle* is 'Tony O'Reilly and the News from Nowhere'. Tracking the rise of the charming rugby-player – as he glides from semi-state enterprise to doing deals with Heinz to managing Heinz, and then to becoming a global media force – O'Toole points up the corporate ruthlessness that operates behind the charm and the rigorously controlled media image. This essay raises obvious questions about economic and media power in an age of global capital and communications. For example, how are people on the ground (various in their needs, their cultures, their histories), and how are individual states, to resist the seemingly irresistible? O'Toole does not pursue such questions, and in a curious way this essay stands alone. Having welcomed the dissolution of Irish particularity into the global mix, how is O'Toole to connect any critique of international corporate power with local political energies and resistance? Once again, as with his internal critique of Ireland in the 1980s, O'Toole offers a sharp critical intelligence disconnected from any potential counterforce.

De-visionism

'In 1996, arguably for the first time in recorded Irish history, it became possible to understand the Republic of Ireland without reference to Britain' (O'Toole 1997: 10). This opening sentence of the introduction to *The Ex-Isle* is both assertive and uncomfortable. Why the reference to recorded history if the Republic has existed only since 1948? Why 'arguably'? The third word of the piece is already preparing a fall-back position. There is a certain pattern here. *Jesse James* presented a journey through Ireland that bypassed any serious engagement with Britain or Northern Ireland. Only in the introduction did O'Toole feel obliged to include issues from H-Block protests North and South, to killings and bombings in Northern Ireland. The essays and articles gathered in *Black Hole*, *Green Card* and *The Ex-Isle* continued to ignore Northern Ireland and Britain except insofar as they appeared in vacuous nationalist rhetoric. While other pundits engaged in Conor Cruise O'Brien-style, single-strand anti-nationalist revisionism, mentioning but not analysing unionism and British power, O'Toole took the master's technique a step further by practising de-visionism: making the entire subject disappear. Only when confident that nationalist ideology is on its last legs does O'Toole begin to mention the personal idealism and probity of many in the first generation of leaders of independent Ireland or to refer to individuals or groups who had opposed political and social orthodoxies before the 1960s. Believing that it is finally dead, he is free at last to discuss the British dimension.

> As they had been constructed historically, the conflicting identities of British Protestantism and Irish Catholicism were statements not just about religious belief or political allegiance or even about the intertwining of the two. They were also – crucially – statements about much more mundane aspects of people's lives. (O'Toole 1997: 14)

What has O'Toole accomplished in these two sentences? The use of the passive in the opening phrase avoids any active narrative. History becomes agentless, so that there is no need to mention questions of power (exercised by whom? in whose interests?); democracy and consent, state sectarianism and violence (before and after the 1801 Act of Union); the level of Protestant leadership of and participation in Irish republicanism and nationalism (such as the United Irishmen, Davis, Mitchell, Butt, Parnell and Hyde); the tension between, on the one hand, the liberating potential of the Protestant language of civil and religious liberty and, on the other, the impossibility of applying that language to the Catholic majority if Protestant power was to be retained; the difference in meaning between Britishness as understood in Britain and as understood by Ulster Protestants; the circumstances of the creation of Northern Ireland; and the difference between Northern Ireland and Britain. Characteristically, O'Toole picks up the issue at the moment of Irish independence and sets up a set of facile oppositions (Irish/British, Catholic/Protestant, rural/urban, and so on) without a history. Characteristically also, he now declares them dissolved – except for some thoroughly nasty intercommunal conflict in Northern Ireland from which the Republic would do well to dissociate itself.

We have seen how Conor Cruise O'Brien, after a period of courageous exploration and questioning, chose for his own reasons to concentrate on one factor in the Northern Ireland equation. 1994 was the year of the Downing Street Declaration, which formally initiated the process that would lead to the multi-party Belfast/Good Friday Agreement. The thinking behind it ran completely counter to the positions of both O'Brien and O'Toole. In that same year, O'Brien brought out *Ancestral Voices*, an ill-written, meandering book which purported to be a study of religion in Irish politics, but which avoided any analysis of Protestantism and power in Britain and Ireland over the centuries, failed to deal with the intertwined history of Protestantism and Catholicism in Ireland and substituted mumbo-jumbo about Catholic ancestral voices and mysticism for analysis. This farrago was declared both stylish and historically sound by no less a figure than the historian Roy Foster.[1]

Only four years later, with O'Brien – true to the logic of the analysis he had set out in the 1970s – having explicitly declared himself happy to be an ally of Ian Paisley, can O'Toole finally achieve critical distance from the master? But it is the Fintan O'Toole who had for so long refused to engage in any depth with the question of Northern Ireland who is now, as chief pundit of Celtic Tiger Ireland, hymning the Belfast Agreement in the *New Yorker* and in the process neutering history (in his passing references to the Act of Union and Partition, for example), omitting what he does not want to think about (the DUP and rejectionist unionism), and painting a simplistic version of his and his contemporaries' attitude to Northern Ireland – under cover of an Ireland for Beginners tone (O'Toole 1998: 54–62) . In addition, we are informed of the happy fact that culture in Ireland has become 'harmless' – which helps to make O'Toole's marketing in the US of Celtic Tiger-period Irish art a risk-free, politically safe activity.

Questions Asked and Unasked

Insofar as intellectuals in the Republic have acted to uncover contradictions in nationalist ideology and to show ambivalence towards violence among the seemingly unambivalent, they have been engaged in a valid and challenging intellectual project. There are questions to be asked, however, of the intellectual integrity of those who, when called on to explain Ireland past and present to the English-speaking world, have confined critical analysis almost entirely to one political tradition. The effect has been to confirm rather than to question stereotypes and to encourage political and historical complacency. In an area so under-examined, it may be useful to be specific. Has British Conservatism needed no reminding of its disregard for the democratic wishes of the majority of Irish people throughout the nineteenth century or of its crucial role, under the leadership of Bonar Law, in encouraging the threat of political violence in Ireland before the First World War? Has the British public in general needed no reminding of Britain's behaviour in the 1912–22 period, Britain's failure to ensure just rule in Northern Ireland before 1968, or its responsibility for the disastrous decision to leave security powers in unionist hands for another two years after August 1969? Has it really occurred to no one that there might be need for a modicum of British and unionist revisionism to accompany the nationalist variety? Did anyone wonder why the intellectual rigour of the *London Review of Books* was suspended in 1995–96 for rambling disquisitions by Colm Tóibín?[2] Why did intellectuals like Tóibín and O'Toole not react when John Lloyd congratulated them in *Prospect* on their status as 'Irish traitors' in the same company as the ex-IRA man Sean O'Callaghan (Lloyd 2000: 36–40)? Is there nothing to be said about the increasing difficulty of distinguishing between the Irish coverage of the *Telegraph* and that of the *New Statesman* (during its spasms of interest)? Should the tone as well as the peculiar content of the Irish references in Eric Hobsbawm's revered *Nations and Nationalism* go unremarked (Hobsbawm 1990)? Why have those who denounce introverted nationalism so often treated the Troubles as a self-enclosed problem that has nothing to say to the history, self-understanding and future of Britain, and of England in particular?

Conclusion

It should now be possible to step back and to perceive the broad pattern to the intellectual culture of Ireland's gateway pundits: the restriction of criticism to one tradition; the failure to activate the positive potential within that tradition; the setting up of false polarities which feed directly into the prejudices of the metropolis; the provincial anxiety to be well thought of in the metropolis that underlies a proclaimed but frequently undemonstrated internationalism; the ingestion of metropolitan standards to the point where genuinely broad-ranging comparative analysis is not pursued; the almost systematic failure to challenge stereotyped thinking in the metropolis; and the fear of history and of active, grounded politics which defuses both critical culture and local resistance to international corporate power and culture.[3]

Notes

1. For analysis of both the O'Brien book and the Foster review see Barra Ó Séaghdha, 'Jump Cuts', *Graph*, second series, No. 1 (1995) pp. 135–9.
2. For an analysis of Colm Tóibín's *London Review of Books* articles see Barra Ó Séaghdha, 'Jump Cuts', *Graph*, second series, no.2 (1996) pp. 132–4 and 139–42.
3. My thanks to Pat Cooke for constructive suggestions during the preparation of this chapter.

10 Broadcasting and the Celtic Tiger: From Promise to Practice

Roddy Flynn

It's cool to be Irish right now. The 'fun side' of economic growth, it is commonly asserted, is the opportunity for increased cultural diversity (not just Japanese sushi bars but Mongolian all-you-can-eats and genuine Romanian cuisine) and a renaissance of indigenous cultural activity. In the latter category politicians point to an intangible but definitive connection between domestic economic success and that of Irish musicians, writers and film-makers on the global stage. Even broadcasting has been said to reap the benefits of success – the Celtic Tiger has banished the two-channel 16-inch black and white portable world of the 1970s and 1980s to the confines of history, replacing it with greater quality and choice.

These twin themes – diversity and renaissance – were established as explicit goals for Irish broadcasting as early as the late 1980s, but the means chosen for achieving these goals – the liberalisation and commercialisation of broadcasting – clearly presaged the Tiger's current neo-liberal policy orthodoxy. Thus in 1988 the Minister for Energy and Communications, Ray Burke, noted Ireland was 'no longer in a situation where the State needs to lay down in detail what the public can have in its radio broadcasting services'. Instead the Minister was seeking to create an environment where 'the talent, capability and investment potential in society' would create 'new dynamic broadcasting services ... and ... allow society to benefit from these'. The thinking was clear: remove the dead hand of the state and let the market deliver what people really wanted.

This chapter illustrates and discusses the consequences for programming quality, and for the larger public service broadcasting mission, of the adoption of a neo-liberal approach to radio and television. The creation of a commercial radio and television sector ended the 62-year-old broadcasting monopoly of the state-owned

Radio Telefís Éireann (RTÉ). It was assumed that – by definition – more channels would mean more choice. Yet the Irish experience suggests that such ideologically motivated pursuit of rather abstract free-market goals, without regard to the specific conditions prevailing in a given broadcasting environment, may (indeed may be expected to) fail to offer viewers diversity or to develop programme-making capacity. Indeed the path followed by broadcasting under the Celtic Tiger suggests that the adoption of such means to achieve such goals may ultimately narrow choice.

Broadcasting and the Irish State: the Historical Context

To understand the state of Irish broadcasting in 1988 one must briefly place it in historical context. From the launch of the first state-owned radio station in 1926 (2RN) until the creation of a national television service in 1961, responsibility for the finance and regulation, and for the day-to-day operation of broadcasting, lay directly in the state's hands. The Department of Posts and Telegraphs (P&T) set up and ran Dublin- and Cork-based stations in the 1920s before establishing the first truly national broadcaster – Radio Éireann – in 1933. The Department did so with some reluctance having had responsibility for broadcasting foisted upon it by a Parliamentary Committee convinced that broadcasting was too important a resource to be left in private hands. P&T's disinclination was based on the cost of broadcasting, which it sought to defray from a licence fee, an import duty on radio sets, and advertising. Despite these, Irish broadcasting was desperately underfunded until the 1940s. Licence fee evasion was rife and in 1932 the service was deprived of import duty income when this was absorbed by the Department of Finance into general exchequer revenues. From this point onwards the broadcasting service was increasingly forced to look to advertising revenue, undermining the financial independence critical to its Reithian public service remit.

Throughout this period, the Minister for Posts and Telegraphs was in theory directly responsible for the minutiae of each day's radio schedule. In this context the Broadcasting Act of 1960 represented a transformation of the broadcasting landscape. Initially prompted by the decision to extend state broadcasting activities into the world of television, the drafters of the Act also took the opportunity to place control of broadcasting in the hands of a semi-state body – RTÉ. Henceforth responsibility for day-to-day activities lay with a Broadcasting Authority which, although appointed by the Minister for P&T, was expected to represent the interests of the public at large.

The apparently unforeseen impact of the introduction of this buffer between the public service broadcaster and the state was the potential for direct state–broadcaster conflict, an outcome made all the more likely by the broadcaster's attempt to reflect the dramatic pace of change in Irish society in the early 1960s. From the mid-1960s on, a series of Fianna Fáil governments and RTÉ came into conflict with increasing frequency, culminating in the sacking of the entire RTÉ authority by then Minister for Posts and Telegraphs, Gerry Collins, in 1972 over the broadcast of an interview with the leader of the Provisional IRA, Seán Mac Stíofáin. The impact of this lesson was chastening – RTÉ adopted a degree of caution with regard to subsequent governments, bordering on an abrogation of its public service responsibilities. Significantly the most notable examples of Irish-related investigative broadcast journalism in the 1980s came almost exclusively from UK broadcasters, especially Granada Television's *World in Action* team whose 'Death on the Rock', Birmingham Six/Guildford Four and Goodman International documentaries arguably had greater political impact in Ireland than they did in the UK. Indeed, the public disquiet which the last of these programmes caused led the Irish parliament to establish a tribunal of inquiry into corruption in the Irish beef export industry.

Liberalising the Airwaves

By the start of the 1980s it was obvious that a single national broadcaster was unable fully to represent or reflect a society still undergoing tremendous social and cultural change. In addition the proliferation of commercially viable pirate radio stations in the 1970s lent credence to the notion that a legal commercial broadcasting sector could be feasible. An Independent Radio Bill was introduced in 1981 but this collapsed along with the Cabinet that promulgated it early in 1982. In 1987 the idea of introducing commercial broadcasting was refloated by then Minister Ray Burke's Sound Broadcasting Bill which envisaged licensing a national radio station, 24 local stations, up to 100 townsize and a further 100 neighbourhood stations, all of which would be in private hands. In announcing this, Burke noted that he was also examining the viability of an independent television service. In the event the Sound Broadcasting Bill was to emerge as two separate acts – the Broadcasting and Wireless Telegraphy Act (which was mainly aimed at shutting down the radio pirates) and the Radio and Television Act. The latter piece of legislation established the Independent Radio and Television Commission, a body with responsibility for awarding licences to and monitoring the activities of an envisaged national radio broadcaster, 24 local radio broadcasters *and* a national television broadcaster. All of these were to be privately owned companies which would rely exclusively on advertising revenues for their survival (while not specifically ruling out the townsize and community stations, the Act made scarce provision for them).

With hindsight a range of objectives – explicit and implicit – appear to have driven the establishment of a commercial broadcasting sector. Significantly improving the range and quality of broadcasting in Ireland was at best only an afterthought – the needs of commerce and of industrial development appear to have been at least as significant. There had long been a constituency within the pirate broadcasting sector that wished to operate on a legal basis. In relation to considerations of industrial development, it was made clear that the introduction of commercial television was at least partly driven by the objective of gaining first-mover advantage for Ireland in the emerging field of MMDS (Microwave Multipoint Distribution System), a television transmission system. The Department of Energy and Communications believed Ireland was in a position to capture the European market for the manufacture of MMDS technology once a home market had been established. The commercial television station would be the only channel to have a 'must carry' status for MMDS operators – hence TV3 was the bait to entice viewers to adopt the new system. There was a further industrial policy objective relating to the development of the infant independent television production sector in Ireland. In 1987 RTÉ's use of independently commissioned programming was sporadic, accounting for a low percentage, in single figures, of its total programme output. Ray Burke envisaged from the outset that the national television channel would make extensive use of this developing resource, adopting the publisher-broadcaster model successfully adopted by Channel 4 in the UK (Brennock 1988).

In passing, one should acknowledge other more clandestine motivations shaping the introduction of commercial broadcasting. It has become commonplace to suggest that part of the shift to commercial broadcasting was driven by a simple desire on the part of the 1987 government to 'nobble' RTÉ, rendering an already far from combative organisation even more quiescent to the government line in its coverage of 'sensitive' political issues (Kenny 1988). This theory would be leant further credence by the 1990 Broadcasting Act which, in the guise of seeking to facilitate the operation of the free market, actually did the opposite, artificially capping the amount of advertising revenue RTÉ could raise. There are even murkier possible motivations: since 1998 Ray Burke has been one of the key figures investigated by an official tribunal of inquiry into political corruption. Initially scrutinised for his role in land-zoning deals, it was subsequently alleged that Burke had been in receipt of substantial sums of money (some tens of thousands of pounds) from the successful promoters of the submission for the national radio licence (Century Radio). Although at the time of writing (August 2001) the tribunal has not yet concluded or published its findings, it has been suggested that Burke received payments in return for forcing RTÉ to reduce its charges to Century for use of its transmission system and/or to ensure that Century secured the licence.[1]

Nonetheless the Radio and Television Act did take at least some account of the need to maintain the quality of Irish broadcasting by including diluted versions of the public service obligation placed on RTÉ by the 1960 Broadcasting Act. According to Section 18, Subsection 3a of the Act, Irish commercial television was to 'be responsive to the needs and interests of the whole community, be mindful of the need for understanding and peace within the whole island of Ireland, ensure that the programmes reflect the varied elements which make up the culture of the whole island of Ireland, and have special regard for the elements which distinguish that culture and in particular for the Irish language'.

Both Bills passed through parliament with relatively few amendments. Once established, the IRTC set about its business with all due speed inviting applications and awarding licences for the local and national radio and television franchises in the six months following October 1988. Over 200 submissions were received for the 24 local radio licences which by any standards would prove to be the most successful results of the 1988 legislation. Although the number of local stations has dwindled over the years (to a total of 16 in mid-2001), those that have survived can generally be regarded as a success both in commercial and programming terms, reflecting local life and culture in a fashion never fully heard on the national broadcasters. Furthermore by offering reduced rates concomitant with their reach[2] these stations have made the airwaves accessible to advertisers who could not previously have considered such expenditure.

TV3: Commercial Fare

Yet there have been far more negative results associated with the efforts to establish national commercial radio and television services. The remainder of this chapter focuses on a case study of television that illustrates this, but it should be made clear at the outset that very similar observations could be made, to a greater or lesser extent, about the national radio licence.

Even most optimistic commentators in 1988 were somewhat nonplussed by the bullishness of Ray Burke's original press release on commercial broadcasting. That there was a market for local radio stations had been clearly demonstrated by the pirates, but there was little evidence of similar financial support for national broadcasting. Commenting on the broadcasting proposals in 1988, one writer noted that 'current political decisions appear to lack recognisable reference points in terms of market data or policy documents such as those prepared by the Hunt or Peacock Committees in Britain' (Kenny 1988).

Notwithstanding this, four groups made a submission for the national radio licence with Century Radio emerging as victor. There was less interest in the television licence, however. When the IRTC met in April 1989 to consider the television licence, they were presented with a submission from just one group – the Windmill Consortium which included U2 manager Paul McGuinness and film producer John Kelleher, and which was financially backed by the Jefferson Smurfit Group. In the absence of any other candidates, the IRTC duly awarded the licence to the consortium, which anticipated commencing operations by September 1990. It would, however, be a further eight years before it actually commenced broadcasting. The support of putative investors proved difficult to transform into actual cash – first the Jefferson Smurfit Group, then their replacement Yorkshire Television, pulled out of the project within 18 months of the awarding of the licence. Both companies had doubts about the viability of establishing a third television station financed by advertising. In an apparent attempt to shore up the station's prospects (or 'to level the playing field' as it was put) Ray Burke introduced a new broadcasting bill in 1990 capping RTÉ's advertising revenue, but even this was insufficient to encourage investors to get behind TV3. (Nor did the 1990 bill aid the struggling Century Radio which ceased operation in 1992.) On top of everything else MMDS, the new distribution system through which TV3 was to reach the population as a whole, failed to develop at the speed originally anticipated. Therefore, in 1991 the IRTC withdrew the TV3 licence on the grounds that the station had not been launched by the deadline originally stipulated. Indeed the IRTC argued that to all intents and purposes the disappearance of backers like Smurfit and Yorkshire meant that there now was no consortium to support. For a few years, the issue of commercial broadcasting on a national scale disappeared.

In 1994, however, the TV3 consortium succeeded in winning back the licence after a Supreme Court decision in its favour. When this was followed by a new investment from Ulster Television, it appeared that the channel might be up and running by 1995. Yet in 1996 UTV also pulled out, unhappy with the level of managerial control its 45 per cent equity state won it. The situation was finally retrieved by the entrance in 1997 of Canadian cross-media giant Canwest Global which purchased the UTV stake in TV3 in its entirety. Canwest brought serious muscle to the TV3 proposition – owning channels or stations in Canada, Australia, New Zealand and Northern Ireland, Canwest had access to substantial programming resources, buying US programmes in bulk and then distributing them to its global arms. Canwest made TV3 a commercially viable operation for the first time. Thus, in September 1998, nearly a decade after first winning the national commercial television licence, TV3 went on the air.

The specific terms of the contract drawn up between the IRTC and TV3 in 1998 bore little resemblance to the service promised in 1989. The IRTC had made its expectations of any new service clear. In November 1988, the chairman, Seamus Henchy, said of the commercial stations that 'token compliance with the requirements to broadcast news and current affairs will not be tolerated' (Anon. 1988). Similarly in January 1989 the then IRTC secretary, Sean Connolly, enunciated the prerequisites for those applying for the national commercial television licence:

> The applicants must show that they are commercially viable and have the initial capital to provide a station that will broadcast news and a percentage of material that is produced by people other than the company itself ... the successful company must also reflect 'an Irishness' ... expected from a national television station' (Tynan 1989).

In its April 1989 submission to the IRTC the Windmill Consortium directly addressed those demands. Consortium chairman James Morris had noted that he expected at least 70 per cent of the new company's share ownership to remain in Irish hands. Moving to content, he stressed that the new channel – named TV3 – 'would not be a mirror image of what was already in existence' but that 'the new service would be both national and local with local interest pro-gramming at times being broadcast to each of four regions in the country simultaneously ... three regional studios would be set up' (Foster 1989).

Morris was supported by Paul McGuinness who stressed the station's putative contribution to the independent production sector: 'There was a newly emergent film production sector and these producers "would be treated as a major resource to give TV3 its distinctive style".' Then, explicitly echoing Ray Burke, he added that 'in many ways it would be like Channel 4 in Britain ...'. McGuinness concluded with the opinion that 'the advent of the new service was "the most significant change in the nation's cultural infrastructure since the foundation of RTE"' (Foster 1989).

By 1998, however, these 'commitments' had been replaced by bare undertakings to carry news and current affairs and to ensure that 15 per cent of broadcasting time consisted of Irish material. According to Section 18, Subsection 3a of the 1988 Radio and Television Act, the IRTC could in theory have insisted on a lot more. In 1989 one commentator had noted that although it was possible that TV3 might well focus on the 'light entertainment/video/film/canned comedy/canned sport end of business' that with the IRTC in charge 'it is unlikely that TV3 will be allowed to marginalise itself in this way' (Anon. 1989). In point of fact this perfectly captures TV3's output to date. On the IRTC website, TV3's mission statement declares its aims as being

> to tap the qualities of community pride, independence, creative talent, humour and determination that are a vital part of Irish society, and, in so doing, to bring to its audience a full representation of life in Ireland and of its interaction with the rest of the world.

This is hardly reflected in the channel Irish audiences watch. The assertion of TV3 chairman James Morris that the channel would not be a mirror of what is available elsewhere is confounded by even the most casual glance at TV3's schedule: *Jerry Springer, The Young and the Restless, Cagney and Lacey, Ricki Lake, VIP, The Love Boat, Emmerdale, Judge Judy, Coronation Street, Charlie's Angels, Cold Feet, Birds of a Feather, Sex and the City, Seinfeld, Mad About You, Heartbeat* and so on, all of which are available on other terrestrial/cable channels. Hardly the stuff of Paul McGuinness's claim that it would lead to a 'significant change in the nation's cultural infrastructure'. This also points to the other major discrepancy between the original proposal and what is currently on offer. It is obvious that the programming above is exclusively sourced from US and UK producers; indeed Canwest is now the largest non-US purchaser of US production material (Brodigan 2001). What then of the commitment to use the independent Irish production sector or indeed simply to screen Irish material?

TV3's 'Irish' output has been limited to the legal minimum – 15 per cent of total broadcast time, rising to 25 per cent after five years. In practice, this has been fulfilled with news programming, one current affairs programme *Agenda* (which as several reviewers have pointed out could essentially be a radio show since it rarely leaves the studio) and the introduction of a studio-based breakfast show (the duration of which was increased by 30 minutes as TV3 approached the end of its third year). Despite appointing a commissioning editor previously held in some esteem within the independent production sector, and despite publishing a programme policy statement committing the station to spending on independently produced programmes 15 per cent (or IR£1.38m – whichever is higher) of the total amount invested in Irish programming, only a handful of programmes have actually been commissioned. This is largely due to a qualification in the station's contract which states that such commissions will only go ahead if the company is breaking even – something which had not been achieved by summer 2001. The highest profile show of those which have been commissioned – *The Weakest Link* – is far from being an innovative contribution to Irish television since it is a direct transplant of the BBC's format. Beyond this are programmes which only appear to be 'home-produced' – *The Pepsi Chart Show* and *20/20* – which to a large extent are international shows with presenter inserts top-and-tailed to suit whichever countries they are screened in. (*20/20* is a show which can be found on several of Canwest's stations across the globe: consequently much of what the Irish audience sees is taken from previous US, Canadian or occasionally Australian editions.) In short, TV3 has adopted the cheapest possible programming as the core of its schedule – US and UK acquisitions.

The programme output reflects TV3's ownership. Far from 70 per cent of the station being in Irish hands, 90 per cent of the company is owned by Canwest and Granada Media (who took a 45 per cent stake in autumn 2000).[3] The arrival of Granada had an immediate impact on the TV3 schedule: *Coronation Street*, the jewel in Granada Television's crown which had been acquired by RTÉ for some decades, was transplanted to its commercial rival where it quickly established itself as a ratings winner. In 2000 TV3's single most successful broadcast won it 301,000 viewers. By summer 2001 *Coronation Street* was attracting 400,000-plus viewers to the channel on a weekly basis.

Regulatory Capture

TV3 has been able to adopt this universalist and culturally unspecific programming because the regulator, the IRTC, has permitted it to.

What is more, the IRTC's generosity extends beyond programming. For example, although TV3 is supposed to pay the IRTC a sum equivalent to 3 per cent of its revenue in return for the right to broadcast, this sum has been reduced to a flat rate of IR£50,000 for the first four years of the station's existence. This is justified by reference to the 'general difficulties of establishing a third television station in Ireland' but also to 'the changed and more unfavourable legislative environment in which TV3 will now operate since the franchise was first awarded'. This, a reference to the 1993 removal of the cap on RTÉ advertising, seems inexplicable given that the cap hadn't even been mooted when TV3 won the franchise in 1989.

The question is why the IRTC of the late 1990s has decided to apply the most relaxed possible interpretation to the statutory requirements placed on the national commercial broadcaster. The answer would appear to be that somewhere along the way the original rationale for introducing a new commercial broadcasting service got lost – words like 'quality' and 'choice' were replaced by 'commerciality' and 'viability'. In particular the collapse of the national commercial radio station, Century, in 1992 has cast a long shadow over the IRTC's subsequent decisions. Having seen one broadcaster collapse, possibly as a consequence of overly prescriptive scheduling requirements, the Commission has been reluctant to remain so dogmatic. Hence Century Radio's successor, Today FM, was allowed to ditch much of its original submission (that the schedule be talk-dominated as opposed to music) after it performed dismally during its first six months (in 1997). TV3 has enjoyed similar leeway.

The relationship between TV3 (and indeed Today FM) and the IRTC is almost a textbook definition of regulatory capture. The phrase, taken from economics, describes the situation whereby a regulated institution comes to dominate the regulator.[4] This can occur for a variety of reasons, but these can generally be reduced to the fact that the views and interests of the consumers are diffuse, inexpert and difficult to express cogently. By contrast, the regulated company has a very specific set of interests and can employ PR firms to articulate them in the most effective fashion possible. Not surprisingly, regulators are generally swayed by the arguments of the latter rather than those of the consumers/citizens on whose behalf such industries are regulated. This is particularly true where states fails to expound any strong line on regulatory policy.

In the Irish context, the fact that TV3 is the only commercial television station clearly lends the company a substantial degree of clout in its dealings with the IRTC. In effect it can dictate its own terms of reference to the Commission – if the IRTC rejects these TV3

can simply say 'then no commercial broadcasting'. The IRTC's negotiating hand is hardly strengthened by the fact that it is financially
supported by contributions from the broadcasters it regulates – in short
its financial position relies on those broadcasters being up and running.

Impact on Public Service Broadcasting

Does it necessarily matter that TV3 has been allowed gradually to
evade the commitments on the basis of which it was originally
awarded the licence? Even if TV3 adds little to the range of choice
available to Irish viewers, does this undermine the broadcasting environment as a whole? Before considering this question, it is worth
recalling the following warning from 1989:

> Over a period of time RTÉ will have to shrink and shrink, a little bit
> at a time, its public service remit in such a way as to meet the com-
> petition. As the new channel becomes more and more successful
> commercially, as it takes audience share, as it takes revenue share,
> nobody else is going to find that money. That's the problem. Once
> you've got competition for revenue, that's the end of public service
> broadcasting. (Michael Grade quoted in Kenny 1989)

What is striking about this quote is its source: it is not RTÉ (although
their 1989 document 'Change and Challenge' made precisely the
same point) or another advocate of state-owned public service broadcasting. Rather it is Michael Grade, then the avowedly
commercially-oriented head of Channel 4. Tellingly, Grade's point
would not generally apply to the UK broadcasting market. The introduction of commercial broadcasting to Britain in 1954 had some
impact on the BBC which began to compete for ratings with less
explicitly Reithian scheduling. Nonetheless, the fact that the BBC was
not directly competing with ITV for a limited advertising revenue pool
insulated the Corporation from having to go down a purely
commercial route.

RTÉ, however, does not have this protection. The state's consistent
unwillingness to fund broadcasting adequately has left broadcasting
reliant on commercial revenues since the early 1930s. The extent of
this problem is difficult to overstate. Approximately 70 per cent of
RTÉ's income is currently derived from advertising, by far the highest
percentage of commercial income of any public service broadcaster
in Europe and one which has increased consistently throughout the
1990s (European Audiovisual Observatory 2000: 158). In autumn

2000, RTÉ sought sanction for an increase in its licence fee from IR£70 to IR£120, a substantial jump but one which reflected the fact that the licence fee in Ireland has not been tied to inflation in the past and had been at the IR£70 figure since 1996 (when it was increased from IR£62, itself a figure which had been frozen for the previous ten years). By any standards the IR£70 licence fee was remarkably cheap – even after the increase Ireland had the lowest fee of any EU member state with the exception of Luxembourg (where there is no public service broadcaster) and Spain and Portugal (where there is no licence fee). Nor was it a question of being 'just behind' the other states – the Irish fee was less than two-thirds of the average fee charged in other EU member states. RTÉ's argument was that an increase to IR£120 would simply bring the Irish figure up to the EU average.

Yet in the public debate about the putative fee increase, a further crucial fact was lost about the public service broadcaster's finances – even if RTÉ were to have achieved the full IR£50 increase, the actual sum of money this would raise would still, for reasons of scale, fall far short of that available to broadcasters from licence fees raised in other European countries. In 1999, there were 1.138m television households in Ireland (Euromonitor 2000: 326). Even assuming no licence fee evasion,[5] the most RTÉ could hope to raise with a IR£120 licence fee would be IR£136.56m. This compares with the next lowest figure in Europe – Finland with an income of IR£263m from licence fees. Meanwhile at the other top end of the scale, German public service channels had access to up to over IR£5bn in licence fees.

The problem is that these enormous disparities in income are not matched by concomitant differences in production costs. Admittedly, average production budgets vary enormously across Europe in deference to the realities of available finance. Television executives and consultants from the larger EU countries often have some difficulty comprehending RTÉ's per hour production costs which are so low as to be regarded as unfeasible. Nonetheless, there are basic minimum expenditures necessary to produce an hour of television regardless of where you produce it. By contrast the cost of *acquiring* shows is directly related to income – for example the fee charged by Warner Television International Sales to RTÉ for a season of *Friends* bears no relation to the fee charged to Channel 4. Warner sets the fee according to the size of the individual broadcaster's potential audience, so the fee is related to population size. In short, even prior to the introduction of commercial broadcasting, RTÉ had little choice but to rely on acquired programming to an extent unusual by

European standards. Now, with the addition of TV3 to contend with, the pressure to do so has increased.

This might be less of a problem if Ireland had a larger population: in the UK it has proved possible to support three channels dependent on advertising revenue because to an extent (most explicitly so in the case of Channel 4) they have established niches for themselves. In Ireland, however, even though advertising expenditure has increased dramatically in the last five years (see Table 10.1), it remains the case that such are the costs of running a television station that it is unrealistic to consider seeking out commercially viable niche markets in a population of 3.7 million people.

Table 10.1 Advertising expenditure in Ireland 1991–2000 (IR£m)

	1991	1992	1993	1994	1995	1996	1997	1998	1999	2000
TV	57	65	72	83	95	n/a	101.9	113.9	136.3	157.2
Print	109	119	126	139	154	n/a	197.9	208.4	231.7	351.1
Radio	20	28	23	28	27	n/a	29.1	34.3	38.4	43.3
Cinema	2	1	1	2	3	n/a	3.1	3.7	4.0	4.8
Outdoor	13	14	13	15	20	n/a	24.5	30.4	37.9	54.8
Total	201	227	235	267	299	n/a	356.5	390.7	448.3	611.2

Sources: *Euromonitor European Marketing Data and Statistics* 1994–98 (1991–95) and IAPI *Adspend* (1996–2000).

Even the spendthrift TV3 needs about IR£32 million in revenues per annum simply to break even (TV3 1998). This means taking roughly one-fifth of the total television advertising spend in 2000. It might appear that winning one-fifth of the total audience might be the way to do that. However, in practice, a disproportionate amount of that advertising expenditure is targeted on shows with the kind of viewership that advertisers really want – that portion of the population with money to spend and which is still undecided about the brand of washing powder they are going to commit to for life. Consequently, TV3 has from the outset explicitly not targeted a previously unserved audience but rather it has delivered a mass-appeal schedule targeting the 15–34-year-old ABC1s for whom advertisers are so hungry. Since RTÉ is already dependent on advertising revenue, TV3's grab for the same audience has effectively forced the public service broadcaster to adjust its own schedules (especially in the case of its second channel, Network 2) to compete for that same narrowly defined audience. In the months before TV3 came on the air, Network 2 underwent a major facelift, producing a primetime schedule based almost exclusively on US network hit shows in a clear attempt to defend market share. Faced with competition for its major revenue source RTÉ is forced to behave in an increasingly commercial fashion, even legitimating the licence fee by reference to ratings rather than to programme quality.

However, the real threat of commercial broadcasting is not to the public service broadcaster – RTÉ as an institution may well be capable of surviving any competition TV3 can offer – but to public service broadcasting in general. This distinction – between defending RTÉ as an institution and defending public service broadcasting in general – is crucial, but it is one successive governments have apparently failed to make. At present the state's position appears to be that if there is a public service broadcaster (RTÉ) then there will be public service broadcasting. Clearly, however, if that broadcaster is driven to act according to commercial dictates as a consequence of state policies (maintaining a low licence fee while introducing competition for its other revenue source) then it becomes a public service broadcaster in name only. In this situation, public service broadcasting – which should offer a range of quality programmes reflecting a wide range of perspectives and addressing viewers as citizens rather than as consumers – may disappear.

That the danger is real is illustrated by the outcome of RTÉ's appeal for a licence fee increase. In May 2001 the Minister opted to award an increase of IR£14.50 – just one-third of that sought, citing (but not publishing) a report by accountants Pricewaterhouse Coopers as a reason for doing so. Already losing audience share, and recording balance sheet losses,[6] RTÉ now faces the need to invest around IR£50 million in developing new digital channels. The content of these channels may offer the most tangible evidence yet of the combined effect of commercial competition and low public funding. For example, the new digital youth channel, although fronted by Irish presenters, will rely on 'material ... acquired from abroad with a focus on celebrities and comedy' (Smith 2001).

Conclusion

In the 13 years since the 1988 Act a remarkable amount has happened within Irish broadcasting: there have been three more broadcasting Acts; RTÉ has begun to commission extensively from the independent television sector through its Independent Production Unit (IPU). And there are now four Irish TV channels: three public service channels and one commercial channel. In some respects the pursuit of commercial broadcasting has had positive impacts – the creation of an independent local radio sector has been a success in programming and commercial terms. Yet looking to the output of TV3 in particular it is difficult to see what positive contribution it makes to Irish cultural life or even towards the industrial policy objectives underlying the creation of the franchise in 1988.

It would be absurd to 'blame' TV3 for this situation or for adopting a strategy aimed at profit maximisation in a small market (something they have proved remarkably successful at, surpassing Network 2's ratings). The fact remains that the shift towards commercial broadcasting was (and arguably still is) a leap into the unknown on the part of successive governments. In making the original decision to introduce commercial broadcasting, no account appears to have been taken on the part of the state as to how this would impact upon public service broadcasting.[7] Nor has there ever been a convincing exposition of why commercial broadcasting is necessary. Even the initial failure of commercial broadcasting failed to engender any reconsideration of the rationale behind the project. As a neo-liberal consensus seeped into Irish politics (right across the political spectrum), the goal shifted from using commercial broadcasting to achieve other policy goals to its becoming an objective in its own right. In effect the means became the end.

However, it is clear that, far from 'freeing' broadcasters to be innovative and experimental, the commercialisation of broadcasting has had the opposite effect, placing very real limits on the scope for creativity and risk-taking. Unable to risk exploring new formats and genres lest they should fail, both state and commercial broadcasting organisations have had to adopt essentially imitative strategies: either acquiring shows with a proven track record elsewhere or purchasing/borrowing successful formats. RTÉ now screens shows like *The Simpsons, Friends, ER, Buffy the Vampire Slayer* and so on, all of which are available on at least two other channels accessible to Irish cable viewers. Meanwhile TV3 has replaced Cilla Black with Twink for their version of *Blind Date* while RTÉ has recalled veteran broadcaster Gay Byrne to play the Chris Tarrant role on *Who Wants to be a Millionaire?*

The net effect of a decade of headlong pursuit of the commercialisation of broadcasting, therefore, has been to narrow the range of programme material available to an Irish audience: more channels has not meant more choice. This narrowing of choice comes at a time when social, political and cultural change would appear to demand an expansion in perspectives. The growing emphasis on imported programming and formats suggests that the potential of Irish television fully to address/represent the cultural specificities of its increasingly diverse audience is diminishing and will continue to do so.

It may finally be that, by making explicit the consequences of long-term governmental failure to take the idea seriously, the introduction of commercial broadcasting will prompt a re-evaluation of the public service ideal. Indeed TV3, by questioning how RTÉ spends its licence fee income and arguing that it is entitled to a share of it to fund its own news and current affairs public service obligations, has drawn attention to the fact that not everything on the public service broadcaster is public service broadcasting. If that engenders a public debate on why so much of the public service broadcaster's output looks increasingly commercial, then commercial broadcasters will have made an unwitting but real contribution to the health of Irish broadcasting.

Notes

1. In this respect one should note that the initial legislation presented in November 1987 made no provision for the appointment of an independent body to award broadcast licences but left the decision to the Minister of the day, Ray Burke. Only after protest from all the opposition parties was the notion of an independent broad-casting authority introduced.
2. However, the two Dublin local stations – 98FM and FM 104 – have access to one-third of Ireland's total population, which means their rates are often far in excess of their non-Dublin counterparts.
3. Even this overstates the power of the Irish shareholders – only Canwest and the Granada directors of TV3 have voting rights. The Consortium Directors – O.J. Kilkenny, Paul McGuinness, James Morris, Denise Collins and Windmill Lane Pictures Ltd have no such rights.
4. The classic text on the phenomenon of regulatory capture is Nobel Laureate George Stigler's article 'The Theory of Economic Regulation' (1971).
5. A far from safe assumption – through the 1990s Ireland consist-ently recorded the highest licence fee evasion figures in Western Europe. On average some 10–15 per cent of television homes did not have a licence in this period. There is little reason to believe figures have improved since.
6. RTÉ is currently sustaining the losses by dipping into cash reserves earned from the sale of its Cablelink cable distribution company. Although substantial, these reserves are not infinite.

7. There is one notable exception to this characterisation – the 1995 publication by the Department of Arts, Culture and the Gaeltacht, during Michael D. Higgins's period as Minister, of a document outlining the issues that public service broadcasting was likely to face in the short and long-term futures. Unfortunately *Active or Passive* (as the document was called) never had the opportunity to find legislative expression.

11 Screening the Green: Cinema under the Celtic Tiger

Debbie Ging

In tandem with the changes wrought by the Celtic Tiger, Irish cinema has experienced a significant metamorphosis since the beginning of the 1990s. Compared with the gritty social realism that characterised the earlier period known as the First Wave (late 1970s to 1980s), the films of the late 1990s and, in particular, early 2000s have tended to portray a more liberal, urban and successful Ireland. The purpose of this chapter is to interrogate the way in which contemporary Irish cinema has addressed Celtic Tiger Ireland, and to contrast national cinema in an era of economic success with that of the earlier period, with specific emphasis on their respective approaches to diversity, multicultural identity and their capacity to accommodate marginalised voices.

One of the most common assumptions made about pre-boom cinema in Ireland is that, on account of its concern with rural narratives, religion, republicanism and dysfunctional family structures, it belongs to an oppressive cultural tradition that has prevented us from moving toward a more modern and innovative engagement with the art form. By looking at aesthetic form as well as thematic content, I aim to demonstrate that the bulk of the films made under the first Film Board (1981–87), rather than espousing the Ireland of official state nationalism, explicitly challenged it. Since the 1990s, however, a booming economy and the onslaught of globalisation have started to erase this type of self-questioning in favour of a more marketable vision of Irishness, whereby Irish identity has become more a global commodity than a means of critical self-questioning. In spite of the recent claims made in official government and industry reports[1] that cinema is a crucial national story-telling form, it seems that there is less concern in contemporary Ireland with reflecting or constructing a sense of national identity through our film culture than with convincing the international audience that we are 'Paddys no more' (Vorm 1982).

Irish Cinema's Golden Age

The term 'First Wave' Irish cinema generally refers to the work – dating from the mid-1970s to the closure of the first Film Board in 1987 – of a group of film-makers including Joe Comerford, Bob Quinn, Cathal Black, Kieran Hickey and Pat Murphy, who were concerned not only with exploring complex narrative themes but also with challenging conventional cinematic forms. Although many of these films have since been written off as experimental or avant-garde and thus of little relevance to what we might now refer to as a national film industry, they marked a significant period in the development of Irish modernity. Their dismissal at thematic level on account of an 'excessive' concern with 'overdone' topics such as religion, violence, Travellers, national identity and feminism is also problematic and frequently the result of a tendency to equate narratives lacking in universal appeal with some form of regressive nationalism. I argue that these films, by taking a non-indigenous artform and reappropriating it to articulate national and local concerns, demonstrated that embracing the global was not necessarily dependent on a rejection of one's own locality or traditions but rather could be mobilised as a powerful means of interrogating the diversity of Irish identities, their relationship with the past and their complex relation to modernity.

Whereas official state nationalism in Ireland has worked to establish difference as a largely negative concept – i.e. everything that is *not* British – cultural nationalism can establish difference with a view to celebrating diversity. In this sense, the repudiation of the Irish past in the name of a cosmopolitan modernity could be seen as a regressive rather than a progressive move. As Jim Smyth and David Cairns recently commented: 'The break with nationalist discourse has been swift and virtually uncontested, but the "spiritual liberation" which Joyce hoped would replace the stifling confines of Catholic nationalism has proved elusive' (Smyth and Cairns 2000: 226). Given that the 'spiritual liberation' offered to us by contemporary cinema thus far, as exemplified by films such as *About Adam* (1999), *Accelerator* (1998) and *Flick* (2000), has been limited by a distinctly uncritical acceptance of global culture, it is possible that the films of Comerford, Quinn, Murphy, Black, O'Sullivan and Hickey are the closest we have come to a body of work that is both distinctively Irish and at the same time progressive. By reworking conventional cinematic form, these films were able to accommodate a diversity of voices that the move toward mainstream cinema has thus far failed to do. Indeed, one of the most striking features of the first period of independent film-making in Ireland was the way in which it treated strangers, outsiders and marginalised characters. Many of the films made during this period expressly challenged the currently fashionable discourses that equate the past with exclusion and the present with inclusion and diversity by giving voice to a wide range of marginalised perspectives. Moreover, they tended to connect with the past in a progressive way, showing how myths of state nationalism and De Valera's Ireland have left a legacy of repression and suffering. But, while on the one hand, they actively challenged preconceived notions about Irishness, they were also deeply engaged with renegotiating national culture rather than abandoning it in favour of a global, culturally amnesiac identity.

The First Wave film-makers worked consciously with the idea that self-questioning and self-understanding were crucial to progressive thinking on a host of issues linked to Irish identity. They looked back in order to scrutinise the present, and they homed in on the local in order to make sense of the universal. Speaking of his own work, Bob Quinn has said:

> Instead of aiming for the broad canvas I have been making notes, sketches, miniatures, documenting small places and small people; instead of dealing with eternal human verities as understood by a homogenous audience of popcorn eaters, I seem purposely to have been making my oeuvres as obscure as possible, in a language little known outside Ireland, in a community equally rather despised by progressive Irish people. (Quinn 2000: 27)

His comment draws attention to the fact that, while Hollywood might make the world a smaller place, it also renders it a simpler and less diverse place as its 'eternal verities' increasingly overlook the lived realities of 'small places and small people'.

According to Kevin Rockett, Quinn's *Lament for Art O'Leary* (1975) was a crucial and radical film in this respect since it was the first independently produced film to be made in Irish (in Rockett et al. 1988: 137–8). Martin McLoone also points out that it was under-pinned by one of the core objectives of Third Cinema as defined by Solanas and Getino, namely 'the participation of people who, until then, were considered spectators' (cited in McLoone 2000: 132). The film takes an element of Ireland's oral tradition (an Irish-language lament from the 1770s) and uses complex intertextual devices to recast it as a play within a film, in which the actors negotiate the inter-pretation of history and argue with the English director, thus mirroring the narrative of the original lament. According to McLoone: 'It was an attempt, in other words, to reinsert, albeit in a more radical and a more secular sense, the nationalism that was in danger of being jettisoned

in the rush toward modernity' (ibid.: 132). In *Poitín* (1978) Quinn
deliberately eschewed the romantic myth of the west by depicting the
dog-eat-dog realities of small-time crime in rural Ireland, while in
Atlantean (1983) he presented a tongue-in-cheek documentary on the
fact that the Celts had come from North Africa, thus challenging the
purism inherent in nationalism's appropriation of Celtic mythology.
More recently, *The Bishop's Story* (1994), based on the 1987 short film
Budawanny, evoked traces of Friel's play *Dancing at Lughnasa* in its
exploration of the clash between formal Catholicism and the remnants
of paganism that lie dormant in some western communities. Quinn's
contention that the pre-modern traditions of Ireland were significantly
more liberal than modern sexual mores finds echo in Joe Comerford's
Reefer and the Model (1988), in which a homosexual encounter at a
local céilidh goes unnoticed by the locals present.

Indeed, one of the central messages running throughout
Comerford's work seems to be that progress is not dependent on a
simple rejection of traditional values and adoption of new ones, but
rather on their mutual illumination and interaction. The four
characters in *Reefer and the Model*, who constitute a shaky surrogate
family of marginalised identities, seemed to encompass many of
Ireland's social and political problems of the time – a pregnant model
with a past involvement in drugs and prostitution, a smuggler and
armchair republican, a homosexual and an IRA man on the run. As
Lance Pettitt suggests, the participation of the two men in the céilidh
in *Reefer and the Model* and the public acceptance of their sexual
intimacy subverts 'mainland codes', suggesting that the pre-Catholic
traditions of rural Ireland (or what Luke Gibbons has called 'radical
memory') have survived in the most Gaelic outposts of the west and
that the moral codes of modernity are, in fact, often more reactionary
than those of the past (Pettitt 1997: 261). Significantly, Pettitt also
points out that it is the army sergeant, a representative of the state,
who tries to suppress their homosexuality. By exposing the contradictions and complexities of Irish identity, Comerford has shattered
accepted myths about cultural nationalism and Irish Catholicism,
while at the same time embracing a vision of Irishness that is at once
progressive, traditional *and* genuinely pluralist.[2]

Comerford's work is also significant in terms of accommodating
marginalised voices. Unlike much contemporary material which deals
with drug abuse and social exclusion in wholly apolitical terms,
Comerford's early shorts gave an authentic voice to Dublin's urban
underclass (*Down the Corner* 1978) and to heroin addicts (*Withdrawal*
1974), without eschewing the social context. His later films, *Reefer
and the Model* (1988) and *Traveller* (1982), were explicitly concerned

with outsiders, offering the spectator the perspectives of their dispossessed and marginalised characters. The plurality of voices (male, female, straight, gay, republican) do not fuse into a single consciousness but rather exist on different registers, generating dialogical dynamism. According to McLoone:

> The idealism and the aspirations that motivate them may be vague and unarticulated – even contradictory and irrational when they are articulated – but the point is that these ideals are a response to the lack of idealism in conventional society. Their elliptical and imprecise nature requires an equally ambiguous cinematic form to allow them to emerge. (2000: 136)

In *Traveller,* Comerford confronts many of the prejudices surrounding Ireland's only indigenous ethnic group (the Travelling community) by refusing to adopt the 'logical' viewpoint of mainstream society. Voice and image are juxtaposed in contradictory ways, so that the woman – who does not play a major narrative function in the visual story – gets to speak of her experience of domestic violence, sexual abuse and marriage. At one point, the images are overlaid with a discourse about settled people's perceptions of Travellers. While in a mainstream film, these aspects of Traveller culture would inevitably be interpreted as negative representations, Comerford avoids this trap by telling the story from their perspective, not just in terms of voice but also camera point-of-view and even narrative logic. Thus the film relays a variety of discourses about Traveller identity which come from both inside and outside that community, unlike *Into the West* (1992) or *The Field* (1990), in which the Travellers are seen and understood (albeit sympathetically) from the perspective of the settled community.[3] Meanwhile, the more recent *Trojan Eddie* (1996) occupies a kind of middle ground in that it confronts many of the misunderstood elements of Traveller culture, while at the same time adopting the standard narrative logic of a mainstream thriller.

Kieran Hickey's *Exposure* (1978) deals explicitly with Irish reactions to the Outsider (who is both woman and foreigner), highlighting the sexual repression and cultural insularity of 1970s Ireland. Unlike many contemporary stories that address the 'foreigner within' theme, for example Eugene Brady's *The Nephew* (1998), Hickey refuses to structure the film as an individual's journey of self-discovery with a narrative closure of acceptance. Instead, the foreigner is ridiculed and exiled, so that the sense of closure established when the woman has been banished and the three men are reunited in the bar has a deeply ironic function. While the female character controls the gaze of the film by photographing the men, and also dominates in the sense that she is the most intelligent and rational character, we are also allowed to enter the male ideological world in order to understand how their misogyny actually functions. Rather than inviting sympathy with their perspective, however, this serves to deconstruct generally accepted 'norms' of male behaviour and to expose jovial male bonding for its fear of sexual difference, foreignness and Otherness.

Like Comerford, Cathal Black has also been concerned with those voices and identities that were omitted from the official rhetoric of Irish nationalism. In *Pigs* (1984), a disparate group of Dublin's homeless underclass set up home in a derelict Georgian house, possibly a metaphor for fragmented identities in an Ireland that is both post-colonial and modern.[4] As in *Reefer and the Model*, these characters function as allegories for the various social problems that modern Ireland has chosen to sweep under the carpet, and provide a powerful corrective to generally accepted notions of progress, tolerance and modernity. Black does not choose to represent these characters sympathetically but rather reminds us that they are an alternative and forgotten-about aspect of contemporary Irish experience. Significantly, their surrogate familial existence is threatened and finally disbanded not by internal strife but by the state authorities from outside. In one particularly striking juxtaposition of ethnic and homosexual discourses, the black pimp challenges Jimmy about his sexuality by saying 'Touch my black skin and say I love you nigger', possibly the most explicit reference to identity politics in Irish cinema until *The Crying Game* (1992) and later Jimmy Smallhorne's *2by4* (1998). Most importantly, there is no mediating voice telling us how to perceive these characters and their identities, nor is their situation resolved. They simply move on so that we are left feeling that their stories remain to be told and indeed, we are still waiting for them to re-emerge in New Irish Cinema.

Likewise, the seeds that were sown for an Irish feminist cinema in the 1980s have not borne mature fruit. Pat Murphy's *Maeve* (1981) and her subsequent feature *Anne Devlin* (1984) were the first explicit attempts to politically empower women's voices and to revise key periods of Irish history from a female perspective. In *Maeve*, sound and image are radically juxtaposed to expose contradictions and reclaim dominant narratives (for example in scenes in which the female protagonist speaks over documentary footage and television reports, thus subverting the official, British, male authorial voice of history). As is the case with many of the films made during this period, their *form* tells us as much about the fragmentary and disharmonious nature of Irish identity as their content, and as such they consciously resist the conventions of First Cinema, with its emphasis on sound–image harmony, its unified, universal perspective and its insistence on narrative closure. In a similar vein, Margo Harkin's *Hush-a-Bye-Baby* (1989) articulated the anxieties surrounding abortion in 1980s Ireland from a distinctively subjective female point of view, providing a corrective to the official broadcast media's treatment of the debate as an issue to be discussed by medical and religious experts. Importantly, Harkin's film made explicit reference to the 'Kerry Babies' case[5] and to the abortion referendum of 1983, thus rooting the narrative in a historical and social reality. As Martin McLoone has recently commented: 'Taken together, these films constituted the outlines of an impressively challenging feminist cinema that also, like the radical film-making already discussed, was to find itself out of favour in the more commercial environment of the 1990s' (McLoone 2000: 142).

Representing the Other

What is particularly striking about this body of work is: 1) it engaged with the past and with Irish identity in progressive and innovative ways and 2) it accommodated a multiplicity of marginalised voices, refusing to allow the spectator a dominant, Hollywood perspective on 'reality'. Speaking of these films, Martin McLoone claims that 'they amount to an impressively adventurous group of films that augured well for a critically engaged indigenous cinema' (2000: 131). While it can be argued that many of the themes explored during this time – Travellers, homelessness, national identity, feminism – no longer appeal to contemporary audiences, it is equally valid to argue that these are issues which continue to pervade the fabric of daily Irish life. Moreover, the formal innovation of the films has much to offer young film-makers overwhelmed by the Hollywood orthodoxy to conform to action-genre conventions and MTV-style editing. According to Luke Gibbons:

> A vigorous national cinema must be judged not solely on its economic performance, or in terms of establishing a native film Industry (crucial though these are), but also on its capacity to engage with the multiple national narratives preoccupying a society, and its specific ways of telling its own stories.[6]

Within the realm of popular culture, however, the currently fashionable approach to multiculturalism is not underpinned by the notion of distinctive voices but rather by the concept of positive/negative representation. If marginalised, ethnic or gay characters are represented in a 'positive', 'normal' or 'acceptable' light, it is assumed that the text advocates cultural tolerance and diversity. The concept of what is 'normal' is not up for debate, and so a dominant or generally accepted view of 'normality' is endorsed that is invariably white, heterosexual, middle-class and Western-centric. Little consideration is given, on the other hand, to how 'alternative' identities are actually *spoken*.

By using Robert Stam's application of Bakhtinian critique to film, it is possible to show that it is not the issue of positive or negative *representation* which matters but rather the multiplicity of – often contradictory – voices that a given film (or body of films) presents to its audience which is at stake. It also becomes clearer that a disavowal of our own cultural identity, rather than accommodating diversity and inclusion, may actually drown out multiple perspectives and mould cinema into an increasingly homogeneous, monovocal form of expression. This critical approach to modernity is best summed up by Bakhtin:

> In the realm of culture, outsideness is a most powerful factor in understanding ... We raise new questions for a foreign culture, ones that it did not raise for itself; we seek answers to our own questions in it; and the foreign culture responds to us by revealing to us its new aspects and new semantic depths. Without one's own questions one cannot creatively understand anything other or foreign. Such a dialogic encounter of two cultures does not result in merging or mixing. Each retains its own unity and open totality, but they are mutually enriched (Bakhtin 1986: 6–7).

Thus Stam's application of Bakhtin's concept of polyphony[7] is useful in distinguishing between cultural texts that pay lip service to diversity and those which speak from genuinely diverse perspectives. As Stam points out:

> The film or television commercial in which every eighth face is black, for example, has more to do with the demographics of market research or the bad conscience of liberalism than with authentic polyphony, because the black voice, in such instances, is usually shorn of its soul as well as deprived of its colour and intonation. (Stam 1991: 263)

A 2001 report commissioned by the Arts Council, the Irish Film Board and Enterprise Ireland states that 'moving images that both mirror and create desires and conflicts at the heart of Irish life are the most influential form of communication we have today' (Connolly and Dillon 2001: 6). But this claim relates more readily to the political and aesthetic strategies of the First Wave films than to the cool cosmopolitanism that the present Irish Film Board endeavours to promote in its 'Ireland: Land of Sex and Violence' trailer.[8] The earlier films genuinely engaged with the conflicts at the heart of Irish life because they refused to brush difficult and contentious aspects of Ireland's past – relating in particular to religion and republicanism – under the carpet. Meanwhile, they addressed the various problems associated with modernity such as drug addiction, homelessness and corruption, indicating that there were no easy solutions to Ireland's newfound status as a modern nation. Most importantly, however, the 'outsiders' in these films spoke their own realities rather than being interpreted through dominant discourses. Instead of satisfying pre-determined desires and expectations, the First Wave films asked questions and exposed contradictions, laying bare the complexities of Irish national identity.

However, just as this 'cinema of resistance' was starting to get off the ground, the growth in multinational investment and our increasing sense of global identity shifted the focus from a concern with popular memory to a concern with constructing a more 'progressive', cosmopolitan identity. As a result, the majority of films that have emerged in recent years tend to fall into two broad categories – on the one hand, a pastiche of hip yet politically vacuous images of 'Ireland as Anyplace' and, on the other, a series of nostalgic Tourist Board images aimed primarily at the American marketplace.

From Traveller to Trainspotting: Irish Cinema Goes Global

According to Kevin Rockett: 'The post-1987 film environment ... witnessed the restoration of the ascendancy of the industrial model for film production over a culturally engaged, critical cinema in Ireland' (Rockett 1994: 127). Although the Ireland of the 2000s has its own distinctive array of social problems, including crime, homelessness and the treatment of immigrants, our national cinema is moving steadily toward easy, globally-digestible narratives. It could also be argued that, given the increased movement of people around the world and the renegotiation of questions of citizenship which surround both indigenous (for example, Traveller) and immigrant groups, Irish identity is becoming increasingly complex and difficult to define. Yet in spite of this, on-screen characters are becoming increasingly stereotypical and bland. They tend to be either simple, fun-loving yokels (*Waking Ned* 1999; *The Nephew* 1998; *The Closer You Get* 2000) or breezy, prosperous urbanites (*About Adam* 1999; *Peaches* 2001), while locations are divided between the rural idyll of the west and the hip cultural capital that is Dublin. As Hugh Linehan notes:

> For the last 40 years the Irish government has had a schizophrenic attitude to promoting its image internationally, torn between presenting itself as a modern, dynamic society ideal for investment by multinational conglomerates, and an idyllic, prelapsarian culture unsullied by the twentieth century. (Linehan 1999: 46)

This polarisation seems to be mirrored by our film culture.

Themes have also become increasingly unadventurous. While some contemporary short-film makers have been tackling homosexuality (Eve Morrisson's short *Summertime* 1995; Barry Dignam's *Dream Kitchen* 1999, and Orla Walsh's short *Bent Out of Shape* 1995), the only feature length film of the 1990s to deal explicitly with this theme is Johnny Gogan's *The Last Bus Home* (1997). Meanwhile, stories about Ireland's underclass, it seems, do not fit with our brash new image of cosmopolitan Dublin. Since Cathal Black's *Pigs* in 1982, Ireland's homeless have failed to make it back onto the big screen. Meanwhile, refugees and immigrants, with the exception of Ian Power's short film *Buskers* (2000), continue to be ignored by our celluloid story-tellers.

The only film that has tackled the issue of hyphenated Irish identity to date is Eugene Brady's *The Nephew* (1998), a film financed almost entirely outside Ireland. Like other recent productions that mobilise a mythicised rural narrative style aimed at the American market (for example, *Into the West*, *Waking Ned* and *The Closer You Get*), *The Nephew* plays on a stereotype of the Irish as quirky and difficult but by no means racist. The younger locals of Inishdaragh are already familiar with Chad's culture thanks to MTV. They are in awe of his clothes and music but there is a kind of benevolent racism at play. A black stranger is introduced and accepted but only on white terms. It is only when Chad sings in Irish at a wake that the local community accepts him, though he has grown up in the street culture of New York. This is the kind of bland, innocuous pluralism that narrows down the potential polyphony of cinema into a unified, homogeneous and essentially white perspective because it is excessively concerned with positive representation. Marginalised characters may still be visible (thus fulfilling the demands of political correctness) but they are no longer speaking in their own voices. Chad is different only insofar as he is American. His 'blackness' is superficial, a fashion issue played out through associations with rap music, dreadlocks, and clothes as opposed to a real political, historical or cultural identity. This is the Benetton version of multi-ethnicity because it makes our lives more colourful as opposed to confronting us with radically different understandings of the world. It is difficult, for example, to imagine the same narrative working if the protagonist were the son of an Irishwoman and a Romanian refugee. Chad is an acceptable hero because he has roughly the same world view as us. Thus, difference is celebrated but within very limited parameters.

Meanwhile, both *Waking Ned* and *The Closer You Get* mobilise a view of rural Ireland as blissfully detached from the real world. The *Ballykissangel* syndrome at work in these films denies that Ireland is a complex and changing nation with a troubled sense of self-identity, pandering instead to a largely mainstream American understanding of Irishness. Complexity, multivocality and diversity of viewpoints are jettisoned in favour of a single, over-simplistic world view that requires a minimum of cross-cultural understanding or critical engagement on the part of the viewer. The desire to provide correctives to these stereotypical Tourist Board images is undoubtedly a healthy one. However, in their strident attempts to disassociate with 'Oirishness', many younger film-makers have opted for story-telling contexts that are determinedly apolitical, free of cultural references and, as a result, increasingly global in their outlook. In the current drive to purge Irish cinema of its demons, the focus seems to be on discarding the old themes and embracing new ones. However, the danger inherent in this trend is that, as the audio-visual scene becomes increasingly dominated by Hollywood conventions, form gradually becomes invisible and thus subordinated to content. As a result, the (American/British) forms adopted to tell local/national stories often do not work, a point driven home by Martin Scorsese when he suggested that Irish film-makers would do better to write what they know instead of trying to recast *Raging Bull* or *Pulp Fiction* in an Irish context.[9]

Returning to my earlier argument about the capacity of the First Wave films to accommodate the voices of the disenfranchised, one might argue that a significant number of contemporary Irish films do in fact deal with outsiders and marginalised groups, for example *Crushproof* (1997), *Flick* (2000) and *Accelerator* (2001). However, in the context of global, post modern culture, the concept of being an outsider has taken on new meanings. Since previously subversive sub-cultures such as the gay rights movement, feminism and ecology have become subsumed into mainstream political, economic and cultural discourses, video directors, advertisers and film-makers have been quick to exploit the bad boy anti-hero of disaffected youth as the new symbol of resistance to 'the system'. This celebration of being an outsider and of rebellion is manifested in everything from ads for Ben Sherman shirts and Sony Playstation ('I've conquered the world') to films such as *Trainspotting* (1995) and *Fight Club* (1999).

This, however, is an illusion of counter-hegemony rather than a genuinely subversive movement, and is totally lacking in social context. The reasons for social marginalisation are not addressed, nor do the protagonists appear to know – or care – what they are rebelling against. Speaking of this cinematic sub-genre in Britain in the 1990s (though it applies equally to Ireland), Claire Monk has noted that

> the youth-oriented films presented young male joblessness and social exclusion as taken-for-granted states with no history, no proposed solution and no expectation of change. With a detached irony, they framed the male underclass not as a 'social problem' but as a subcultural 'lifestyle' with certain attractions for a young, post-political male audience. (Monk 2000: 160)

In much the same way, films such as *Accelerator, Flick* and *Crushproof* address social exclusion as a subcultural style, dispensing with the kind of multivocality or polyphony that the First Wave films used to explore Traveller, homeless, gay and feminist identities. In the vein of earlier films such as *The Disappearance of Finbar* (1996), *Snakes and Ladders* (1996) and *Drinking Crude* (1997), they speak a sort of universal youth culture that is as apolitical as it is location-unspecific. This is a vision of marginalisation that is not only fashionable but may also inadvertently serve to depoliticise the status of those who are genuinely marginalised. It says young people should have attitude but nobody seems to know what about.

Kieron J. Walsh and Roddy Doyle's *When Brendan Met Trudy* (2001)[10] is a far more self-conscious attempt to break into a modern narrative tradition, but in its efforts to embrace modernity and laugh off the past, it runs into certain difficulties. In particular, the famine village sequence and the multicultural party/refugee subplot come across as fairly heavy-handed attempts to redefine contemporary Irish identity. If Doyle is saying that we are becoming a vibrant, youthful, multicultural society for whom the memory of the famine has little relevance, the fact that the two are posited as mutually exclusive is problematic. Again, it seems to be more a case of 'right-on', politic-ally-correct pluralism than an attempt to deconstruct the complexities and contradictions of the new Ireland. However, unlike Gerry

Stembridge's *About Adam*, *When Brendan Met Trudy* at least engages with cultural specificity rather than implying that Dublin is just the same as any other city – a cosmopolitan centre in which multicultural characters provide a colourful backdrop to the central plot. Speaking of the inevitability of his film being compared with Stembridge's *About Adam*, Walsh has said:

> I gather Gerry Stembridge's intention was to depict a new Dublin and a contemporary Ireland that was on a par with any other good place to live. I didn't have that in mind at all. There's a backdrop of things in this film which are very specifically Irish. It wasn't Roddy's intention or mine to sell Dublin as a great place to live.[11]

In addition to those films that seek to represent the cappuccino culture of contemporary Ireland, the past decade or so has also produced a surprising number of films that are set in the past. Indeed, one of the most consistent criticisms levelled at mainstream Irish cinema is that it is excessively caught up in the past, and young filmmakers are frequently heard lamenting the dearth of contemporary narratives that speak to the new generation. However, although many of these films are dismissed as heritage or nostalgia pieces (*Circle of Friends* 1995; *This Is My Father* 1998; *Angela's Ashes* 1999; *Dancing at Lughnasa* 1998; *Agnes Brown* 1999; *The Last of the High Kings* 1996; *Rat* 2000, and *A Love Divided* 1999), there is an argument that they are conscious attempts to make sense of the present by re-evaluating the past. In particular, *Korea* (1995), *The Butcher Boy* (1997) and Kevin Liddy's *Horse* (1993) and *Country* (2000), though set in the 1950s and 1960s, are anxious meditations on modernity. As Luke Gibbons points out (Chapter 6) the anachronisms present in films such as *Michael Collins* (1996) are deliberate devices that serve to connect past events with their continuing impact on contemporary politics. Thus, by moving beyond the representational paradigm, it is possible to reinterpret many of these narratives as unheard voices from the past that still have something to say to the present.

From Here to Post-modernity

In addition to the globalisation process that affects all cultures, there are a number of other reasons for the changes that have affected Irish cinema. First, the production context in which most films are made in Ireland has changed radically. Tax incentives such as those offered by Section 481 (formerly Section 35) have been instrumental in luring in large-budget American productions.[12] However, although they have provided employment for large numbers of Irish crews, many of the films produced represent mainstream American notions of Irishness rather than articulating the realities of Irish existence, past or present. Films such as *Waking Ned* and *The Closer You Get* either focus on mythical (re)visions of the past or pretend that nothing has changed, and are geared largely toward the US market's fantasy of soft primitivism. This, combined with audiences' prolonged exposure to American audio-visual product, has effectively shaped Irish people's preconceptions of what a film should look like. According to Bob Quinn:

> Even the growing number of vaguely home-made 'Irish' films are in the main simply lookalike mainstream Americana with Irish accents. Odd how we never get ideas from the biggest film industry in the world – that of India ... nor from Egypt ... or Russia ... or China ... or Poland ... or Italy ... . (2000: 27)

Meanwhile, there has been a steady move toward co-production with other European countries, in particular through the initiatives offered over the past ten years by the MEDIA programme, which funds high-budget European co-productions that can compete with Hollywood products. According to Martin McLoone, the result is often a kind of Euro-pudding in the vein of *Spaghetti Slow* (1996) or *The Disappearance of Finbar* (1996), in which the locations and nation- ality of the cast are heavily influenced by the funding territories (though *The Last Bus Home* (1997) has proved a notable exception) and he suggests this as a reason why so many Irish films fail. Ruth Barton, on the other hand, maintains that without co-production there would be no Irish film industry,[13] while Rod Stoneman, chief executive of the Irish Film Board, claims that attempts to ape Hollywood will fail and that we must move toward Europe, Latin America, Africa, to build alliances which accept and celebrate scale, diversity and difference of artisan production.[14] However, there is little evidence to date that this is actually happening.

Another important factor to be considered is the shifting categor- isation of cinema. Third Cinema no longer serves the same function that it did in the 1970s since the socio-political structures that supported it have radically changed (McLoone, 2000). While European arthouse comes increasingly under the influence of Hollywood, mainstream American film-makers such as Scorsese and the Coen brothers have started looking to European cinema for stylistic inspiration. Meanwhile, the problematisation of identity politics articulated in many theories of post-modernism, coupled with the move toward an increasingly post-nationalist concept of identity have been reflected on our screens by a shift away from national pre-occupations toward individual ones. However, this does not always mean that the resultant films have nothing to do with contemporary Irish experience. As McLoone points out: 'Even if these films are not politically engaged, they can be engaged with politically' (2000: 168). That said, there is still an important distinction to be made between films such as *The Butcher Boy* (1997) and *Korea* (1995) – which deal specifically with the impact of modernity and global culture on trad-itional Ireland – and a film like *About Adam*, which is essentially a Hollywood-style romantic comedy made by an Irish director and set in Ireland but with little or nothing to say about Ireland (except, perhaps, that it is like anywhere else in the Western world). Moreover, in this increasingly post-political culture, the impact of British laddism (as seen in *Trainspotting* 1995; *Twin Town* 1997; *Lock, Stock and Two Smoking Barrels* 1999, and *Snatch* 2001) is also beginning to cross-fertilise with other styles. For example, it could be argued that recent Irish films such as Paddy Breathnach's *I Went Down* (1998), Fintan Connolly's *Flick* (2000), Conor McPherson's *Saltwater* (2000) and Vinny Murphy's *Accelerator* (1998) are inspired by a mixture of Hollywood, arthouse and new-lad influences.

Angela McRobbie sees in post-modern culture the potential articu-lation of voices which 'were historically drowned out by the (modernist) meta-narratives of mastery' (McRobbie 1994: 15). While she might welcome these developments as part of post-modernism's inevitable tendency toward diversity, hybridity and cross-fertilisation, there is also an argument for a more critically measured response to what is happening. I contend that, in spite of the post-feminist and post-modern discourses that surround issues of gender, globalisation and modernity, Irish people are not as unconcerned with Ireland and Irishness as our globalised cultural output would suggest. In other words, although the culture industries actively trade in global images because they are more commercially viable, Irish people do not ne-cessarily live in the celluloid global village that they see projected on their cinema screens. For example, the argument that Ireland's failure to develop genre cinema indicates that we no longer have any national preoccupations is a precarious one. If we look at the daily newspapers, watch current affairs programmes or listen to the radio, it is clear that we have a great number of national preoccupations. Indeed, it would seem that issues of identity now concern Irish people more than ever before, and that the definition of 'Irishness' has never been more contentious. These incongruities between lived experience and the cinematic images being consumed would seem to indicate that we are actively embracing the idea of globalisation, 1) because it is more profitable and 2) in our bid to join the ranks of the world's modernised, we feel that it is also necessary to rid ourselves of cultural memory. If this is indeed the case, then perhaps cultural nationalism, as a means of analysing cinema, is simply obsolete, in which case critics, policy-makers and funding bodies should stop pretending that there is an important link between film and national identity and submit to the notion that the culture industries are myth-makers and creators of fantasies that have little to do with our lived existence.

New Irish Cinema – Coming Soon?

The drive in the 1990s toward financing bigger-budget productions has posed a considerable threat to multivocality. Of the top 50 films at the Irish box office in 2000, only one, *Angela's Ashes*, was Irish.[15] Clearly, as Rod Stoneman has suggested, the strategies of aping Hollywood and/or British cinema are not working. In spite of a handful of notable exceptions (*November Afternoon* 1996; *The Fifth Province* 1997; *2by4* 1998; *I Could Read the Sky* 1999), the cinevisual landscape is becoming increasingly dominated by lad culture, 'chic flicks' and Oirish mysticism. The recently released *Peaches* (2001) would suggest that the immediate future does not look bright. Described as an Irish film (in that it is funded by the IFB and shot in Dublin by an Irish director), it is diegetically located in London with British actors. Indeed, both Damien O'Donnell's *East is East* (2000) and Paddy Breathnach's latest offering *Blow Dry* (2001) signal a depressing trend in which promising Irish directors are finding narrative inspiration as well as production money in the UK. Meanwhile, official reports such as that published by the Film Industry Strategic Review Group (1999) imply that the wealthier, the more modern and the more cosmopolitan Ireland becomes, the more chance we have of developing a healthy film industry (through tax incentives and foreign investment). However, this concept of a healthy cinema is a purely economic one and on the whole incongruous with the notion, also espoused by the 1999 Report, that national cinema is the predominant way in which a culture 'tells its own stories'. As Bob Quinn recently pointed out: 'The report stressed that "Film and TV are the most powerful contemporary means of cultural expression", yet it still emphasised the multinational industrial perspective, that government money be in the main used as a pump-primer to lure Mel Gibson and the likes in' (2000: 28).

On the whole, the celluloid stories that Ireland is telling itself and others are becoming increasingly universal. At present, it seems that *The Corrs, Riverdance* and *Angela's Ashes* are sufficient markers of Irishness to satisfy both domestic and foreign audiences. The fact that they are globally exportable is generally seen as a plus, a reminder that we too can make it in the outside world without really losing our identity. The fact that these cultural images are more about Irishness as perceived from middle America than the diverse experiences of Irishness coming out of contemporary Ireland (and indeed the Irish diaspora) is rarely questioned. If we can no longer speak as ourselves but rather adopt the increasingly homogeneous language and visual styles of the metropolitan centre, it is equally unlikely that Ireland's immigrants, Travellers, homeless and diaspora will find a voice (or voices) through the medium of film. Looking at the cinema of the Celtic Tiger to date, there is little evidence to suggest that post-modernism heralds a plurality of marginalised voices. If we are to resist the increasing trend toward more formally conservative film-making, it is important that the Film Board and other funding bodies continue to invest not only in productions that can guarantee global appeal but also in narrative forms and themes that are specific to Irish experience, whether native, immigrant or diasporic.

Notes

1. See the *Final Report of the Film Industry Strategic Review Group* (1999) and *Developing Cultural Cinema in Ireland* (2001).
2. According to Lance Pettitt (1997), Comerford's original treatment described Badger as a northern Presbyterian, which makes his liaison with the Irish soldier all the more transgressive.
3. This departure from positive representation in favour of the mar-ginalised speaking for themselves is reminiscent of Australian film-maker Tracey Moffat's approach in her short films *Night Cries* and *Nice Coloured Girls*. In *Night Cries*, Moffat rejects the notion of an authentic Aboriginal experience that can be somehow objectively presented to the Western onlooker. In *Nice Coloured Girls*, by overlaying the image track with a male (colonial) voice-over and 'speaking' the subjectivity of the Aboriginal women through subtitles, she delivers a powerful commentary on the way in which Aboriginal reality has trad-

itionally been *spoken from* a white perspective as well as *spoken to* a white perspective.

4. The characters in the house comprise of a prostitute, her black pimp, a schizophrenic, a homosexual and a drug dealer.

5. In 1984, a baby was found stabbed to death in a plastic fertiliser bag on a beach in Co. Kerry. Although a young single woman, Joanne Hayes, confessed to murdering her child, it was later discovered that she had given birth to a different baby, which was found buried in her garden. The incident became known as the "Kerry Babies" affair.

6. Luke Gibbons, 'The Esperanto of the Eye? Re-thinking National Cinema' in *Film Ireland*, Issue 55 (October–November 1996), p. 22.

7. In *Problems of Dostoevsky's Poetics* (1984), Bakhtin argues that Dostoevsky is not to be identified with one or another voice within his novels, but rather with the agency that orchestrates a multiplicity of distinct and even antithetical voices. This view of texts as a polyphonic play of voices shifts the emphasis away from realism and positive/negative representation to one of voices and discourses.

8. The trailer in question is a skilfully edited series of clips from Irish films, set to a fast-paced contemporary score, which promotes New Irish Cinema as sexy and modern.

9. Scorsese gave a public interview at Ardmore Studios in May 1998 after a screening of student work, much of which clearly imitated his own oeuvre.

10. The film was written by Roddy Doyle and directed by Kieron J. Walsh.

11. Kieron J. Walsh in interview with Hugh Linehan, 'The Ticket', supplement to the *Irish Times*, 7 March 2001, p. 2.

12. Section 481 tax incentives provide film-makers with cost-saving methods of making films as well as a return on profit for investors. The legislation requires that a minimum of 75 per cent of the work on the production of the film be carried out in the state. However, the Minster with responsibility for culture may specify a lower percentage level of not less than 10 per cent, subject to certain guidelines.

13. Ruth Barton, 'The Smaller Picture? Irish Cinema: Funding, Figures and the Future', conference paper delivered at the inaugural conference of the European Cinema Research Forum, University of Wales, Bangor, January 2001.

14. Rod Stoneman, 'Under the Shadow of Hollywood: the Industrial versus the Artisanal' in *Kinema: A Journal for Film and Audiovisual Media*, Spring 2000 (http://www.arts.uwaterloo.ca/FINE/juhde/kinemahp.htm, accessed 20.08.01).
15. *Angela's Ashes* is an Irish/American production with a British director and British stars playing the leading roles.

12 Conclusions and Transformations

Peadar Kirby, Luke Gibbons and Michael Cronin

Culture is a kind of ethical pedagogy which will fit us for political citizenship by liberating the ideal or collective self buried within each of us, a self which finds supreme representation in the universal realm of the state.

Terry Eagleton (2000: 7)

The foregoing chapters have mapped the contours of the reinvented Ireland of the 1990s. In doing this, they have laid bare the foundations left by the Celtic Tiger on which to build Irish society over the coming decades. This chapter begins by drawing out some key elements of this reinvented Ireland and how it understands itself, as revealed by the book's contributors. In doing this, it makes explicit the dominant structures and values on which Irish society is currently based. Yet, hidden within and behind these, there exist subversive potentials that hold the promise of a transformed future. These are also made explicit, again on the basis of the contributions to this book. In its second part, the chapter explores in more detail the socially transformative potential of these dimensions of the Irish experience, since the editors believe that the radical transformation of Irish society – indeed its reinvention in a far more thorough way than has happened in the 1990s – is too urgent and important a task to be left to aspiration alone. The political and material potential is therefore analysed more rigorously and the links between culture and political, economic and social transformation brought into sharper focus. The role attributed to culture in the opening quote above is thus our point of departure, though it is obvious that the state as currently embodied under late capitalism, let alone under the Celtic Tiger, is far removed from such emancipatory ideals. The important point, however, is that true universalism liberates the potential *within* particular cultures, a

196

potential that remains buried if it is impervious to diversity, and to an encounter with other cultures.

Reinvented Ireland

A common theme of many chapters in this book is that the reinvented Ireland of the Celtic Tiger is based on the creation of a 'modern, liberal, progressive, multicultural' image fashioned according to the need for international acceptance rather than through engagement with Ireland's past (Chapter 2); indeed, fashioning this 'image' has entailed a denial of the past and its representation in negative terms (Chapters 6 and 9). In denying that past, contemporary Ireland has also denied sources of creative tension out of which a better future could be built, such as religious critique (Chapter 8), an engagement with and representation of the 'others' of Irish life (Chapter 6 and 11), or the social struggles out of which Ireland was invented a century ago (Chapter 2).

Also denied have been the darker sides, not only of Ireland's past (such as the psychological legacy of colonialism identified in Chapter 7), but also of Ireland's present. For, according to Cronin (Chapter 4), as time takes precedence over place in the new Ireland, it generates spatial contradictions and categories of exclusion, and we run the risk of a generalised amnesia since 'the faster you go, the quicker you forget'. Similarly, as Ging shows in Chapter 11, Irish film during the Celtic Tiger has moved from the engagement with the excluded 'others' of Irish life that characterised the New Wave cinema of the 1970s and 1980s, to adopting increasingly the homogenous language and visual styles of the metropolitan centre in order to fashion a more antiseptic and 'successful', and therefore more marketable, image of Irishness.

Another theme running through the chapters is that this sanitised version of Ireland is functional to the political economy of the Celtic Tiger, and in particular to its interlinked dynamics of elitist capital accumulation and growing social inequality (Chapter 2). Indeed, Peillon (in Chapter 3) argues that socio-economic critique is losing its institutional basis as most forms of cultural production, not to mention politics itself, are now integrated into the economy, either as production or consumption. As a result, the very possibility of a critical stance is suppressed or not even entertained. Also, as Flynn illustrates in his examination of broadcasting (Chapter 10), though free market liberalisation was justified as a means to achieving greater diversity and quality, it has in fact failed to achieve either. He concludes that the market has now become an end in itself. In Chapter 5, Dunne draws attention to the implications for a robust sense of citizenship of this dominant ethic of individual consumption and freedom and he warns that the public sphere needs to be grounded in strong communal solidarities, and notions of freedom that generate respect for – and attachment to – others, rather than just granting a licence to ourselves.

However, many authors also identify subversive potentials in this situation. Indeed, the very functionality of this created 'image' to the economic success of contemporary Ireland offers its own counter-possibilities of challenging the dominant social order through challenging its dominant meaning. For example, in Chapter 6 Gibbons concludes that the ability to look outward, and particularly to identify with the plight of refugees and asylum-seekers, may be best served by reclaiming those lost narratives of Ireland's past which generate new solidarities in the present. Moane (Chapter 7) also identifies a legacy of resistance, creativity, courage and determination whose roots lie in the struggles of many Irish people against colonial rule. She argues that, as well as the pathologies inherited from colonialism, these strengths manifest themselves in today's Ireland and urges a sustained commitment to their liberatory potential. Pilkington returns to a tradition of social critique within the Irish Catholic Church and argues that the ethical strength of both the Church of Ireland and the Catholic Church lies in a deliberate and critical separation from state power (Chapter 8).

In these ways, therefore, the chapters contain the seeds of social transformation. They also locate within the movements and actors of civil society the principal agency of such transformation. However, the specific means through which such transformation can be brought about requires further elaboration. This is addressed in the remainder of this chapter.

Sites of Resistance and Transformation

In focusing on the importance of culture for social transformation, the work of Karl Polanyi provides a useful theoretical framework. His classic work, *The Great Transformation* (1944),[1] traced the emergence of industrial society in Britain in the early part of the nineteenth century as 'the outcome of a conscious and often violent intervention on the part of government which imposed the market organisation on society' (1957: 249). The social destruction that this wrought was not primarily economic (in the sense that it increased economic exploitation) but cultural, in that it resulted in the 'disintegration in the cultural environment of the victim' (ibid.: 157). For Polanyi, this cultural environment was made up of the institutions and mores that give status and meaning to social existence. As he put it: 'Almost invariably professional status, safety and security, the form of a man's [sic] life, the breadth of his existence, the stability of his environment were in question' (ibid.: 154). In the reaction of society to the process whereby economic forces colonise ever more social spaces, Polanyi identified a 'double movement' through spontaneous social counter-movements which seek to protect the coherence and values of society from the inroads of a commodifying market logic. These attempts by society to restore 'the fullness of life to the person' (Polanyi 1969: 72) are, for Polanyi, essentially cultural processes. For him, a key resource through which the colonisation of the market can be resisted is an engagement with our own society and history as a source of moral community and a recovery of our social imagination (Inayatullah and Blaney 1999: 331).

This process of reaction against the inroads of market forces well describes what happened in Ireland in the last decade of the nineteenth century and the first decades of the twentieth as culture helped constitute sites of resistance to the dominant order, drawing on history to recover social imagination. This is an essential dimension of the invention of Ireland entirely missed by Rory O'Donnell in his notion of Ireland's reinvention – namely, that it happened through the mobilisation of social and cultural forces *against* the dominant social – i.e. colonial – order. Through the action of these social and cultural forces a new nation was imagined and then created, akin to the process described by Benedict Anderson in his celebrated book *Imagined Communities* (1991). As described briefly in Chapter 2, this involved a rich array of different social movements, promoting visions of a new social order linking economics, politics, social conditions, education, language revival, industry, religion, sports, theatre, rural life, music, even international order. Of course, there were tensions within these as radical, liberal and conservative currents jostled for dominance. That, following independence in 1922, an essentially liberal-conservative social order emerged from this ferment of social invention should not blind us to the potential of the process; as Polanyi reminds us, it was establishing institutions and mores that gave a new and more vital meaning to social existence, thus laying the foundations of a stable and secure social order. One of Anderson's main insights is that victorious nation-states attempt to convert chance – the contingencies of history – into destiny, as if events could only have turned out that way. It is thus in the interests of new social orders to airbrush out the competing social visions which stood in the way of their own ascent to power, to impose an all-embracing narrative of the nation on what were, in fact, highly contested episodes and events whose outcome was not at all preordained at the time. Thus, our interest in this book in the roads not taken in the past, if only to draw attention to the fact that similar possibilities of alternative routes to growth and development exist in the present.

The main lesson to be learnt from this history is that contemporary Ireland is badly in need of such contestatory social activism if we are to imagine and create a new social order. This directly contradicts the claim that the Celtic Tiger can in some way be equated to the social order then being created. For it bears much more similarity in essence to the violent imposition by government of a market organisation on society that Polanyi described in the Britain of the Industrial Revolution. Many dimensions of the resultant cultural destruction and its social impact have been identified and described in the chapters of this book, from the chrono-politicisation of contemporary Ireland (Chapter 4), to the amnesia towrds the hidden injuries of progress (Chapter 6), and to the commodification of Irish identity for the world market through contemporary Irish cinema (Chapter 11). Similarly, Polanyi's 'double movement' describes some of the spontaneous reactions happening in the Ireland of the Celtic Tiger against this destruction, among them strong public sector strikes and the No vote in the Nice Treaty. In these ways sites of resistance are being opened and the legitimacy of the dominant order is beginning to be contested.

The task of fashioning a new social order requires a lot more, however. The invention of Ireland a century ago reminds us that resistance must move to creation and that creation requires imagination. The raw materials for imagining a different social order for Ireland are found through an engagement with our past, rediscovering in its many muted voices values and aspirations contrary to those that dominate the social order of the Celtic Tiger. In this way, radical strands of egalitarianism, popular democracy, social economy, ecological spirituality, an internationalism attentive to the plight of the poor and exploited of the earth, a robust feminism, cultural regeneration and an indigenous language world lie waiting to be tapped into as rich sources of imagining a radically different, more humane and just social order. This is not to imply that a return to these sources is not well underway already; clearly many political, social and cultural movements in today's Ireland draw inspiration from elements of our past. But much remains to be done to emulate the way Irish people of 100 years ago fashioned an entirely new sense of their future out of their critical and radical engagement with the past.

This means of transforming our social order embodies Eagleton's notion of culture as utopian critique, as referred to in Chapter 1. Does it, however, meet his criterion that a desirable future must be a feasible one, growing out of the transformative forces at work in the present order? For, if not feasible, it runs the risk of making matters worse, of destroying society and people's lives in the name of improving them. This is implied in O'Donnell's view that the economic success of the Celtic Tiger has resulted from 'closing off illusory alternatives [which] forced all to engage in realistic discussion of change' (2000b: 211). Are the alternatives proposed in this chapter illusory and is its discussion of change unrealistic?

O'Donnell's view reflects one widely held in economic and political circles today, namely that success derives from accommodation to the demands of international competitiveness and from internalising the disciplines of the market. Such a view is heard not only from neo-classical economists but also from social democratic leaders such as Tony Blair. It is the dominant orthodoxy explaining the success of the Celtic Tiger and rests on a presumption that economic interests are the dominant motivating factors for individuals. However, as Polanyi put it: 'Nothing obscures our social vision as effectively as the econo-mistic prejudice' (1957: 159). As illustrated in Chapter 5, Polanyi's point finds strong echoes in dominant visions of society under the Celtic Tiger where the economic is regarded as the ultimate criterion of success despite the fact that this success is achieved through a loss of equality and solidarity which undermines the basis for common citizenship. The conceptual divisions between the economic, the political and the social were much criticised by Polanyi as leading to 'a warped vision of social and political history' (ibid.: 157). Such a warped vision fails to recognise the interdependence of market and state and neglects the fundamental tensions and even contradictions that exist between the requirements of economic and of social success. As a result, in its headlong rush for economic growth the dominant economistic vision of society undermines fatally the conditions for longer-term social sustainability.

Recognising the severe limitations of any social vision based on pri-oritising the economic over the social helps explain what seem immense contradictions in today's social order. On the one hand, unprecedented peace and prosperity is the lot of the world's most developed states. Yet, side by side with this, we have collapsing states in which the very basis of peaceful coexistence among neighbours has been brutally undermined perhaps irrevocably, we have growing poverty amid abundant plenty, we have an emerging powerful and semi-democratic political right in many developed countries, and we have vocal dissent emerging at the very nature of our present world order. Perhaps, however, there is no contradiction here. For as John Gray has reminded us of the conflicting currents in today's global order,

> a global free market engenders new varieties of nationalism and fundamentalism even as it creates new elites. By eating away the foundations of bourgeois societies and imposing massive instability on developing countries, global capitalism is endangering liberal civilisation. It is also making it harder for different civilisations to live in peaceful coexistence. (Gray 1999: 210)

Or as historian Filipe Fernández-Armesto predicts in the epilogue to his magisterial survey of the millennium just ended: 'Western liberalism, enfeebled by its inconsistencies, seems bound to be wishy-washed away ... Communism and fascism have been dismissed as extinct dinosaurs, but they will be back, clawing at one another in the streets, like revivified clones out of Jurassic Park' (Fernández-Armesto 1995: 700–1). These are indeed apocalyptic warnings. The surest way to avoid them coming true is to attend urgently to the need to construct a social order that can show in practice that it is serving the well-being of the majority, rather than the Jurassic morality of the Celtic Tiger, 'clawing one another in the streets'.

Galbraith has drawn attention to the fact that it was the left, with its concern for social justice and equality, that saved capitalism from itself. He writes:

> [T]he survival of the modern market system was, in large measure, our accomplishment. It would not have so survived had it not been for the successful efforts of the social left. Capitalism in its original form was an insufferably cruel thing. Only with trade unions, pensions for the old, compensation for the unemployed, public health care, lower-cost housing, a safety net for the unfortunate and the deprived and public action to mitigate capitalism's commitment to boom and slump did it become socially and politically acceptable. Let us not be reticent: we are the custodians of a political tradition that saved classical capitalism from itself. (Galbraith 1997: 5)

The point would be widely accepted now, though we might less concerned today about saving capitalism from its own internal logic. It reminds us, however, that the realists are not those who preach the virtues of ever greater productivity and international competitiveness but those who attend to the social costs of economic liberalisation and the need to ensure that the market serves society and not vice versa. Clearly the lessons of the twentieth century tell us that neither the extremes of the free market nor of state action serve social good. The challenge is to find the conditions under which the dynamism of economic production and exchange can be used for the good of society without being allowed destroy society. The realists are those who respond to this challenge, rather than those fundamentalists who treat the market as a moral absolute – indeed the only absolute left in a world disenchanted of all other meaning. Political absolutism was overthrown in the age of the Enlightenment only to be reinstated in economic form in the dismal guise of the market and the commodity. The aim of a reconfigured politics at the dawn of a new century should be to disenchant in turn these new cargo-cults of globalisation, to restore – or create – agency and self-determination where it has all but vanished into the chimera of consumer choice.

This is where social activism comes in. For a balance between the needs of society and the needs of the market cannot be elaborated through the theoretical recipes so beloved of neo-classical economists but emerges from the struggles of an activist civil society drawing on the values and social imagination of its own history. This is why France led the way in the reaction to neo-liberal reform in the early 1990s through a determined wave of strikes, or why Denmark holds so strongly to its traditional social model based on high taxes and high social spending. This is why a return to the lessons of the invention of Ireland a century ago holds vital clues and resources to help us construct a better social order for the Ireland of tomorrow. One of the main differences is that today we are struggling not just for a national social order but to provide a building block for a better world order, in keeping with the expanding global horizons of the nation itself. In a more integrated and yet dispersed world, this will require new, robust forms of social regulation on the market and it is as yet very hard to see what these will be. One version may be a more federalised system. Another element, drawing on one emerging strain of development thinking (see, for example, Korten 1999), would be to emphasise the coherence of local communities, returning economic and social power as much as possible to the local level. The shape of tomorrow's world is far from clear and will almost certainly contain elements of both of these approaches. What we can be sure of is that social institutions, adequate to the requirements of social stability and cohesion, to the sense of cultural belonging that underpins a successful society will not emerge without a process of social mobilisation and creativity within each national society. Each has its own essential contribution to make drawing on its own traditions of social struggle. In this regard, Ireland

has much to offer. It is, therefore, those who argue that market disciplines are the condition for social success who are unrealistic; the lessons
of the past show this has led to social destruction. It is those who argue
for an activist society mobilised and proposing alternative social
projects who are the harbingers of the social order of the future.

Towards a Cultural Politics of 'Dynamic Rootedness'

A recurrent difficulty for individuals in contemporary societies is that
they are constantly told they have never had it so good in terms of the
freedoms they enjoy but their life world is increasingly characterised
by uncertainty, unpredictability and ceaseless change. The formal
freedoms appear limitless but effective freedom is sharply circumscribed. The affluent Irish city-dweller can choose between 20
different kinds of cheese but has no idea whether his/her job will be
there next week. This is the dilemma described by Zygmunt Bauman
where he sees a wide and growing gap between the condition of individuals *de jure* and the possibility of their becoming individuals *de facto*.
By the latter is meant the ability of individuals to have control over
their fate and to be able to make choices they genuinely desire. As
Dunne argues in Chapter 5, the individual as consumer is pampered,
petted and praised while the individual as citizen is left increasingly
powerless to effect change in the immediate political and economic
environment. Part of this powerlessness comes from the construction
of citizenship itself where individuals see themselves as part of the
problem rather than part of society. In other words, as Ulrich Beck
observes, 'how one lives becomes a biographical solution to systemic
contradictions' (Beck 1992: 137). Unemployment, poverty, disadvantage, powerlessness are individualised as problems and the
solutions on offer are the therapeutic services provided to privatised
paying customers (Gibbons, Chapter 6). The individual solutions are
predictably no match for the social problems, so imaginary answers
are produced to mask the democratic deficit. In Bauman's analysis,

> all 'solutions', in order to seem sensible and viable, must be in line
> with and on a par with the 'individualisation' of tasks and respon-
> sibilities. There is therefore demand for individual pegs on which
> frightened individuals could hang collectively, if only for a brief
> time, their individual fears. Our time is auspicious for scapegoats –
> be they politicians making a mess of their private lives, criminals
> creeping out of the mean streets and rough districts, or 'foreigners
> in our midst'. Ours is a time of patented locks, burglar alarms,

barbed-wire fences, neighbourhood watch and vigilantes. (Bauman 2000: 38)

One of the fears of the first advocates of capitalism in the eighteenth century was that a polite and commercial society would bring about an end to heroism, valour and military prowess through the professionalisation of a standing army. They need not have worried, for the market soon turned war itself into a business, with catastrophic consequences for the last century. Under late capitalism, however, there is a genuine fear that society is being reduced to an economy and that politics itself is devolving onto a professional elite – transforming civic culture, as Dunne again reminds us, into an extension of the debased managerial skills designed for running large neo-feudal corporations. Parodying Villiers de L'Isle-Adam, the proclamation for a modern republic could now read: 'As for democracy, our representatives will do that for us.' This is the context in which to view the underworld of corruption, clientelism and sharp practice that some commentators fondly imagine to be the residue of a bygone parish-pump politics. It is in fact perfectly consistent with a new deracinated politics in which, as Dunne puts it, accountability has given way to accountancy – and creative accountancy at that. There is indeed an invisible hand guiding the market – but if the Celtic Tiger is anything to go by, it is more likely to be handing over a brown paper bag, or spiriting profits to some equally invisible offshore account in some speck in the Atlantic ocean.

It is one the paradoxes of political change that individuals can only fully realise their individuality if they go beyond the individual in seeking transformation of their circumstances. In an era of aggressive privatisation of social experience and deregulation in the economic sphere, supra-individual collective action can appear difficult or remote, particularly when the only communal ideal presented to a population is unfettered self-enrichment. In such circumstances, an impoverished civil society not only leads to a weaker body politic (high levels of electoral abstentionism, cynicism with respect to the political process) but greatly limits the scope for individual action in effecting change. Irish society in late modernity faces two classic problems of liberal democratic societies. Firstly, as Alexis de Tocqueville famously observed, the individual is not always the citizen's best friend. The single-minded pursuit of personal gain and self betterment can generate an indifference to society itself and a disengagement from a non-instrumental shared life with others. The danger here is that the society will implode through a lack of values other than those relating to individual egotism. The second difficulty is that as Ireland becomes an increasingly multicultural society, how is it to allow different communities to coexist and take part in a shared sense of purpose without the country becoming a collection of mutually indifferent or, at worst, fractiously intolerant cultures (Mesure and Renaut 1999: 195–6)

One response is to make the public arena a neutral, procedural space where respect for fundamental principles of law guide interactions between individuals and communities. All are equal before the law and what is held in common is the law itself. Versions of this response are already with us in the marked increase in litigation in Ireland in recent years and the emergence of a thriving 'tribunal' culture where abuses of power or privilege are investigated in a legal framework. The exponential increase in committees, procedures, paperwork throughout the public service under the name of 'accountability' and 'transparency' is another dimension of the juridical organisation of interaction with others (the procedures are as much a preventative measure against any future litigation as a genuine commitment to openness). Though such a procedural conception of a democracy has its obvious uses, it can only with difficulty be seen as enabling vision for a society, betraying as it does a fundamental lack of trust between the individuals in that society and leading to an instrumentalisation of their relationships.

In proposing a cultural politics of *dynamic rootedness* we want to argue for a political engagement with cultural possibility that looks to radical, transformative energies in the Irish past and present. In linking radical, dissenting, alternative traditions in the Irish past to individuals and groups and movements which contest the present neo-liberal orthodoxy in Ireland, a critical culture can emerge that allows people to situate themselves not only in place and time but in a shared community of liberation. In such a project, there is a fundamental commitment not to the shibboleths of modernisation but to the radical potential of critical modernity. In advancing the notion of critical modernity here, we do not intend this in the sense of what Frank Kermode has described as schismatic modernity (Kermode 1968: 93–124), a radical sundering from the past where history is repudiated in the name of the revolutionary *tabula rasa*. Rather, modernity as we understand it is intended in the sense of a self-aware and self-critical continuity with those traditions and movements in Irish life which have contested or continue to contest the monopoly of power and resources by élites, whether pre- or post-colonial. As Ireland moves from a land of emigration to a land of immigration, such a conception of placed modernity allows for the repudiation of a facile and exploitative culture of consumerist multiculturalism in favour of a radical and transformative engagement with new immigrant communities. It is through foregrounding the internal diasporic and dissident energies in Irish culture that a genuine openness towards others can thus be effected. It is perhaps in this sense, as Eagleton reminds us in the epigraph to this chapter, that 'culture is a kind of ethical pedagogy which will fit us for political citizenship by liberating the ideal or collective self buried within each of us' – by virtue precisely of our rootedness in the cultures we lay claim to, and which lay claim to us. The essentialising universalism of legalism and the dogmatic differentialism of ethnocentrism need not be the only political models on offer. In arguing for a form of modernity which contests exploitative forms of modernisation, the aim is not to substitute a reified past for an uncertain present but to provide a space of utopian possibility for the radical forces in Irish society.

Valuing Interdependence

Richard Sennett concludes his *The Corrosion of Character: The Personal Consequences of Work in the New Capitalism* with the simple observation that, 'a regime which provides human beings no deep reasons to care about one another cannot long preserve its legitimacy' (Sennett 1998: 148). Dehumanising work practices on Irish high-tech assembly lines or in the teleservices sector, indifference to the values of service and commitment in 'downsizing' mergers and acquisitions, a ruthless narrow-gauge functionalism driving educational policy, are simply some elements among many which deprive citizens of the structures and the motives to care deeply about their other fellow citizens. When surprise is expressed about the coldness, the lack of warmth, the aggressive selfishness of Celtic Tiger culture in Ireland, what is surprising is the surprise. The consequences, both personal and social, of the new capitalism as currently practised in Ireland mean that the situation could hardly be otherwise. This is a system which, after all, makes the individual consumer the paragon of civic virtue. Alasdair MacIntyre makes the following observation in his work *Dependent Rational Animals*:

> We human beings are vulnerable to many kinds of affliction and most of us are at some time afflicted by serious ills. How we cope is only in small part up to us. It is most often to others that we owe our survival, let alone our flourishing, as we encounter bodily illness and injury, inadequate nutrition, mental defect and disturbance, and human aggression and neglect. (MacIntyre 1999: 1)

For MacIntyre, the history of thought from Plato to Moore has been curiously uninterested in the connection between human affliction and our dependence on others, and he claims that

> when the ill, the injured and the otherwise disabled *are* presented in the pages of moral philosophy books, it is almost always exclusively as possible subjects of benevolence by moral agents who are themselves presented as though they were continuously rational, healthy and untroubled. (1999: 3; original emphasis)

The denial of dependency leads to the fetishisation of autonomy that not only disguises real and disabling forms of economic and political subjection but deprives the political sphere of the potential to use connectedness to others as a way of levering political change. In exploring different lines of connections and filiations in Irish society, the hope is to demonstrate that the most potent manifestations of *independence* are always at some level forms of *interdependence*.

As has been amply demonstrated in our arguments drawing on political economy, there is a materialist dimension to our critique, so often lacking in the aspirational idealism which bedevils particular kinds of cultural critique in Ireland. We further wish to argue that it is necessary to go beyond state-centred intellectual approaches that are doubly obsessed by security in social control and reductionist cost-benefit analysis in policy-making. In this the intention is not to be antagonistic to the public sector in the manner of right-wing anti-state intellectuals, but to posit that the relationship between state and intellectuals must at some level be repeatedly antagonistic if only to champion civil society against the instrumentalisation of the state and the economy for the benefit of the few. Max Weber once spoke of the iron cage of bureaucratic rationality which all but incarcerated Western culture in a prison of its own making. It is time to put the Celtic Tiger back into that cage and release Irish society from such predatory designs on its own progress into the future.

Note

1. The 1957 edition of this work is referenced here.

Bibliography

Acheson, Alan (1997) *A History of the Church of Ireland 1691–1996* (Blackrock, Co. Dublin and Dublin: The Columba Press and APCK).

Adam, Heribert (2000) 'Divided Memories: Confronting the Crimes of Previous Regimes', *Telos*, Vol. 118, winter 2000, pp. 83–108.

Adorno, Theodor (1973) *Negative dialectics* (London: Routledge and Kegan Paul).

Adorno, Theodor (1998) 'The Meaning of Working through the Past', *Critical Models: Interventions and Catchwords* (New York: Columbia University Press), pp. 89–103.

Aiken, Frank (1959) *Ireland at the United Nations: Speeches by Mr. Frank Aiken* (Dublin: Brún agus Ó Nualláin).

Airey, Siobhán (1999) *Challenging Voices, Pathways to Change: A Study on Justice and Spirituality* (Ballinasloe: Sisters of Mercy Western Province).

Allen, Kieran (1999) 'The Celtic Tiger, Inequality and Social Partnership', *Administration*, Vol. 47, No. 2, pp. 31–55.

Allen, Kieran (2000) *The Celtic Tiger: The Myth of Social Partnership in Ireland* (Manchester: Manchester University Press).

Amnesty International (2000) *Asylum Law and Policy in Ireland: A Critical Guide* (Dublin: Amnesty International).

Anderson, Benedict (1991) *Imagined Communities* (London: Verso, revised edition)

Anon. (1988) 'Independent Stations subject to "the full rigours of the law"', *Irish Times*, 7 November 1988.

Anon. (1989) 'RTÉ Beware: TV3 is Cominatcha', *Aspect*, May 1989, pp. 20–5.

Anon. (2001) *The Glenstal Book of Prayer: A Benedictine Prayer Book* (Blackrock, Co. Dublin: The Columba Press).

Antze, Paul and Lambek, Michael (1996) eds, *Tense past, cultural essays in trauma and memory* (London: Routledge).

Arendt, Hannah (1958) *The Human Condition* (Chicago: University of Chicago Press).

Bakhtin, Mikhail (1984) *Problems of Dostoevsky's Poetics* (Minneapolis: University of Minnesota Press).

Bakhtin, Mikhail (1986) *Speech Genres and Other Late Essays*, trans. Vern W. McGhee (Austin: University of Texas Press).

Barrett, Alan, John Fitzgerald and Brian Nolan (2000) 'Earnings Inequality, Returns to Education and Low Pay' in Brian Nolan, Philip J. O'Connell and Christopher T. Whelan, eds, *Bust to Boom? The Irish Experience of Growth and Inequality* (Dublin: IPA), pp. 127–46.

209

Barrett, Sean D. (1997) 'Policy Changes, Output Growth and Investment in Irish Tourism 1986–96', *Irish Banking Review*, Autumn, pp. 39–48.

Barry, Frank (1999) 'Irish Growth in Historical and Theoretical Perspective' in Frank Barry, ed., *Understanding Ireland's Economic Growth* (Basingstoke: Macmillan), pp. 25–44.

Barton, Ruth (1999a) 'Feisty Colleens and Faithful Sons: Gender in Irish Cinema', *Cineaste*, Contemporary Irish Cinema Supplement, Vol. XXIV, Nos 2–3, 1999, pp. 40–5.

Barton, Ruth (1999b) 'Family Narratives and Irish Cinema', *Irish Journal of Feminist Studies*, Vol. 3, No. 2, pp. 22–31.

Bauman, Zygmunt (1998) *Globalization: The Human Consequences* (Cambridge: Polity Press).

Bauman, Zygmunt (2000) *Liquid Modernity* (Oxford: Blackwell).

Beck, Ulrich (1992) *Risk Society: Towards a New Modernity* (London: Sage).

Bell, Daniel (1974) *The Coming of the Post-Industrial Society: A Venture in Social Forecasting* (London: Heinemann).

Bell, Daniel (1979) *The Cultural Contradiction of Capitalism* (London: Heinemann).

Bew, Paul, Ellen Hazelkorn and Henry Patterson (1989) *The Dynamics of Irish Politics* (London: Lawrence and Wishart).

Bolger, Dermot (1992) *A Dublin Quartet* (London: Penguin).

Bowen, Kurt (1983) *Protestants in a Catholic State: Ireland's Privileged Minority* (Kingston and Montreal, Ca.: McGill-Queen's University Press).

Bracken, Patricia, Liam Greenslade, B. Griffin, and M. Smyth (1998) 'Mental health and ethnicity: an Irish dimension', *British Journal of Psychiatry*, Vol. 172, pp. 103–5.

Bradley, John (2000) 'The Irish Economy in Comparative Perspective' in Brian Nolan, Philip J. O'Connell and Christopher T. Whelan, eds, *Bust to Boom? The Irish Experience of Growth and Inequality* (Dublin: IPA), pp. 4–26.

Bradshaw, Brendan (1989) 'Nationalism and Historical Scholarship in Modern Ireland', *Irish Historical Studies*, Vol. 36, No. 104, pp. 329–51.

Brady, Ciaran (1994) ed., *Interpreting Irish History: The Debate on Historical Revisionism* (Dublin: Irish Academic Press).

Brennan, Tim (2001) 'Cosmopolitanism and Internationalism', *New Left Review*, Vol. 7, January–February 2001, pp. 75–84.

Brennock, Mark (1988) 'TV relay system to carry new channel', *Irish Times*, 22 February 1988.

Brett, David (1996), *The Construction of Heritage* (Cork: Cork University Press).

Brewer, John. D. with Gareth I. Higgins (1998) *Anti-Catholicism in Northern Ireland, 1600–1998: The Mote and the Beam* (Basingstoke: Palgrave).

Brodigan, Catherine (2001) 'TV3 and Cultural Imperialism', unpublished BA dissertation, Dublin City University.

Brown, Terence (1985) *Ireland: A Social and Cultural History 1922–1985* (London: Fontana).

Butler, Hubert (1986) *Escape from the Anthill* (Mullingar: The Lilliput Press).

Callan, Eamonn (1998) *Creating Citizens: Political Education and Liberal Democracy* (Oxford: Oxford University Press).

Cantillon, Sara, Carmel Corrigan, Peadar Kirby and Joan O'Flynn (2001) 'Towards More Robust Equality Objectives' in Sara Cantillon, Carmel

Corrigan, Peadar Kirby and Joan O'Flynn, eds, *Rich and Poor: Perspectives on Tackling Inequality in Ireland* (Dublin: Oak Tree Press in association with the Combat Poverty Agency), pp. 301–13.

Cantillon, Sara, Carmel Corrigan, Peadar Kirby and Joan O'Flynn (2001) eds, *Rich and Poor: Perspectives on Tackling Inequality in Ireland* (Dublin: Oak Tree Press in association with the Combat Poverty Agency).

Carr, Patricia (1998) 'The Cultural Production of Enterprise: Understanding Selectivity as Cultural Policy', *Economic and Social Review*, Vol. 29, No. 2, pp. 33–55.

Carson, Julia (1990) ed., *Banned in Ireland. Censorship and the Irish Writer* (Athens, Georgia: University of Georgia Press).

Castells, Manuel (1997) *The Power of Identity* (Oxford: Blackwell).

Castells, Manuel (1998) *End of Millennium* (Oxford: Blackwell).

Catalyst (1999) *Sectarian Divisions and the Church of Ireland Synod: What Now?* (Belfast: Catalyst).

Central Statistics Office (1991) *Census of Population*, Vol. 6, Table 3 (Dublin: Stationery Office).

Central Statistics Office (1996) *Census of Population*, Vol. 7, Table 8 (Dublin: Stationery Office).

Central Statistics Office (2000) *That was Then, This is Now: Change in Ireland, 1949–1999* (Dublin: CSO).

Cohen, Stanley (2001) *States of Denial: Knowing about Atrocities and Suffering* (Cambridge: Polity Press).

Collins, Stephen (1998) 'Is it any wonder the farmers are revolting?', *Sunday Tribune*, 1 November 1998.

Conference of Religious in Ireland (1999) *Resources and Choices: Towards a Fairer Future* (Dublin: CORI Justice Commission).

Connolly, Neil and Maretta Dillon (2001) *Developing Cultural Cinema in Ireland* (Report commissioned by the Arts Council, the Irish Film Board and Enterprise Ireland in association with the Northern Ireland Film Commission, 2001).

Connolly, S.J. (1995) *Religion, Law and Power* (Oxford: Oxford University Press).

Coughlan, Denis (1988) 'June deadline set for Bill on commercial TV', *Irish Times* 28 April 1988.

Coulter, Carol (1988) 'Church of Ireland reassessment of links with loyalism overdue' *Irish Times*, 25 July.

Council of Europe (2000) *Crime and Justice in Europe* (Strasbourg: Council of Europe).

Cronin, Michael (1993) 'Translating Technology: Languages in the Reticular Economy', *Teagluim*, Vol. 1, pp. 16–18.

Cronin, Michael (1998), 'Gulliver's Isles', *Graph*, Vol. 3, No. 1, pp. 4–5.

Crouch, Colin (1999) *Social Change in Western Europe* (Oxford: Oxford University Press).

Curtis, Liz (1994) *The Cause of Ireland; From the United Irishmen to Partition* (Belfast: Beyond the Pale Publications).

Danieli, Yael (1998) ed., *International Handbook of Multigenerational Legacies of Trauma* (New York: Plenum Press).

Dentith, Simon (1995) *Bakhtinian Thought: An Introductory Reader* (London; New York: Routledge).

Department of Arts, Culture and the Gaeltacht (1995) *Active or Passive: Broadcasting in the Future Tense* (Dublin: Government Publications).

Devereaux, Eoin (1997) 'The Theatre of Reassurance? *Glenroe*, Its Audience and the Coverage of Social Problems' in Mary J. Kelly and Barbara O'Connor, eds, *Media Audiences in Ireland* (Dublin: University College Dublin Press), pp. 35–47.

Devlin, Martina (1998) 'Is the Celtic Tiger mutating into the Celtic Ostrich?' *Irish Independent*, 17 November 1998.

Dillon, Michèle (1993) *Debating Divorce. Moral conflict in Ireland* (Lexington: University Press of Kentucky).

Dillon, Michèle (1998) 'Divorce and cultural rationality' in Michel Peillon and Eamonn Slater, eds, *Encounters with Modern Ireland* (Dublin: IPA), pp. 127–33.

Dirlik, Arif (2000) 'Globalization as the End and the Beginning of History: The Contradictory Implications of a New Paradigm', *Rethinking Marxism*, Vol. 12, No. 4, pp. 4–26.

Doyle, Roddy (1988) *The Commitments* (London: Minerva).

Dunne, Joseph (1995) 'What's the Good of Education?' in P. Hogan, ed., *Partnership and the Benefits of Learning* (Dublin: ESAI), pp. 60–82.

Dunne, Joseph (1997) *Back to the Rough Ground: Practical Judgement and the Lure of Technique* (Notre Dame and London: University of Notre Dame Press).

Dunne, Joseph (1998) 'Identity and Difference in the "New Europe": A View from the Periphery' (Occasional Papers Series, Centre for Western European Studies, University of California at Berkeley).

Dunne, Joseph (2000) 'Culture, Citizenship and the Global Market: Challenges to Education in the "New Europe"' in F. Crawley, P. Smeyers and P. Standish, eds, *Universities Remembering Europe* (Oxford: Berghahn), pp.157–84.

Eagleton, Terry (2000) *The Idea of Culture* (Oxford: Blackwell).

Eames, Robin, 'The Great Famine: Address by Most Reverend Dr Robin Eames, Archbishop of Armagh, Primate of All Ireland', Church of Ireland Press Office, 31 August 1995.

Euromonitor (various years, 1991–2000) *European Marketing Data and Statistics* (London: Euromonitor Publications).

European Audiovisual Observatory (2000) *Statistical Yearbook 2000.* (Strasbourg: European Audiovisual Observatory).

Fahey, Tony (1998) 'The Catholic Church and Social Policy' in Seán Healy and Brigid Reynolds, eds, *Social Policy in Ireland: Principles, Practice and Problems* (Dublin: Oak Tree Press) pp. 411–30.

Fallon, Brian (1998) *An Age of Innocence: Irish Culture 1930–1960* (Dublin: Gill & Macmillan).

Fanon, Frantz (1952) *Black Skin, White Masks* (New York: Grove Press; London: Pluto Press) original French edition, 1952.

Fanon, Frantz (1967) *The Wretched of the Earth* (London: Penguin) original French edition, 1961.

Ferguson, Harry (2000) 'Learning from the past: Child abuse and institutional care in historical perspective' in L. Mac Aodha, ed., *Child Abuse in Institutional Care: Learning from the Past and Hoping for the Future* (Dublin: National Conference of Priests of Ireland), pp. 22–40.

Fernández-Armesto, Felipe (1995) *Millennium: A History of Our Last Thousand Years* (London: Black Swan).

Final Report of the Film Industry Strategic Review Group (The Strategic Development of the Irish Film and Television Industry 2000–2010) (August 1999). Ireland Film and Television Network website (www.iftn.ie).

Fitzgerald, John (2000) 'The Story of Ireland's Failure – and Belated Success' in Brian Nolan, Philip J. O'Connell and Christopher T. Whelan, eds, *Bust to Boom? The Irish Experience of Growth and Inequality* (Dublin: IPA), pp. 27–57.

Forde, Walter (1999) 'Losing our sense of community', *Irish Times*, 17 August.

Foster, Hal (1985) ed., *Postmodern Culture* (London: Pluto Press).

Foster, Roy F. (1988) *Modern Ireland 1600–1972* (London: Penguin).

Foster, R.F. (1993) *Paddy and Mr Punch* (London: Allen Lane).

Foster, Ronan (1989) 'Hearing told that TV station would go on air next year', *Irish Times*, 5 April.

Gailey, Andrew (1987) *Ireland and the Death of Kindness: The Experience of Constructive Unionism* (Cork: Cork University Press).

Galbraith, John Kenneth (1997) 'Preface', *New Political Economy*, Vol. 2, No. 1, pp. 5–9.

Garvaghy Residents (1999) *Garvaghy: A Community Under Siege* (Belfast: Beyond the Pale Publications).

Gellner, Ernest (1994) *Encounters with Nationalism* (Oxford: Blackwell).

George, Susan (1998) 'Fast Castes' in Jeremy Millar and Michiel Schwarz, eds, *Speed: Visions of an Accelerated Age* (London: Whitechapel Art Gallery), pp. 115–18.

Gibbons, Luke (1988) 'Coming out of Hibernation? The Myth of Modernity in Irish Culture' in Richard Kearney, ed., *Across the Frontiers: Ireland in the 1990s* (Dublin: Wolfhound), pp. 205–18.

Gibbons, Luke (1996a) *Transformations in Irish Culture* (Cork: Cork University Press).

Gibbons, Luke (1996b) 'The Esperanto of the Eye? Re-thinking National Cinema' in *Film Ireland*, No. 55, pp. 20–2.

Gibbons, Luke, 'Guests of the Nation: Ireland, Immigration and Post-Colonial Solidarity' (unpublished paper).

Gray, John (1999) *False Dawn: The Delusions of Global Capitalism* (London: Granta Books).

Green, Roy (2001) 'Social partnership needs new pay strategy', *Irish Times*, 18 May.

Greene, Sheila and Geraldine Moane (2000), 'Growing Up Irish', *Irish Journal of Psychology*, Vol. 21, Nos 3–4, pp. 122–37.

Healy, Seán and Reynolds, Brigid (1998) 'Progress, Paradigms and Policy' in Seán Healy and Brigid Reynolds, eds, *Social Policy in Ireland: Principles, Practice and Problems* (Dublin: Oak Tree Press).

Herman, Judith (1992) *Trauma and Recovery* (New York: Basic Books).

Hobsbawm, Eric J. (1990) *Nations and Nationalism since 1780* (Cambridge: Cambridge University Press).

Honohan, Iseult (forthcoming) *Civic Republicanism* (London: Routledge).

Hutchinson, Bertram (1969–70) 'On the Study of Non-Economic Factors in Irish Economic Development', *Economic and Social Review*, Vol. 1, No.4, pp. 509–29.

Inayatullah, Naeem and David L. Blaney (1999) 'Towards an Ethnological IPE: Karl Polanyi's Double Critique of Capitalism', *Millennium*, Vol. 28, No. 2, pp. 311–40.

Industrial Policy Review Group (1992) *A Time for Change: Industrial Policy for the 1990s* (Dublin: Stationery Office).

Institute of Advertising Practioners of Ireland (1997–2001) *Adspend* (Dublin: IAPI).

Inter-Departmental Policy Committee (1999): *Social Inclusion Strategy* (Dublin: Stationery Office).

Irish Catholic Bishop's Conference (1999) *Prosperity with a Purpose: Christian Faith and Values in a Time of Rapid Economic Growth* (Dublin: Veritas).

Jacobsen, John Kurt (1994) *Chasing Progress in the Irish Republic* (Cambridge: Cambridge University Press).

Jaouen, Hervé (1990) *Journal d'Irlande 1977–1983; 1984–1989* (Rennes: Éditions Ouest-France).

Jessop, Bob and Ngai-Ling Sum (2001) 'Pre-disciplinary and Post-disciplinary Perspectives', *New Political Economy*, Vol. 6, No. 1, pp. 89–101.

Jones, Howard (1987) *Mutiny on the Amistad* (Oxford: Oxford University Press).

Jordan, Neil (1996) *Michael Collins: Film Diary and Screenplay* (London: Vintage).

Joyce, James (1977) *Ulysses* (Harmondsworth: Penguin).

Kane, Eileen (1977) *The Last Place God Made: Traditional Economy and New Industry in Rural Ireland* (New Haven, CT: Human Relations Area Files Inc.).

Keatinge, Patrick (1978) *A Place Among the Nations: Issues of Foreign Policy* (Dublin: IPA).

Kennedy, Liam (1992–93) 'Modern Ireland: Post-Colonial Society or Post-Colonial Pretensions', *Irish Review*, Vol. 13, winter 1992–93, pp. 107–21.

Kenny, Colum (1988) 'Irish Broadcasting's leap in the dark', *Irish Times*, 24 May.

Kenny, Colum (1989) 'Michael Grade, Channel 4 and the Irish', *Irish Times*, 25 January.

Kenny, Vincent (1985) 'The Post-Colonial Personality', *Crane Bag*, No. 9, 70–78.

Keogh, Dermot (1998) *Jews in 20th Century Ireland: Refugees, Anti-Semitism and the Holocaust* (Cork: Cork University Press).

Kermode, Frank (1968) *The Sense of an Ending: Essays in the Theory of Fiction* (Oxford: Oxford University Press).

Kiberd, Declan (1993) 'Douglas Hyde: A Radical in Tory Clothing?', *Irish Reporter*, No. 11, pp. 18–20.

Kiberd, Declan (1995) *Inventing Ireland* (London: Jonathan Cape).

Kirby, Peadar (2000) 'Growth with Inequality: The International Political Economy of Ireland's Development in the 1990s', unpublished PhD thesis, London School of Economics.

Kirby, Peadar (2001) 'The Role of Interests and Identity in Constituting Security: Charting the Shifts, Theorising the Links', paper given to workshop in Gothenburg University, Sweden, 2 June.

Kirby, Peadar (2002) *The Celtic Tiger in Distress: Growth with Inequality in Ireland* (Basingstoke: Palgrave).

Korten, David C. (1999) *The Post-Corporate World: Life after Capitalism* (West Hartford: Kumarian Press and San Francisco: Berrett-Koehler Publishers).

Kundera, Milan (1996) *Slowness* (London: Faber & Faber).

Laffan, Brigid and Rory O'Donnell (1998) 'Ireland and the growth of international governance' in William Crotty and David E. Schmitt, eds, *Ireland and the Politics of Change* (London: Longman), pp. 156–77.

Laïdi, Zaki (1998) *A World without Meaning: The Crisis of Meaning in International Politics* (London: Routledge).

Lash, Scott and John Urry (1994) *Economies of Signs and Space* (London: Sage).

Layte, Richard, Bertrand Maitre, Brian Nolan, Dorothy Watson, James Williams and Barra Casey (2000) 'Monitoring Poverty Trends: Results from the 1998 Living in Ireland Survey' (Dublin: ESRI Working Paper No. 132).

Layte, Richard, Brian Nolan and Christopher T. Whelan (2000) 'Trends in Poverty' in Brian Nolan, Philip J. O'Connell and Christopher T. Whelan, eds, *Bust to Boom? The Irish Experience of Growth and Inequality* (Dublin: IPA), pp. 163–78.

Leddin, Anthony and Brendan Walsh (1997) 'Economic Stabilisation, Recovery, and Growth: Ireland 1979–1996' (Working paper WP97/8, Department of Economics, UCD).

Lee, Joseph (1989) *Ireland 1912–1985: Politics and Society* (Cambridge: Cambridge University Press).

Lee, Joseph (1999) 'A Sense of Place in the Celtic Tiger?' in Harry Bohan and Gerard Kennedy, eds, *Are We Forgetting Something?: Our Society in the New Millennium* (Dublin: Veritas), pp. 71–93.

Linehan, Hugh (1999), 'Myth, Mammon and Mediocrity: the Trouble with Recent Irish Cinema', *Cineaste*, Contemporary Irish Cinema Supplement, Vol. XXIV, Nos 2–3, pp. 46–9.

Lloyd, David (1999) *Ireland after History* (Cork: Cork University Press).

Lloyd, John (2000) 'Good Traitors', *Prospect*, January, pp. 36–40.

Lyons, F.S.L. (1973) *Ireland since the Famine* (London: Fontana).

Lyons, F.S.L. (1979) *Culture and Anarchy in Ireland 1890–1939* (Oxford: Clarendon Press).

MacConnell, Sean (1998) 'Demise of farming would affect more than rural Ireland', *Irish Times*, 30 November 1998.

MacCurtain, Margaret (1987) 'Women and the Catholic Church', Keynote Address, Third International Interdisciplinary Congress on Women, Dublin

MacDonagh, Oliver (1983) *States of Mind: Two Centuries of Anglo-Irish Conflict 1780–1980* (London: Pimlico).

MacIntyre, Alisdair (1999) *Dependent Rational Animals: Why Human Beings Need the Virtues* (London: Duckworth).

MacLachlin, Malcolm and Michael O'Connell (2000) *Cultivating Pluralism: Psychological, Social and Cultural Perspectives on a Changing Ireland* (Dublin: Oaktree Press).

Mac Laughlin, Jim (1994) *Ireland: The Emigrant Nursery and the World Economy* (Cork: Cork University Press).

Mac Laughlin, Jim (1997) 'Ireland in the Global Economy: An End to a Distinct Nation?' in Ethel Crowley and Jim Mac Laughlin, eds, *Under the Belly of the Tiger: Class, Race, Identity and Culture in the Global Ireland* (Dublin: Irish Reporter Publications) pp. 1–19.

Martín-Baró, Ignacio (1994) *Writings for a Liberation Psychology: Essays, 1985–1989*, A. Aron and S. Corne, eds (Cambridge, MA: Harvard University Press).

McCarthy, Conor (2000) *Modernisation, Crisis and Culture in Ireland, 1969–1992* (Dublin: Four Courts Press).

McCormack, William J. (1986) *The Battle of the Books. Two Decades of Irish Cultural Debate* (Mullingar: The Lilliput Press).

McGoldrick, Monica (1996) 'Irish families' in Monica McGoldrick, ed., *Ethnicity and Family Therapy* (New York: Scribner).

McLoone, Martin (2000) *Irish Film: The Emergence of a Contemporary Cinema* (London: British Film Institute).

McRobbie, Angela *Postmodernism and Popular Culture* (London: Routledge).

Meaney, Geraldine (1991) *Gender and Nationalism*, LIP pamphlet (Dublin: Attic Press).

Memmi, Albert (1967) *The Colonizer and the Colonized* (Boston: Beacon Press) original French edition, 1957.

Mercier, Vivian (1994) *Modern Irish Literature: Sources and Founders* (Oxford: Clarendon Press).

Mesure, Sylvie and Alain Renaut (1999) *Alter Ego: les paradoxes de l'identité démocratique* (Paris: Aubier).

Moane, Geraldine (1994) 'A Psychological Analysis of Colonialism in an Irish Context', *Irish Journal of Psychology*, Vol. 15, Nos 2–3, pp. 250–65.

Moane, Geraldine (1996) 'Legacies of Colonialism for Irish women: Oppressive or Empowering?', *Irish Journal of Feminist Studies*, Vol. 1, No. 1, pp. 100–18.

Moane, Geraldine (1999) *Gender and Colonialism: A Psychological Analysis of Oppression and Liberation* (London: Macmillan).

Monk, Claire (2000) 'Men in the 90s' in Murphy, Robert, ed., *British Cinema of the 90s* (London: BFI), pp. 156–66.

Mulhall, Daniel (1999) *A New Day Dawning: A Portrait of Ireland in 1900* (Dublin: The Collins Press).

Mullarkey, Kieran (1999) 'Ireland, the Pope and Vocationalism: the impact of the encyclical *Quadragesimo Anno*' in J. Augusteijn, ed., *Ireland in the 1930s: New Perspectives* (Dublin: Four Courts Press), pp. 96–116.

Mulqueen, Eibhir (1998) 'Riverdance to tap new markets', *Irish Times*, 16 October.

Murphy, Bernadette (2001) 'Will Irish literature survive prosperity?' *Los Angeles Times*, 14 March.

Nandy, Ashis (1983) *The Intimate Enemy: Loss and Recovery of Self* (Oxford: Oxford University Press).

NESC (1999) *Opportunities, Challenges and Capacities for Choice* (Dublin: NESC, Report No. 105).

Nolan, Brian, Bertrand Maitre, Donal O'Neill and Olive Sweetman (2000) *The Distribution of Income in Ireland* (Dublin: Oak Tree Press in association with the Combat Poverty Agency).

Nolan, Brian, Philip J. O'Connell and Christopher T. Whelan (2000) 'Introduction' in Brian Nolan, Philip J. O'Connell and Christopher T. Whelan, eds, *Bust to Boom? The Irish Experience of Growth and Inequality* (Dublin: IPA), pp. 1–3.

O'Brien, Conor Cruise (1972) *States of Ireland* (London: Hutchinson).

O'Brien, Conor Cruise (1994) *Ancestral Voices: Religion and Nationalism in Ireland* (Dublin: Poolbeg).

O'Carroll, Ide and Collins, Eoin (1995), eds, *Lesbian and Gay Visions of Ireland, Towards the Twenty-First Century* (London: Cassells).

ÓCinnéide, Séamus (1998) 'Democracy and the Constitution', *Administration*, Vol. 46, No. 4, pp. 41–58.

O'Connor, Barbara (1998) 'Riverdance' in Michel Peillon and Eamonn Slater, eds, *Encounters with Modern Ireland: A Sociological Chronicle 1995–1996* (Dublin: Institute of Public Administration), pp. 51–60.

ÓCroidheáin, Caoimhghin (2001) 'Language from Below: The Irish Language, Ideology and Power in 20th Century Ireland', unpublished PhD dissertation, Dublin City University.

O'Donnell, Ian and Eoin O'Sullivan (2001) *Crime Control in Ireland: The Politics of Intolerance* (Cork: Cork University Press).

O'Donnell, Rory (1999) 'Reinventing Ireland: From Sovereignty to Partnership', Jean Monnet Inaugural Lecture, UCD, 29 April.

O'Donnell, Rory (2000a) 'Public Policy and Social Partnership' in Joseph Dunne, Attracta Ingram and Frank Litton, eds, *Questioning Ireland: Debates in Political Philosophy and Public Policy* (Dublin: IPA), pp. 187–213.

O'Donnell, Rory (2000b), 'The New Ireland in the New Europe' in Rory O'Donnell, ed., *Europe: The Irish Experience* (Dublin: IEA), pp. 161–214.

O'Donnell, Rory and Damian Thomas (1998) 'Partnership and Policy-Making' in Seán Healy and Brigid Reynolds, eds, *Social Policy in Ireland: Principles, Practice and Problems* (Dublin: Oak Tree Press), pp. 117–46.

Ó Gráda, Cormac (1998) *Black 47: The Great Irish Famine in History, Economy and Memory* (Princeton: Princeton University Press).

O'Hearn, Denis (1998) *Inside the Celtic Tiger: The Irish Economy and the Asian Model* (London: Pluto Press).

O'Hearn, Denis (2000) 'Globalization, "New Tigers", and the End of the Developmental State? The Case of the Celtic Tiger', *Politics & Society*, Vol. 28, No. 1, pp. 67–92.

O'Leary, Don (2000) *Vocationalism and Social Catholicism in Twentieth-Century Ireland: The Search for a Christian Social Order* (Dublin: Irish Academic Press).

O'Mahony, Patrick and Gerard Delanty (1998) *Rethinking Irish History* (Basingstoke: Macmillan).

O'Neill, Kathleen (1992) *Telling It Like It Is: Poverty in a North Dublin Suburb* (Dublin: Combat Poverty Agency).

Ó Riain, Seán (1997a) 'An Offshore Silicon Valley? The Emerging Irish Offshore Industry', *Competition & Change*, Vol. 2, pp. 175–212.

Ó Riain, Seán (1997b) 'The Birth of a Celtic Tiger', *Communications of the ACM*, Vol. 40, No. 3, pp. 11–16.

Ó Riain, Seán (2000a) 'The Flexible Developmental State: Globalization, Information Technology, and the "Celtic Tiger"', *Politics & Society*, Vol. 28, No. 2, pp. 157–93.

Ó Riain, Seán (2000b) 'Soft Solutions to Hard Times' in Eamonn Slater and Michel Peillon, eds, *Memories of the Present. A Sociological Chronicle of Ireland, 1977–1998* (Dublin: Institute of Public Administration), pp. 237–45.

Ó Riain, Seán and Philip J. O'Connell (2000) 'The Role of the State in Growth and Welfare' in Brian Nolan, Philip J. O'Connell and Christopher T. Whelan, eds, *Bust to Boom? The Irish Experience of Growth and Inequality* (Dublin: IPA), pp. 310–39.

O'Sullivan, Mary (2000) 'Industrial Development: A New Beginning?' in J. W. O'Hagan, ed, *The Economy of Ireland: Policy and Performance of a European Region* (Dublin: Gill & Macmillan), pp. 260–85.

O'Sullivan, Roddy (1998) 'Meeting told traffic congestion could curb economic growth', *Irish Times*, 25 November.

O'Toole, Fintan (1987) *The Southern Question* (Dublin: Raven Arts Press).

O'Toole, Fintan (1990) *A Mass for Jesse James* (Dublin: Raven Arts Press).

O'Toole, Fintan (1994) *Black Hole, Green Card* (Dublin: New Island).

O'Toole, Fintan (1996) 'In the Land of the Emerald Tiger' *Irish Times*, 28 December 1996.

O'Toole, Fintan (1997) *The Ex-Isle of Erin* (Dublin: New Island Press).

O'Toole, Fintan (1998) 'The Meanings of Union', *New Yorker*, 27 April–4 May, pp. 54–62.

O'Toole, Fintan (1999) 'Working Class Dublin on Screen: The Roddy Doyle Films', *Cineaste*, Vol. 24, Nos 2–3, pp. 36–9.

O'Toole, Fintan (2000) 'In Terms of Kindness, Rich Ireland's Budget is Poverty-Stricken', *Irish Times*, 9 December.

O'Toole, Fintan (2001) 'The phoney war on tax cheats splutters on', *Irish Times*, 5 May.

Ó Tuama, Seán (1972) 'The Gaelic League Idea in the Future' in Seán Ó Tuama, ed., *The Gaelic League Idea* (Cork: Mercier Press), pp. 98–109.

Palan, Ronen (2000): 'New trends in global political economy' in Ronen Palan, ed., *Global Political Economy: Contemporary Theories* (London: Routledge), pp. 1–18.

Patterson, Orlando (1982) *Slavery and Social Death* (Cambridge, MA: Harvard University Press).

Peck, Deborah (2000) 'An Gorta Mór: The Great Famine and its Aftermath', doctoral dissertation, Massachusetts Professional School of Psychology.

Peillon, Michel (1982) *Contemporary Irish Society: An Introduction* (Dublin: Macmillan).

Pettitt, Lance (1997) 'Pigs and Provos, Prostitutes and Prejudice: Gay Representation in Irish Film, 1984–1995' in Éibhear Walshe, ed., *Sex, Nation and Dissent in Irish Writing* (Cork: Cork University Press), pp. 252–84.

Pettitt, Lance (2000) *Screening Ireland: Film and Television Representation* (Manchester and New York: Manchester University Press, 2000).

Phillips, Adam (1993) *On Kissing, Tickling and Being Bored* (London: Faber & Faber).

Phoenix, Eamonn (1994) *Northern Nationalism: Nationalist Politics, Partition, and the Catholic Minority in Northern Ireland 1890–1940* (Belfast: Ulster Historical Foundation).

Pilkington, Lionel (2001) *Theatre and the State in Twentieth-Century Ireland: Cultivating the People* (London and New York: Routledge).

Plunkett, Horace (1905) *Ireland in the New Century, with an Epilogue in Answer to Some Critics* (London: John Murray).

Pocock, J.G.A. (1975) *The Machiavellian Moment: Florentine Political Thought and the Atlantic Republican Tradition* (Princeton NJ: Princeton University Press).

Polanyi, Karl (1957) *The Great Transformation: The Political and Economic Origins of our Time* (Boston: Beacon Press).

Polanyi, Karl (1969): 'Our Obsolete Market Mentality' in George Dalton, ed, *Primitive, Archaic, and Modern Economies: Essays of Karl Polanyi* (Boston: Beacon Press), pp. 59–77.

Power, Carla (2001) 'What Happened to Irish Art?', *Newsweek*, 20 August.

Quinlan, Kathleen (1995) *Research and Development Activity in Ireland. A Spatial Analysis* (Maynooth: Centre for Local and Regional Development).

Quinn, Bob (2000) 'Recycled Rants', *Film West*, Issue 42, Winter, pp. 26–30.

Radio Teilifís Éireann (1989) *Change and Challenge: The Future for Broadcasting in Ireland* (Dublin: RTÉ Publications).

Raftery, Mary and O'Sullivan, Eoin (1999) *Suffer the Little Children, the Inside Story of Ireland's Industrial Schools* (Dublin: New Island Books).

Readings, Bill (1997) *The University in Ruins* (Cambridge, MA: Harvard University Press).

Reece, Bob (1998) 'The Irish and the Aborigines', *Quadrant*, January–February 1998, pp. 27–32.

Regan, John M. (1999) *The Irish Counter Revolution 1921–1936* (Dublin: Gill and Macmillan).

Robbie, Angela (1994) *Postmodernism and Popular Culture* (London: Routledge).

Robbins, Bruce (1999) *Feeling Global: Internationalism in Distress* (New York: New York University Press).

Rockett, Kevin (1994), 'Culture, Industry and Irish Cinema' in J. Hill, M. McLoone and P. Hainsworth, eds, *Border Crossing: Film in Ireland, Britain and Europe* (Belfast: Institute of Irish Studies), pp. 126–39.

Rockett, Kevin, Luke Gibbons and John Hill (1988), *Cinema and Ireland* (London: Croom Helm).

Rodiger, David R. (1991) *The Wages of Whiteness: Race and the Making of the American Working Class* (London; New York: Verso).

Sandel, Michael (1998) *Democracy's Discontents: America in Search of a Public Philosophy* (Cambridge, MA: Belknap Press).

Scott, James (1990) *Domination and the Arts of Resistance: Hidden Transcripts* (New Haven: Yale University Press).

Sennett, Richard (1998) *The Corrosion of Character: The Personal Consequences of Work in the New Capitalism* (New York: W.W. Norton).

Shanahan, Ella (1987) 'Bill proposes new independent radio structure', *Irish Times*, 21 November.

Sheehan, Erica (2000) ed., Frank Murphy and Cathleen McDonagh (Compilers) *Travellers: Citizens of Ireland: Our Challenge to an Intercultural Irish Society in the 21st Century* (Dublin: Parish of the Travelling People).

Sheerin, Emer (1998) 'Heritage Centres' in Michel Peillon and Eamon Slater, eds, *Encounters with Modern Ireland* (Dublin: IPA), pp. 39–48.

Skelly, Joseph Morrison (1997) *Irish Diplomacy at the United Nations, 1945–1965: National Interest and the International Order* (Dublin: Irish Academic Press).

Sloterdijk, Peter (1998) 'Modernity as Mobilisation' in Jeremy Millar and Michiel Schwarz, eds, *Speed: Visions of an Accelerated Age* (London: Whitechapel Art Gallery), pp. 43–52.

Smith, Jamie (2001) 'New digital channels to cost £40m a year', *Irish Times*, 27 July.

Smyth, Gerry (1997) *The Novel and the Nation: Studies in the New Irish Fiction* (London: Pluto Press).

Smyth, Jim and Cairns, David (2000) 'Dividing Loyalties: Local Identities in a Global Economy' in Michel Peillon and Eamonn Slater, eds, *Memories of the Present: A Sociological Chronicle, 1997–1998* (Dublin: Institute of Public Administration), pp. 225–34.

Smyth, Sam (1996) *Riverdance: The Story* (London: André Deutsch).

Solanas, Fernando and Octavio Getino (1976) 'Towards a Third Cinema' in Bill Nichols, ed., *Movies and Methods* (Berkeley: University of California Press), pp. 44–64.

Stam, Robert (1991) 'Bakhtin, Polyphony, and Ethnic/Racial Representation' in Lester D. Friedman, ed., *Unspeakable Images: Ethnicity and the American Cinema* (Urbana and Chicago: University of Illinois Press), pp. 251–76.

Stigler, George (1971) 'The Theory of Economic Regulation', *Bell Journal of Economics*, Vol. 2, No. 1, spring, pp. 3–21.

Stoneman, Rod (2000) 'Under the Shadow of Hollywood: the Industrial versus the Artisanal' in *Kinema: A Journal for Film and Audiovisual Media*, Spring (http://www.arts.uwaterloo.ca/FINE/juhde/kinemahp.htm, accessed 20 August 2001).

Sturken, Marita (1998) 'The Remembering of Forgetting: Recovered Memory and the Question of Experience', *Social Text*, Vol. 57, Winter, pp. 103–26.

Taussig, Michael (1987) *Shamanism, Colonialism and the Wild Man: A Study in Terror and Healing* (Chicago: University of Chicago Press).

Taylor, Charles (1989) *Sources of the Self: The Making of the Modern Identity* (Cambridge, MA: Harvard University Press).

Taylor, Charles (1992) *The Ethics of Authenticity* (Cambridge, MA: Harvard University Press).

Taylor, Charles (1997) 'Invoking Civil Society', in *Philosophical Arguments* (Cambridge, MA: Harvard University Press), pp. 204–24.

Tovey, Hilary (1999) 'The Co-operative Movement in Ireland: A Movement for Modernity?', paper to the second regional conference on social movements and change, University College Cork, April.

Tucker, Vincent (1992) 'The Myth of Development' (Department of Sociology, University College Cork: Occasional Papers in Irish and World Development).

Tucker, Vincent (1997) 'A Cultural Perspective on Development' in Vincent Tucker, ed., *Cultural Perspectives on Development* (London: Frank Cass), pp. 1–21.

TV3 (1998) *Programme Policy Statement*, Ninth Schedule of Licence issued by Director of Telecommunications Regulation to the IRTC dated 15 September.

Tynan, Maol Muire (1989) 'Welsh TV in bid for new channel', *Irish Times*, 18 January.

United Nations Development Programme (2001) *Human Development Report* (Oxford: Oxford University Press).

Varley, Tony and Chris Curtin (1999) 'Defending Rural Interests Against Nationalists in 20th Century Ireland: A Tale of Three Movements' in D. Davis, ed., *Rural Change in Ireland* (Belfast: Institute of Irish Studies), pp. 58–83.

Varley, Tony and Chris Curtin (forthcoming) *The Few and the Many: Organising People for Collective Action in the West of Ireland* (Assen, The Netherlands: Van Gorcan).

Virilio, Paul (1977) *Vitesse et Politique* (Paris: Galilée).

Vorm, William (1982), ed., *Paddy No More: Modern Irish Short Stories* (Dublin: Wolfhound Press).

Walzer, Michael (1984) *Spheres of Justice: A Defence of Pluralism and Equality* (New York: Basic Books).

Walzer, Michael (1995) 'The Argument from Civil Society' in Ronald Beiner, ed., *Theorizing Citizenship* (Albany: State University of New York Press), pp. 153–74.

Waters, John (1998) 'Irish racism expresses sense of inferiority', *Irish Times*, 27 January.

'What is Catalyst', *Church of Ireland Gazette*, 27 November 1998.

Whelan, Kevin (1990) 'Clio agus Caitlín Ní hUallacháin', *Oghma*, Vol. 2, pp. 9–19.

White, Jack (1975) *Minority Report: The Anatomy of the Southern Irish Protestant* (Dublin: Gill and Macmillan).

Whyte, J.H. (1971) *Church and State in Modern Ireland* (Dublin: Gill and Macmillan).

Wilkinson, Sue (1996) *Feminist Social Psychologies* (Buckingham: Open University Press).

Williamson, Judith (1986) 'Woman is an Island: Femininity and Colonization' in Tania Modleski, ed., *Studies in Entertainment: Critical Approaches to Mass Culture* (Bloomington: Indiana University Press), pp. 99–118.

Wilson Foster, John (1991) *Colonial Consequences: Essays in Irish Literature and Culture* (Dublin: Lilliput Press).

World Health Organisation (2001a) *European School Survey Project on Alcohol and other Drugs* (Stockholm: World Health Organisation).

World Health Organisation (2001b) *Health for all Statistical Base* (Stockholm: World Health Organisation).

Wren, Maeve-Ann (2000a) 'EEC was ally Ireland had been seeking for centuries', *Irish Times*, 16 May.

Wren, Maeve-Ann (2000b) 'Relative poverty deepens despite Celtic Tiger', *Irish Times*, 19 May.

Yeats, William Butler (1972) *Memoirs: Autobiography – First Draft, Journal*, ed., Denis Donoghue (London: Macmillan).

Yee, Chiang (1953) *The Silent Traveller in Dublin* (London: Methuen).

Contributors

Michael Cronin is Senior Lecturer in the School of Applied Language and Intercultural Studies and Dean of the Joint Faculty of Humanities, Dublin City University. He is co-editor of *Tourism in Ireland: A Critical Analysis* (Cork University Press, 1993) and author of *Translating Ireland: Translation, Languages, Cultures* (Cork University Press, 1996) and *Across the Lines: Travel, Language, Translation* (Cork University Press, 2000). He was co-editor of *Graph: Irish Cultural Review* from 1986 to 1999.

Joseph Dunne teaches philosophy in the Education and Humanities programmes at St Patrick's College Dublin. He is author of *Back to the Rough Ground: Practical Judgement and the Lure of Technique* (Notre Dame and London: University of Notre Dame Press, 1997) and co-editor (with Frank Litton and Attracta Ingram) of *Questioning Ireland: Debates in Political Philosophy and Public Policy* (Dublin: IPA, 2000).

Roddy Flynn is the Chair of Film and Television Studies at the School of Communications, Dublin City University, where he lectures on political economy of the media. He has also written extensively on the Irish and European audiovisual and telecommunications industries. He has formerly worked as a journalist and as a research consultant. He holds a PhD from Dublin City University.

Luke Gibbons is Professor of English, and Film, Theatre and Television, at the University of Notre Dame, Indiana, and formerly taught at Dublin City University. He has written extensively on Irish literature, the visual arts and popular culture. He is author of *Transformations in Irish Culture* (Cork University Press, 1996) and is an editor of the forthcoming *Routledge Encyclopedia of Irish Culture*, and his next book, *Edmund Burke and Ireland: Aesthetics, Politics and the Colonial Sublime, 1750–1850* (Cambridge University Press), is due for publication in 2002.

Debbie Ging is a lecturer in communications at Dublin City University. She has also taught at the Institute of Technology, Tallaght, and at the Dublin Institute of Technology. Research interests include Irish cinema, the psychological functioning of sound in cinema, gender studies and multiculturalism and the media. She is currently engaged in doctoral research on the subject of popular culture and the construction of Irish masculinity, and is a regular contributor to *Film West*.

Peadar Kirby is a senior lecturer in the School of Communications, Dublin City University. A former journalist, he has published extensively on issues of development, in Ireland and Latin America. Among his recent books are *The Celtic Tiger in Distress: Growth with Inequality in Ireland* (Palgrave, 2002) and *Poverty Amid Plenty: World and Irish Development Reconsidered* (Trócaire and Gill & Macmillan, 1997). He holds a PhD from the London School of Economics.

Geraldine Moane teaches Psychology, Women's Studies and Equality Studies in University College Dublin and in community settings, and has been active in the women's movement since 1976. She is the author of *Gender and Colonialism: A Psychological Analysis of Oppression and Liberation* (Macmillan, 1999), and has also published on violence, health care, lesbian issues, colonialism and ancient Ireland. Her primary interest is in transforming the impact of oppressive social conditions.

Barra Ó Séaghdha has contributed essays, reviews and interviews in the areas of literature, art, music, history and cultural politics to a variety of magazines and newspapers. He was co-editor of the Irish cultural review *Graph*. He works in the EFL sector.

Michel Peillon was born and educated in Paris and has, since the 1970s, been lecturing in Sociology at the National University of Ireland, Maynooth. He has written extensively on many aspects of Irish society in the last twenty years. He has written or edited five books and has published numerous articles in Irish and international journals. He is at present co-editing the series *Irish Sociological Chronicles*.

Lionel Pilkington is a lecturer in English at the National University of Ireland, Galway, and is a member of the Church of Ireland congregation of St Nicholas's Collegiate Church. He is the author of *Theatre and the State in Twentieth-Century Ireland: Cultivating the People* (Routledge, 2001) and of various articles on Irish culture and politics.

Index

Compiled by Sue Carlton

Aboriginal peoples, Australia 102
abortion 119, 183
About Adam (Stembridge) 12, 178,
   186, 189, 191
Accelerator (Vinny Murphy) 178,
   187, 188, 191
Adam, Heribert 91
Adorno, Theodor 44, 97
Aiken, Frank 103, 104
air travel 57–8
Airey, Siobhán 58, 61, 62
alcohol and drug consumption 110,
   117–18
Allen, Kieran 5
Amongst Women 11, 96
An t-Éireannach 133, 152
Anderson, Benedict 199
Angela's Ashes 96, 192, 193
Anglo-Irish Agreement (1987) 146
Anne Devlin (Pat Murphy) 182
Apocalypse Now (Coppola) 95
Apprentice Boys 145
Aristotle 74, 75
arts
   and social change 44
   and versions of past 10–12
   see also cinema; culture
asylum-seekers 61, 62–3
Atlantean (Quinn) 180

Bakhtin, Mikhail 184
Ballroom of Romance, The
   (O'Connor) 10, 96
Barton, Ruth 190
Bauman, Zygmunt 58, 61, 204–5
Beaumont, Seán Nelson 133
Beck, Ulrich 204
Behan, Brendan 132
Belfast Agreement 157
Bell, Daniel 42, 47

Bent Out of Shape (Walsh) 186
Bernard, John Henry 128
Bew, Paul 15
Big House 27, 133
Bishop's Story, The (Quinn) 180
Black, Cathal 178, 182
   see also Korea; *Pigs*
Black Hole, Green Card (O'Toole)
   155, 156
Blair, Tony 126
Blow Dry (Breathnach) 192
Bolger, Dermot 7
Bourke, Jim 64
Bowen, Elizabeth 133
Bowen, Kurt 131, 133
Bradshaw, Brendan 27
Brady, Eugene 181, 186
Breathnach, Paddy 191, 192
broadcasting 160–75
   advertising expenditure 172
   commercial 162–75
   historical context 161–2
   liberalisation 162–4
   licence fee 171
   public service obligation 164,
      170–3, 175
   regulation 168–70
Broadcasting Acts 98, 161, 163,
   164
Broadcasting and Wireless
   Telegraphy Act 162
Brown, Terence 131, 134
Budawanny 180
Burke, Ray 160, 162, 163, 164,
   165
Buskers (Power) 186
Butcher Boy, The (Jordan) 10–11,
   96, 98, 189, 191
Butler, Hubert 131
Byrne, Gay 174

Cairns, David 178
Canwest Global 166, 167, 168
Carr, Patricia 51
Casement, Roger 100–1
Castells, Manuel 31
Catalyst 134
Catholic Action 136
Catholic Church 99, 124, 132–3
    domination of 45, 114, 119, 121
    impeding modernisation 124–5,
        129, 137–8, 144, 147
    and Irish State 42–3, 135–7, 198
    weakening influence 89, 111,
        154, 155
Catholic vocationalism 135–6
Celtic mythology 180
Celtic Tiger 35, 197–8
    alternatives to 201
    approaches to 4–9, 22
    cultural responses to 9–15
    and Drumcree crisis 127–8
    historical bases for 21, 29–33
censorship 45, 128
Century Radio 164, 165, 169
Channel 4 (UK) 163
Chiang Yee 54, 55
chrono-politics 57–8, 60, 65
Church of Ireland 133, 134–5, 138
    and commemoration of Famine
        129–30
    and Drumcree crisis 126, 128,
        134
    and liberalism 127–31
    support for unionism 134–5
    see also Protestantism
cinema 92–4, 95, 97–8, 177–93
    American influence 187, 190
    and cultural diversity 183–4,
        186–7
    European co-productions 190
    feminist 182–3
    First Wave 177, 178–85, 187
    foreign investment 192–3
    globalisation 177, 185–9, 191–2
    and homosexuality 186
    and national identity 177–80,
        183, 185–7, 188–9, 191–2, 193
    and post-modernism 191, 193
    and revaluation of past 96, 189

and social exclusion 186, 187–8,
    193
    stereotyping 185–6
citizenship 40, 69–88, 185, 204
    classical conception of 74–6
    and democracy 76, 78
    and economic agency 78–80
    educating for 69–71, 75–6, 85–6
    and freedom 77–8
    and individuality 205–6
    and patriotism 73
    and rights 76–7, 80–1
    and solidarity 71–2
    see also civil society; interdepen-
        dence
civic humanism 74, 76
civil society 28, 29, 72, 81–4, 205
    and solidarity 83–4
    and state 84–6
Civil War 116
Clann na Talmhan 136
Closer You Get, The 186, 187, 190
Coen brothers 190
Cohen, Stanley 89, 94
Collins, Gerry 162
Collins, Michael 122
colonialism 91–2, 94, 109
    domination 111, 112, 113
    psychological legacies of 111–13,
        114, 117–22
    and resistance 111, 120–2
    see also history
Comerford, Joe 178, 180–1, 182
Commitments, The (Parker) 10, 92–4
Connolly, James 25
Connolly, Sean 166
Conradh na Gaeilge (Gaelic
    League) 25
contraception 119
co-operative movement 24, 84
Coppola, Francis Ford 95
CORI (Conference of Religious in
    Ireland), Justice Commission
    137
cosmopolitanism 100–4
Coulter, Carol 130
Country 189
creativity 23–4, 121
credit union movement 84
Cronin, Michael 23

Crouch, Colin 48
Crushproof 187, 188
Crying Game, The (Jordan) 182
cultural modernity 42
cultural political economy 22, 33
culture 12–17, 38–53, 158, 196–7, 207
  commodification of 46–7, 50
  definition of 39
  diversity 16, 40, 160
  as factor of production 47–50
  as means of consumption 50
  and 'negative practices' 43, 52, 53
  and politics 17
  renaissance 160
  and social criticism 43–6, 52–3
Cumann na nGaedheal 131, 133
Curran, John 84
Curtin, Chris 136
Cushing, Richard 103

Dancing at Lughnasa (Friel) 93, 180
Davitt, Michael 102, 103
De Valera, Eamon 26, 28, 79, 92, 129, 133, 136, 179
de-differentiation 46
de-visionism 156–8
'Death on the Rock' 162
Delanty, Gerard 40
democracy 32, 39, 76, 137, 205
Department of Posts and Telegraphs (P&T) 161
Desart, Ellen, Countess of 132
Dillon, Michèle 40
Dirlik, Arif 100
disabled 61, 62
Disappearance of Finbar, The 188, 190
discrimination, anti-catholic 130–1, 134
divorce 119
Doherty, Moya 64
Douglass, Frederick 95
Downing Street Declaration (1994) 157
Doyle, Roddy 10, 11, 92–4, 188
Dream Kitchen (Dignam) 186
Drinking Crude 188
Drumcree crisis 125–8, 130, 134

Dublin 54–5
Dudley Edwards, Ruth 148
Dulles, Foster 103
Durcan, Paul 129
Dworkin, Ronald 81
dynamic rootedness 207

Eagleton, Terry 13, 15–16, 196, 200, 201, 207
Eames, Robin 130
East is East (O'Donnell) 192
East Timor Solidarity Group 26
Eat the Peach 10
economic growth
  and alcohol consumption 118
  and education 70
  and inequality 8
  and role of cultural change 12–15
  social impact of 4–5, 10, 27–9, 33–4, 109–10, 137, 202–3
economic modernity 42
Eden, Maud 133
education
  for citizenship 69–70, 75–6, 85–6
  and equality 70–1, 83
  universities 57
EEC membership 151
egalitarianism 25–6
emigration 26, 33, 149, 155
entrepreneurship 43, 50–1
equality 70–2, 75, 202
  and civil society 82–3
Esmonde, Sir Thomas Grattan 132
ethnic cleansing 73
European Central Bank 64
European Credit Transfer System (ECTS) 57
European Union 31, 56, 58, 64, 110, 152
Ex-Isle of Ireland (O'Toole) 63, 155, 156
exclusion 32, 33, 136
  see also cinema; social exclusion; poverty
exports 56
Exposure (Hickey) 181

Fahey, Tony 134
Fallon, Brian 65
Family (Winterbottom) 11

Famine 96, 111, 113, 114–15, 116, 129–30
Fanon, Frantz 112
farmers 58–60
Faulkner, Pat 64
Fenians 152
Fernández-Armesto, Felipe 201
Fianna Fáil 131, 136, 150–1, 153, 155, 162
Fianna Fáil/PD coalition 62
Field, The (Sheridan) 96, 181
Field Day tendency 91
Fight Club 188
Film Industry Strategic Review Group 192
Fitzgerald, John 12, 29
Flick (Connolly) 178, 187, 188, 191
Focus 129
Fogarty, Michael 136
foreign investment 104, 149
Foster, Ronan 6
Foster, Roy F. 27, 91, 132, 148, 157
free-market liberalism 8, 202–3
freedom 204
    and citizenship 70, 71–2, 76, 77–8, 81
    and civil society 82
    freedom of contract 79
Friel, Brian 10, 93, 180

Gaelic Athletic Association 84
Gaeltacht (Irish-speaking) areas 41
Gailey, Andrew 131
Galbraith, J.K. 201
Garvaghy Road Residents' Association 127
gateway pundits 143, 145, 159
gays and lesbians 61, 123
'General, The', cult of 11
geo-politics 55–6
George, Susan 60
Getino, Octavio 179
Gibbons, Fiachra 124, 125, 138
Gibbons, Luke 24, 40, 180, 183, 189
global capitalism 202
    domination of 112, 120, 122
    resistance to 111, 122, 123

globalisation 12, 21, 26–7, 29–31, 97, 104, 154–6
    cinema 177, 185–9, 191–2
    and cultural diversity 100
    and local identity 14
    and mobility 58
Goodman International 162
Grade, Michael 170
Granada Television 162, 168
Gray, John 201
Great Hunger, The (Kavanagh) 10
Green Berets, The 95
Gregg, John A.F. 128, 129
Gregory, Isabella Augusta, Lady 124
Guardian 124, 125, 138
guilt 89–91, 115

H-Block hunger strikes 146, 156
Harkin, Margo 183
Haughey, Charles 60, 150
Hayes, Fr John 136
Hazelkorn, Ellen 15
Healy, Séan 137
Hegel, G.W.F. 43, 99
Henchy, Seamus 166
Hickey, Kieran 178, 181–2
history
    psychological legacies of 110–23
    psychosocial legacies 117–22
    revisionism 90–2
    see also colonialism; past
Hobsbawm, Eric 158
Holocaust survivors 115–16
homeless 186
homosexuality 186
Horse (Liddy) 189
Hourihane, Anne Marie 105
Hush-a-Bye-Baby (Harkin) 183
Hutchinson, Bertram 40
Hyde, Douglas 25

I Went Down (Breathnach) 10, 191
ideological franchising 14
immigration 105, 111, 186, 206–7
Independent Production Unit (IPU) 173
Independent Radio and Television Commission (IRTC) 162, 164, 165, 166, 167–9

Industrial Development Authority (IDA) 40
industrialisation, and education 69–70
inequality 30–1, 34, 110
and post-colonial state 111
intellectuals, conceptual borrowing 14–15
interdependence 207–8
International Financial Services Centre 56
international issues, awareness of 26–7
Into the West 181, 186
IRA 145–6, 155
Ireland
bases of reinvention 29–33
and Britain 156–7
conflicting dynamics 42–3
and Europe 29, 152, 155
foreign policy 103
independence 55
industrial development 40–1
international outlook 26–7
invention of 23–9
national identity 27
see also cinema; national identity
parliamentary democracy 39
reinvention of 21, 35, 197–8, 199
sense of history 27
service sector 47–50, 56
shifts in power relations 111–12
social projects 24–5, 28
understandings of past 6–7, 109
Irish Catholic Bishops' Conference 137
Irish Countrywomen's Association 84
Irish Farmers' Association (IFA) 59
Irish language 14, 25, 28, 34, 117
and broadcasting 164
and cinema 179
Gaeltacht areas 41
Irish Renaissance 23, 24
Irish State 5, 9, 43, 50–2, 51
Irish Times 23, 59

Jacobsen, John Kurt 27
Jaouen, Hervé 6

Jefferson Smurfit Group 165
Jefferson, Thomas 78
Jessop, Bob 22
Joyce, James 12, 54, 55, 73, 96, 178

Kane, Eileen 41
Kavanagh, Patrick 10, 11, 129–30
Keegan, Trevor 54
Kelleher, John 165
Kennedy, John F. 104
Kennedy, Liam 90, 91–2
Kenny, Vincent 118
Kermode, Frank 205
Kerry Babies case 183
Kiberd, Declan 1, 21, 23, 27, 45
Kilkenny case 116
Kirby, Peadar 5, 13, 31
Korea (Black) 10, 96, 97–8, 189, 191
Kundera, Milan 65

Ladies Land League 152
Laïdi, Zaki 35
Lament for Art O'Leary (Quinn) 179
Last Bus Home, The (Gogan) 186, 190
Law, Andrew Bonar 158
Leader 28
League of Nations 26, 152
Lee, Joseph 14–15, 28
Lemass, Sean 6
Liddy, Kevin 189
Linehan, Hugh 186
literacy 110
Literary Revival 96
literature
inspiration from past 96–7
and social criticism 45
Little Big Man 95
Lloyd, John 158
Lodge, Cabot 103
London Review of Books 158
Los Angeles Times 99
Lyons, F.S.L. 6, 27

McCarthy, Conor 6, 7
McCarthy, Thomas 129
McColgan case 116
McCourt, Frank 96
McCreevy, Charlie 8

McDonagh, Martin 11, 129
MacDonagh, Oliver 6
McDyer, Fr James 136
McGahern, John 10, 11, 90
McGuinness, Frank 129
McGuinness, Paul 165, 167
MacIntyre, Alasdair 207–8
McLoone, Martin 179, 181, 183, 190, 191
McPherson, Conor 191
McQuaid, John Charles 136
Macra na Tuaithe 84
McRobbie, Angela 191
McVeigh, Timothy 99
Madden, R.R. 102
Maeve (Pat Murphy) 182
Major, John 56
Manichean world view 23, 109, 112, 118, 123
marginalisation 58, 61, 111
market forces, resistance to 198–200, 203
Marxism 5
Meaney, Geraldine 119
media
  and pluralist projects 24–5
  pundits 143–59
  and social concern 8
  see also broadcasting; cinema
MEDIA programme 190
Memmi, Albert 112
Mercier, Vivian 131
Michael Collins (Jordan) 12, 98, 189
missionaries 26
Mitchel, Angus 101
MMDS (Microwave Multipoint Distribution System) 163, 165
modernisation 6–8, 14, 151, 153
  and acceleration 63–4
  backlash 144
  and critical modernity 206–7
  and foreign capital 149
  and globalisation 100
  and identity 23–4
  uneven modernity 39, 40–1
Monk, Claire 188
Moran, D.P. 24, 28
Morris, James 166–7
Morrison, Toni 95
Morrisson, Eve 186

Muintir na Tíre 84, 136
multiculturalism 34, 105, 183–4, 206–7
Murphy, Bernadette 89, 90
Murphy, Pat 178, 182
Murphy, Tom 10
My Left Foot (Sheridan) 11
Myers, Kevin 148

National Anti-Poverty Strategy (NAPS) 26
National Economic and Social Council (NESC) 1
nationalism 6–7, 27, 43, 94, 104–5, 156
  and Celtic mythology 180
  and citizenship 69, 73–4
  and identity 34
  militant 145–6
  versus neo-liberalism 33–5
Ne Temere decree 132
neo-corporatism 52
neo-liberalism 7–8, 34–5
Nephew The (Brady) 181, 186
Network 2 172–3
new social orders 199–200, 202–3
New Statesman 158
Newsweek 11, 89, 90, 96, 105
Nice Treaty (2001) 32, 35, 200
1916 Rising 116
nomadism, licit and illicit 59–60, 63
Northern Ireland
  attitude of Republic to 144, 145–6, 153
  and Britain 157, 158
  Catholic minority 134
  nationalists 145–6, 148
  understanding conflict 143–4
  see also Troubles
nostalgia 10, 94, 96

O'Brien, Conor Cruise 6, 145–8, 157
O'Brien, Edna 10
O'Callaghan, Sean 158
Ó Cinnéide, Séamus 31–2
O'Connor, Barbara 64
O'Donnell, Damien 192

O'Donnell, Rory 1, 4–5, 12–13, 21,
    22–3, 24, 29, 199–200
Offences Against the State Act 9
O'Hearn, Denis 5, 22
O'Mahony, Patrick 40
Orange Order 126, 127, 128, 130,
    134
O'Reilly, Tony 155
Ó Riain, Seán 4–5, 22, 34, 51
O'Sullivan, Thaddeus 178
O'Toole, Fintan 7, 23, 60, 63, 90,
    92, 119–20, 148–58
Ó Tuama, Seán 25

Paisley, Ian 126, 157
Paris, Texas (Wender) 12
past
    legacies of 94–9, 105, 109
    see also history
patriotism 72–3
Patterson, Henry 15
Peace Process 111
Peaches 186, 192
Peck, Deborah 114, 115
peripherality 56, 57
persecution 102
Pettitt, Lance 180
Phelan, Jim 59
Phillips, Adam 65–6
Phoenix, Eamon 134
Pigs (Black) 182, 186
Pius IX, 134
Plunkett, Horace 125, 138
Poitín (Quinn) 180
political modernity 42
Polyani, Karl 198–9, 200
poverty 30–1, 34, 58, 60–2
    see also exclusion
Power, Carla 96, 99
primary education 39
prison population 9
Prospect 158
prosperity
    and guilt 89–91
    see also economic growth
Protestantism
    and Anglo-Irish Ascendancy 131,
        132, 133
    impeding modernity 127–9

privileged treatment of 131–2,
    134
    see also Church of Ireland
Public Order Act 9

Quiet Man, The (Ford) 10
Quinn, Bob 178, 179, 190, 192

racism 34, 119, 186
radio 160–3, 165, 169
Radio Éireann 161
Radio Telefís Éireann (RTÉ)
    161–2, 164, 168
    cap on advertising 163, 165, 169
    and public service broadcasting
        170–1, 172–3, 175
Radio and Television Act 162, 163,
    167
Reagan, Ronald 26
Reece, Bob 102
Reefer and the Model (Comerford)
    180–1, 182
Refugee Act 9, 62, 63
Refugee Applications Commissioner
    62
refugees 61, 62–3, 186
religion 124–39
    see also Catholic Church; Church
        of Ireland
republicanism 74, 76, 78–9
research and development 48
Reynolds, Brigid 137
Riverdance 63–4, 193
road congestion 64–5
Robinson, Lennox 128, 133
Robinson, Mary 63
Rockett, Kevin 179, 185
Royal Ulster Constabulary (RUC)
    126, 130, 131, 134

Saltwater (McPherson) 191
Save the West campaign 136
Scorsese, Martin 187, 190
SDLP (Social Democratic and
    Labour Party) 146
Second World War 55–6
Sennett, Richard 207
sexuality 119
Simms, George Otto 129

Sisters of Mercy 60
Sloterdijk, Peter 57, 65
Smyth, Jim 178
Snakes and Ladders 188
social activism 203–4
social irresponsibility 119–20
social partnership 5, 21, 29–30,
    31–2
social solidarity 33
software industry 51, 56
Solanas, Fernando 179
Soldier Blue 95
solidarity 33, 70, 71–2, 121–2, 123
    and shared history of oppression
    100–4
Somerville, Edith 133
Sound Broadcasting Bill 162
Spaghetti Slow 190
speed 55, 59–60, 63–4, 65
Stam, Robert 184
state
    and civil society 84–6
    see also Irish State
Stíofáin, Seán Mac 162
Stoneman, Rod 190, 192
Stopford Green, Alice 101
Sturken, Marita 91
Sum, Ngai-Ling 22
Summertime (Morrisson) 186
survivor guilt 115
Synge, J.M. 96

tachocracy 59
Taissig, Michael 101
tax evasion 9
telecommunications technology
    56–7
Telegraph 158
television
    acquired programming 171–2,
    174
    commercial 164–70
    see also broadcasting
Thatcher, Margaret 146
Thérèse of Lisieux, Saint 124, 138
Third Cinema 179, 190
This is My Father (Quinn) 96
Today FM 169
Toíbín, Colm 148, 149, 158

Tocqueville, Alexis de 205
Tovey, Hilary 25
Trainspotting (Boyle) 188
transport 61–2, 64–5
traumatic memory 95–9, 114–16
    denial and doublethink 116, 118
    and premature closure 99–100
    retraumatisation 116
Traveller (Comerford) 180–1
Travelling community 34, 59, 61,
    123, 181
Trevor, William 10
Trimble, David 126
Trócaire 137
Trojan Eddie 181
Troubles 143–8
    cultural representations of
    11–12
    understanding 143–4, 150
    see also Northern Ireland
Tucker, Vincent 21, 24
TV3 163, 164–70, 172–3, 174, 175
    regulatory capture 168–70
2x4 (Smallhorne) 182
Tynan, Maol Muire 166

Ulster Special Constabulary 134
Ulster Television (UTV) 166
Ulster Unionist Party 130
unionism 145–8, 156
United Irishmen 152
United Nations 26, 102, 152
United States 26, 80, 149, 151,
    152

Varley, Tony 136
Vicious Circle 11
Vietnam War 95, 96
Virilio, Paul 55
vision, importance of 123

Waking Ned 186, 187, 190
Walsh, Kieron J. 188, 189
Walsh, Orla 186
War of Independence 116
Warner Television International
    Sales 171
Weber, Max 208
welfare fraud 9

welfare state 30, 31, 80, 85
West, Trevor 131
Whelan, Kevin 27
When Brendan Met Trudy (Walsh)
    188, 189
Whitaker, T.K. 6
White, Jack 132
Wild Bunch, The 95
Williamson, Judith 10
Windmill Consortium 165, 166

women 62
    and citizenship 76
work, attitudes to 41
world-systems theory 5

Yeats, W.B. 124, 128, 131, 138
Yorkshire Television 165
Young Ireland 152

zero tolerance 9